Jesus the Radical

Jesus the Radical

The Parables and Modern Morality

Raymond Angelo Belliotti

LEXINGTON BOOKS
Lanham • Boulder • New York • Toronto • Plymouth, UK

Published by Lexington Books
A wholly owned subsidiary of The Rowman & Littlefield Publishing Group, Inc.
4501 Forbes Boulevard, Suite 200, Lanham, Maryland 20706
www.rowman.com

10 Thornbury Road, Plymouth PL6 7PP, United Kingdom

Copyright © 2013 by Lexington Books

All rights reserved. No part of this book may be reproduced in any form or by any electronic or mechanical means, including information storage and retrieval systems, without written permission from the publisher, except by a reviewer who may quote passages in a review.

British Library Cataloguing in Publication Information Available

Library of Congress Cataloging-in-Publication Data

Library of Congress Cataloging-in-Publication Data Available

ISBN 978-0-7391-8765-4 (cloth : alk. paper)—ISBN 978-0-7391-8766-1 (electronic)

∞™ The paper used in this publication meets the minimum requirements of American National Standard for Information Sciences Permanence of Paper for Printed Library Materials, ANSI/NISO Z39.48-1992.

Printed in the United States of America

For
Marcia, Angelo, and Vittoria
Il cuore ha le sue ragioni e non intende ragione
("The heart has reasons that reason does not understand")

Contents

Preface	ix
Acknowledgments	xi
Introduction	xiii
Notes	xix

1   The Good Samaritan: "And Who Is My Neighbor?"   1
    Interpretation of the Parable   2
    Who is the Priest?   3
    Who is the Levite?   4
    Who is the Samaritan?   5
    Moral Lessons   9
    Parallels in Secular Philosophy   13
    Radical Impartiality   17
    The Personal Moral Perspective   19
    Should We Be Partial to Family and Friends?   20
    Partialism versus Impartialism as General Benevolence   23
    Partialism versus Impartialism as Affectionate Difference   28
    Notes   34

2   The Prodigal Son: "All That I Have Is Thine"   37
    Interpretation of the Parable   38
    The Paradoxes of Agapic Love   45
    Parental Agape   49
    Agape and Abstraction   52
    Erotic Agape   54
    Notes   57

3   The Laborers in the Vineyard: "Whatsoever Is Right, That Shall Ye Receive"   59
    Interpretation of the Parable   60
    Moral Lessons   66
    The Notion of Desert   67
    Freedom of Contract   74
    Proportionate Reward   75
    Notes   79

4   The Unforgiving Servant: "Shouldest Not Thou Also Have Had Compassion?"   81
    Interpretation of the Parable   82

	The Concept of Forgiveness	83
	The Concept of Mercy	97
	The Parable, Forgiveness, and Mercy	106
	Notes	113
5	The Rich Fool: "Then Whose Shall Those Things Be?"	115
	Interpretation of the Parable	115
	Who Were the Cynics?	118
	Was Jesus a Cynic Philosopher?	125
	The Case in Favor of Identifying Jesus with Cynicism	125
	The Case against Identifying Jesus with Cynicism	138
	Notes	143
6	The Unjust Steward: "Because He Had Done Wisely"	145
	Interpretation of the Parable	146
	What Is the Context of Jesus' Moral Message?	152
	Sex and Marriage	154
	Family Relations	159
	Associating and Identifying with Undesirables	163
	Unsettling Established Rituals	165
	Interrogating Prevailing Norms of Just Distribution	166
	Material Minimalism	168
	Notes	172

Bibliography	175
Index	179
About the Author	183

Preface

I was raised a Roman Catholic. I attended parochial school from kindergarten through eighth grade. During my religious training—and religion was always the focus of the first session of every school day—we spent considerable time on the parables of the New Testament. This was unsurprising in light of the moral lessons contained in those stories. The transmission of moral lessons was, of course, the raison d'être of parochial school.

One day, when I was in fifth grade, we were ruminating over the Parable of the Laborers in the Vineyard. During recess, I sidled over to our teacher, a nun in the order of St. Joseph and enthusiastically offered my judgment, "Sister, I think that Jesus was wrong on this one." The nun made no effort to conceal her shock. As Jesus could never be wrong, just who was I to call his teachings into question?

A wiser student would have apologized for his impertinence, marched resolutely back to his seat, and cut his losses. Unfortunately, a ten-year-old boy with a big mouth and a curious, undisciplined mind rarely recognizes, much less embraces, prudent strategy. Predictably, I doubled down on what I took to be my wisdom. First, I outlined the reasons, expressed exquisitely and articulately in my judgment, why I thought that Jesus' conclusions were erroneous. Second, I accepted the nun's challenge and provided an account of how Jesus *could* be wrong: given that according to Catholic theology he was at once the son of God and a human being, he was susceptible to mistakes when and only when his human side was in play. Thus, he could be wrong when enunciating a parable if and only if during the rendering his human fallibility clouded his typically flawless divine judgment. This, undoubtedly, must have occurred during his account of the Parable of the Laborers in the Vineyard.

You must remember that this encounter occurred in the 1950s, when the Catholic Church was even less accommodating to quasi-heretical utterances than it is today. The nun acted swiftly; she convened a meeting which was attended by the parish priest, herself, my parents, and me. This unpleasant religious intervention had only one agenda item: a host of authority figures would confront an incorrigible youth and get his mind straight.

As always, my parents privately counseled a pragmatic stance: Maybe you are on to something, but do not get kicked out of school; make whatever atonements you must and get on with your education; for goodness' sake (that was not the phrase they used), do not turn stubborn on this matter. So I sat, listened, was unconvinced, but feigned contrition, and returned to the good graces of the parish. The Church was always a sucker for a sinner who had seemingly seen the light and offered repentance. But I remained unconvinced that Jesus' conclusions were right. (I now understand that one of the paramount points of the parable is its reformative aspiration: the story is not designed to reflect the conventional economic wisdom of society but to call for the transformation of dominant ideas. Thus, that I, using conventional economic wisdom, concluded that Jesus was "wrong" is unsurprising. What I missed then was Jesus' enjoinment to renounce conventional economic wisdom for a nobler standard. Even if we decide, all things considered, to reject the loftier norm, Jesus was not "wrong" for the reasons I advanced when I was ten years old.)

In any event, I always enjoyed contemplating the parables of the New Testament, whether inspired by a priest's sermon or the classroom instruction of my nuns (who throughout the remainder of my parochial school years cast suspicious glances my way whenever parables were recounted in class; word about me spread quickly).

About fifteen years later, I was enrolled as a graduate student in philosophy at the University of Miami. My chosen specializations within that field were ethics, political philosophy, and philosophy of law. At some point in my matriculation, one of my professors remarked that every philosopher that he knew who specialized in ethics had a strong religious background. Perhaps they had later strayed from organized religion or were even strident atheists, but they all shared at least one characteristic: they were exposed thoroughly to religion and its theological underpinnings throughout their formative years.

My years as a philosophy professor have only confirmed my mentor's view. I have retained my appreciation of the parables and find that when I recall them today they raise uncommonly interesting philosophical issues. Now, as I labor midway into my seventh decade on earth, the time seems appropriate to connect my abiding curiosity in the New Testament parables and critical issues in my chosen profession. Such is the genesis of this work.

Acknowledgments

Numerous people contributed to this work directly or indirectly. As always, my family comes first. Thanks to my parents, Angelo and Luisa Leonardo Belliotti, for carefully guiding me through the labyrinth that was parochial school education in the 1950s and for providing the ballast of my moral education. My wife, Marcia, as always, provided immeasurable emotional support and critical commentary as I undertook this project. An eighteenth-century Italian playwright, Carlo Goldoni, wrote *"Muore per metà chi lascia un' immagine di se stesso nei figli."* ("He only half dies who leaves an image of himself in his sons.") I am fortunate to have spawned and raised a son, Angelo, who extravagantly exceeds my image in every important way. I am blessed twice by having also a daughter, Vittoria, whose unwavering sense of justice, boundless capability to love, and intense family pride are prized by all who know her. As always, that this book will long outlive its author and my words will be available to torment my children when I am no longer here warms my spirit.

Thanks to Jana Hodges-Kluck, acquisitions editor, who, as always, added her expertise to the production process and who dealt patiently and considerately with an author who was too often impatient and annoying. Also thanks to Stephanie Brooks for her excellent supervision of the typesetting of this work and her invariable good cheer. Finally, thanks to Joanne Foeller, an expert of book formatting who corrected my numerous errors and prepared the manuscript with unmatched efficiency and grace.

Finally, I thank the following publishers for their permission to reprint and adapt material from my books: University Press of Kansas for *Good Sex* (1993) and *Seeking Identity* (1995); and Rodopi Editions for *Jesus or Nietzsche: How Should We Live Our Lives?* (2013).

Introduction

Understanding Jesus' teachings and trying to apply them to contemporary contexts requires some comment on how to perceive the historical Jesus. This is no easy task. The historical Jesus has been interpreted in numerous ways. For example, Jesus has been viewed as a Jewish Cynic peasant philosopher firmly convinced that embracing material minimalism and dismissing conventional societal values were required for personal salvation;[1] as an apocalyptic prophet who was convinced that the arrival of a cosmic judge, the Son of Man, was imminent on earth and that he would render judgment, transvalue the dominant values of the world, and inaugurate the Kingdom of God;[2] as the Son of God, sent as savior to suffer and die in order to redeem all human beings;[3] as an advocate of violent revolution who aspired to liberate the Jews from Roman domination;[4] as a politically leftist social reformer who urged his followers to strive for a radically egalitarian society in which goods were distributed according to need;[5] as a proto-feminist concerned with gender equality and easing the oppression of women;[6] as an accomplished magician capable of performing extraordinary deeds;[7] and as a teacher in the Essene Jewish tradition.[8]

How a person interprets the historical Jesus affects numerous issues, including how much in the canonical Gospels can be understood as the words of Jesus and how much should be viewed as embellishments crafted by early Christians to advance their religious fervor. In any case, the parables contained in the Gospels are among the teachings attributed to Jesus that are among the most uncontroversial in this regard: under every plausible interpretation of Jesus offered by scholars, the parables are taken to be among the words most likely to have been spoken by Jesus and not concocted by well-meaning followers. Thus, the parables provide fertile fruit from which to harvest Jesus' moral message.

Jesus invokes the "Kingdom of God" throughout his preaching. Interpreters understand the precise meaning of that phrase in accord with how they view the historical Jesus. For example, those who take the historical Jesus to be a Jewish Cynic peasant philosopher conclude that the Kingdom of God is a metaphor for the good human society, the ultimate salutary human community. Some interpreters in this camp take the phrase to be purely secular. Thus, Don Cupitt writes:

> [The Kingdom of God] is a dream of all-round freedom and dignity for the ordinary citizen . . . a dream that continues as a guiding ideal in the

> present and as a future hope . . . a human world in which people live without *ressentiment*, and are completely easy with each other . . . a world in which God has disappeared into human hearts, a human social world in which we are all of us in fully open communication — indeed, communion — with each other.[9]

On this view, the Kingdom of God is not intended to advance doctrinal teachings about divinity, but instead describes the better world to arrive on earth through the social transformation generated by putting into practice Jesus' moral message.

Others who view the historical Jesus as a Jewish Cynic peasant philosopher take a slightly different approach. They understand the Kingdom of God as an ethical condition such that human beings live in the present as if God's force and will were fully in control. John Dominic Crossan describes the vision of the Kingdom of God thusly:

> [Wisdom is required] for discerning here and now in this world, one can so live that God's power, rule, and dominion are evidently present to all observers. One enters the kingdom by wisdom or goodness, by virtue, justice, or freedom. It is a style of life for now rather than a hope of life in the future. This is therefore an ethical kingdom . . . [Jesus] taught and acted, theorized and performed against social oppression, cultural materialism, and imperial domination.[10]

Those who understand the historical Jesus to have been an apocalyptic prophet interpret the Kingdom of God as a future eventuality where God will rule on earth as God already rules in the transcendent realm. A cosmic judge, the Son of Man, would soon arrive to render judgment and transvalue values — those enjoying power and privilege will be humbled and those who are currently oppressed and disenfranchised will be exalted — as a prelude to the establishment of the Kingdom of God on earth. In this vein, Bart Ehrman writes:

> When Jesus talks about the Kingdom [of God], he appears to refer principally to something here on earth — where God will at some point *begin* to rule as he already *does* rule up above . . . Jesus . . . evidently thought that God was going to extend his rule from the heavenly realm where he resides down here to earth. There would be a real, physical kingdom here, a paradisal world in which God himself would rule his faithful people, where there would be eating, drinking, and talking, where there would be human co-regents sitting on thrones and human denizens eating at banquets. This future kingdom stands over against the present evil kingdoms to which God's people are now subjected, kingdoms of hatred, want, and oppression. In the future kingdom, God's people will be rewarded with a utopian existence.[11]

On this approach, the Kingdom of God is neither metaphorical nor extant. Instead, its future inauguration is assured and human beings are advised to live now in ways that prefigure the ideals of the coming kingdom. That is, understanding the nature of the coming Kingdom of God allows human beings to derive proper courses of conduct today.

> In the Kingdom there would be no more war. Jesus' disciples were not to engage in acts of violence *now*. In the Kingdom there would be no more poverty. Jesus' disciples were to give away all they had and give to the poor *now*. In the kingdom there would be no more oppression or injustice. Jesus' disciples were to treat all people equally and fairly now—even the lowest classes, the outcasts, the destitute; even women and children . . . The ways Jesus' disciples were to live in the present in preparation for the coming Son of Man reflected life as it would be when the Kingdom fully arrived.[12]

Mainstream Christians who understand the historical Jesus as the Son of God sent to redeem the world from sin by the sacrifice of his life take the Kingdom of God to embody love, peace, and harmony. The Kingdom began with Jesus' death and resurrection, is expanded by human beings who live by Jesus' example and teachings, and will attain perfection when Jesus returns at the end of time. Jesus will then render Final Judgment: only those who are judged righteous will enjoy God's reign forever, while the wicked shall be punished. At Final Judgment, the forces of evil will be forever extinguished. As such, the Kingdom of God can be viewed as God's ultimate intention.

For my purposes, regardless of how one understands the historical Jesus, how one interprets the Kingdom of God, and how one views the timing of the Kingdom of God (as present in those acting according to God's will, as an inevitable future wrought by the Son of Man and God, or as beginning with the death and resurrection of Jesus and expanding through the actions of people of good will), the critical conclusion is that human beings in the present should act in accordance with the supposed values and ideals of the Kingdom. Thus, regardless of one's allegiances to the perplexing questions surrounding the true understanding of the historical Jesus, the values and ideals of the Kingdom of God that Jesus articulated should guide human action today, at least for those who accept Jesus as an exemplary moral teacher (if not more).

Although numerous early Christians, including St. Paul and the writers of the canonical Gospels, stressed that belief in Jesus (and especially in his death and resurrection) was critical for a felicitous entrance into the Kingdom of God, Jesus emphasized appropriate action to alleviate the oppression of the poor, needy, and disenfranchised. For example, "For I was an hungred, and ye gave me meat: I was thirsty, and ye gave me drink: I was a stranger, and ye took me in . . . as ye have done it unto one of the least of these my brethren, ye have done it unto me" (Matt. 25:35, 40); "I say unto you, Inasmuch as ye did it not to one of the least of these [those in need], ye did it not to me" (Matt. 25:45). There is an ongoing Christian debate about the relative importance of belief in the salient parts of Jesus' life and death, the performance of praiseworthy deeds for the needy, and the receipt of saving grace for entering eternal life. However, to deny that the historical Jesus highlighted the role of human compassion for and action to benefit the oppressed in attaining the Kingdom of God is difficult.

Debate also centers on the meaning of the phrase the "Son of Man" and on whether the historical Jesus actually used that expression or whether the phrase was attributed to him by early Christians as an expression of their conviction that Jesus was divine. Those who interpret Jesus as an apocalyptic prophet take the phrase to connote the cosmic agent of divine judgment who will ensure soon the total victory of the forces of good over the forces of evil presently dominating the world and who will begin the process through which the Kingdom of God will be realized. Those who interpret Jesus as a Jewish Cynic peasant philosopher take the "Son of Man" to be Jesus' way of identifying himself with his audience, as sharing their common identity as oppressed human beings. Christians who interpret Jesus as divine take the "Son of Man" as Jesus' assurance that he will return to render final judgment and inaugurate the Kingdom of God. In short, whether Jesus was referring to himself as the Son of Man in those instances where the words are attributed to him in the canonical Gospels and whether he uttered the expression at all are highly disputed issues.

Unlike academic philosophers, religious reformers and custodians of societal traditions do not craft sophisticated deductive arguments to prove their moral conclusions. They do not seek to persuade through logical legerdemain; instead, these influential paragons tell stories. Thus, the Bible is rich with imaginative parables that press themselves upon our minds, stir our deepest emotions, and teach us moral lessons in unforgettable contexts. Likewise, Aesop's fables cascade through generations with greater social impact than any syllogism or categorical moral imperative. The power of parables and folklore arises from their accessibility, colorful cast of characters, and magical allure. Events occur in stories that transcend the natural laws of reality: animals are active moral agents, supra-human beings intervene, and miracles spring up at propitious occasions. Moreover, comedic and tragic artistic considerations often demand the inclusion of episodes that require the audience to execute astounding leaps of faith. After all, parables and folklore are exquisitely more entertaining than a painstaking, pedantic philosophical demonstration. But parables and folklore are also less rigorous than philosophical arguments: conflict, tension, and outright contradiction pervade biblical parables and Aesop's fables when each set of moral tales is considered as a whole. Perhaps that is their greatest lesson: the human condition resists neat, fully coherent explanations and principles that might capture the complexity of our moral life.

In chapter 1, I interpret the Parable of the Good Samaritan. After describing and analyzing the character and actions of the priest, Levite, and Samaritan, I set forth the moral lessons of the story. The paramount issues are of enduring concern: Who is my "neighbor"? How far must my moral circle of concern extend? Does Jesus' rendering of the love commandment require that I undertake as much risk, sacrifice, effort, and time in service to strangers (and even "enemies") in need as I would on behalf of myself and those close to me? Does Jesus require not only the proper deeds but also the proper disposition while performing those deeds? Next, I explain and dissect the philosophical views of Mo Tzu, Peter Singer, and James Rachels in order to demonstrate the debate between impartialists, who argue that needs must be fulfilled by those able to do so whosoever might embody those needs, and partialists, who champion the conventional moral wisdom that we owe more to those with whom we share intimate relationships than we owe to strangers. Finally, I highlight the similarities and differences between Jesus' version of impartialism and contemporary philosophical renderings. Typically, Jesus' prescriptions vary strikingly from the conventional moral wisdom of his day and of our own.

In chapter 2, I interpret the Parable of the Prodigal Son. In that story, a patriarch embodies and expresses unconditional love for his two sons, each of whom at various points responds with ingratitude and insult. Unconditional love presumably bestows value upon, as opposed to recognizes value within, the beloved and persists regardless of the reactions and character of the beloved. The philosophical analogue is the nature of agape, the unconditional love that engenders deep paradox. How can a lover genuinely love a *person* if the beloved's attributes, properties, deeds, and responses are irrelevant to the existence of the affection? Stripped of all constitutive characteristics, what remains of the beloved to serve as an object of affection? Is agape possible for only God or, perhaps, parents? Did Jesus prescribe that we should love all other human beings unconditionally? Unraveling and softening the paradoxes of agape is instructive because doing so deepens our understanding of human relationships and the phenomenology of human affection.

In chapter 3, I interpret the Parable of the Laborers in the Vineyard. There Jesus forces us to confront the limitations of social distribution of goods grounded in personal desert and material production. Jesus challenges our common moral intuitions and urges us to reconsider the scope of moral principles such as the notion of desert, freedom of contract, and proportionate reward. Moreover, Jesus asks us to question our own motivations when we respond ungraciously to the good fortune of others. After explaining the differences between two often competing claims of justice—desert and entitlement—I argue that Jesus' moral message can be summarized as follows: "where all receive that to which they are entitled, but where some receive more than they deserve, any resentment toward those more fortunate is misplaced and demonstrates a deficiency of character." Finally, I subject that message to critical scrutiny.

In chapter 4, I interpret the Parable of the Unforgiving Servant. After having an enormous debt waived by his master's generosity, a servant fails to pass that good will forward when dealing with a colleague who owes him money. In the story, Jesus manifests the importance of forgiveness and mercy. I analyze philosophically the concepts of forgiveness and mercy, carefully describing the elements of each. Then, I sketch the similarities and differences between Jesus' understandings of forgiveness and mercy, and prevalent contemporary interpretations. Finally, I describe the extent to which Jesus prescribed that forgiveness and mercy should be our virtual default mind-sets, while retaining a robust place for repentance and remorse.

In chapter 5, I interpret the Parable of the Rich Fool. Oblivious to the needs of others and to his own need for salutary relationships, the landowner of the story seemingly has only one pressing concern: how to manage his overwhelmingly good fortune and ever-expanding material bounty. God deals with his moral obtuseness harshly. The critical issue is the role of material resources in attaining personal salvation. This leads to a discussion of whether the historical Jesus should best be understood as a Jewish peasant Cynic philosopher, instead of as an apocalyptic prophet or as the divine Son of God. Like Jesus, the Cynics were renowned material minimalists and shared a host of other similarities to Jesus that have led some thinkers to identify the two movements. After carefully considering the most important, conflicting evidence, I conclude that portraying Jesus as a Hellenistic philosopher is misguided.

In chapter 6, I interpret the Parable of the Unjust Steward. After having squandered his patron's money, either through malfeasance or incompetence, a steward hatches a plan to wheedle his way back into the landowner's good graces. Through fraud and guile, he maneuvers the situation between the landowner and his clients such that the landowner's self-interest is tied to a reduction of the clients' lease payments that the steward has already orchestrated. As a result, the landowner applauds the steward's ingenuity and aplomb in turning an adverse situation to the steward's practical advantage. The difficulty is reconciling the steward's presumed "wisdom" with the arts of fraud and deception. After offering a better approach that the steward might have taken, I use the parable as a point of departure to analyze more fully Jesus' approach to sex and marriage; family relations; associating and identifying with social undesirables; unsettling established rituals; interrogating prevailing norms of just distribution; and material minimalism. Finally, I discuss the role that the words of Jesus played in a Sicilian Christian-Socialist movement in the late nineteenth century, and conclude by underscoring the dissonance between those words and much contemporary Christian practice.

Accordingly, the book connects the lessons of six parables of the New Testament with philosophical issues structured around morality and the art of leading a good human life. In this manner, I hope to highlight just how radical was the historical Jesus' moral message and how enormous a challenge he raised to the conventional wisdom of his time. More important, I aspire to demonstrate how deeply opposed is Jesus' moral message to the dominant moral understandings of our time. Although our conventional morality is generally profoundly influenced by Judeo-Christianity, several of Jesus' revolutionary insights have been marginalized. By imagining how our world would appear if those insights were highlighted, we can perceive more clearly the people we are and the people we might become.

NOTES

1. John Dominic Crossan, *Jesus: A Revolutionary Biography* (San Francisco: HarperSanFrancisco, 1994); *The Historical Jesus: The Life of a Mediterranean Jewish Peasant* (San Francisco: HarperSanFrancisco, 1991); F. Gerald Downing, *Jesus and the Threat of Freedom* (London: SCM Press Ltd., 1987); B. Mack, *A Myth of Innocence* (Philadelphia: Fortress, 1988).
2. Bart D. Ehrman, *Jesus: Apocalyptic Prophet of the New Millennium* (New York: Oxford University Press, 1999); E. P. Sanders, *The Historical Figure of Jesus* (London: Allen Lane/Penguin Books, 1993): John P. Meier, *A Marginal Jew* (New York: Doubleday, 1994).
3. This is the standard account of Christian religions. See, for example, Michael J. Wilkens and J. P. Moreland (eds.), *Jesus under Fire* (Grand Rapids, MI: Zondervan Publishing House, 1995).
4. S. G. F. Brandon, *Jesus and the Zealots* (New York: Scribner Books, 1967); G. W. Buchanan, *Jesus: The King and His Kingdom* (Macon, GA: Mercer University Press, 1984).
5. Richard A. Horsley, *Jesus and the Spiral of Violence* (Minneapolis, MN: Fortress Publishers, 1987).
6. Elisabeth Schussler Fiorenza, *In Memory of Her* (New York: Crossroad, 1983).
7. Morton Smith, *Jesus the Magician* (San Francisco: Harper & Row, 1978).
8. B. Thiering, *Jesus and the Riddle of the Dead Sea Scrolls* (San Francisco: HarperSanFrancisco, 1992).
9. Don Cupitt, *Jesus & Philosophy* (London: SCM Press, 1988), 25, 69, 70.
10. Crossan, *Jesus: A Revolutionary Biography*, 56, 121.
11. Ehrman, *Jesus: Apocalyptic Prophet of the New Millennium*, 142, 143.
12. Ibid., 181.

ONE

The Good Samaritan: "And Who Is My Neighbor?"

And, behold, a certain lawyer stood up, and tempted [tested] him, saying, Master, what shall I do to inherit eternal life? He said unto him, What is written in the law? How readest thou? And he answering said, "Thou shalt love the Lord Thy God with all thy heart, and with all thy soul, and with all thy strength, and with all thy mind; and thy neighbor as thyself" [Lev. 19:18]. And he said unto him, Thou hast answered right: this do, and thou shalt live. But he, willing to justify himself, said unto Jesus, And who is my neighbor? And Jesus answering said, A certain man went down from Jerusalem to Jericho, and fell among thieves, which stripped him of his raiment, and wounded him, and departed, leaving him half dead. And by chance there came down a certain priest that way: and when he saw him, he passed by on the other side. And likewise a Levite, when he was at the place, came and looked on him and passed by on the other side. But a certain Samaritan, as he journeyed, came where he was: and when he saw him, he had compassion on him, And went to him, and bound up his wounds, pouring in oil and wine, and set him on his own beast, and brought him to an inn, and took care of him. And on the morrow when he departed, he took out two pence [two denarii—equivalent to two days of wages for a day laborer] and gave them to the host, and said unto him, Take care of him; and whatsoever thou spendest more, when I come again, I will repay thee. Which now of these three, thinkest thou, was a neighbor unto him that fell among thieves? And he said, He that shewed mercy on him. Then said Jesus unto him, Go, and do thou likewise.

(Luke 10:25–37)

INTERPRETATION OF THE PARABLE

Whether the lawyer's initial question to Jesus is a test designed to evaluate Jesus' understanding of Jewish law or a sincere inquiry that assumes Jesus embodies wisdom that might advance the lawyer's understanding of Jewish law or a probing overture fashioned to discover Jesus' self-image is not critical to my project.[1] The lawyer's deepest motivation for posing the question to Jesus fades in significance when compared to the radical answer Jesus advances.

The lawyer's ostensible goal is to learn or confirm what he must do to "inherit eternal life." This might mean what faithful believers must do to earn admittance to eternal bliss after death, or what they should do now to prepare for their participation in the new age of the Kingdom of God on earth. These possibilities need not be taken as mutually exclusive. The crucial issue is what the lawyer, and all other faithful believers, should do in order to live their lives in accord with divine imperatives, thereby conforming their wills to that of God's.

Jesus' first answer is unsurprising: obey Jewish law. The formalistic rendering of Jewish law is straightforward: Love God completely and love your neighbor as yourself. As always, Jesus begins in revealed scripture and Jewish law. Of course, this approach is especially pertinent when responding to a question posed by a lawyer. But incisive *interpretation* of scripture and law remains paramount. Again, the lawyer's deepest motivation for asking his second question, "And who is my neighbor?" is relatively unimportant. The lawyer intuits acutely that the expression "my neighbor" is not self-executing. How many other people must his circle of concern include? Only those people within geographic proximity? All and only those members of his religious and ethnic tribe, the Jews? All and only *righteous* Jews? Or must his circle of concern expand beyond tribal boundaries?

The answer to this question is of monumental importance. If the lawyer is required to expand his concern beyond the righteous would he not thereby be a condoner or even an enabler of sin? If he is required to love those outside of his religion would he not thereby be providing consolation for the godless? The lawyer seeks guidance on the number and types of people to whom he owes moral obligations of care.

Even after having established the proper answer to the question of the appropriate scope of a person's concern, other questions would emerge. What does it mean to "love" one's neighbor as oneself? Does that mean that the lawyer must risk as much to preserve the endangered life of a "neighbor" as he would sacrifice to maintain his own life? Does it imply that a neighbor has as great a claim on the lawyer's material resources as does the lawyer? Does it mean that a neighbor has as great a claim on the lawyer's time, effort, and consideration as does the lawyer? Does "loving" one's neighbor require not only performing the appropriate *deeds* but also having the proper *disposition* toward others? Must the lawyer not only fulfill his obligations to others but do so from the only appropriate emotion: love?

Clearly, the answers to such questions cannot be extracted neatly from the plain meaning of the text of Jewish religious law. Indeed, what it means to love God with one's entire "heart, soul, strength, and mind" also requires interpretation. But the focus of this parable is the meaning of "Love your neighbor as yourself." To render an interpretation of the phrase, Jesus might have advanced a host of moral principles, policies, and theories designed to illustrate the scope of "neighbor" and the extent to which loving a neighbor requires our sacrifice, risk, forbearance, and intervention. However, as do all great teachers of morality who reside outside the classrooms of higher education, Jesus appreciates that a story can more vividly and effectively convey moral conclusions and stimulate further reflection.

So a "certain man" travels from Jerusalem to Jericho and is attacked by thieves. We should assume that the man is a Jew, although once his clothes are taken from him by the robbers that would not necessarily be apparent to others. Jerusalem is high above sea level, about seventeen miles from Jericho, which lies about eight hundred feet below sea level. The journey from Jerusalem to Jericho drops more than two hundred feet per mile and the land is virtually barren. Thieves forged numerous hideouts in the treacherous terrain.

WHO IS THE PRIEST?

Bandits rob and wound the traveler, leaving him "half dead." A priest spots the distressed traveler but "passed him by on the other side." Why might the priest have so acted? First, the priest might have been influenced by the prohibition of defilement: contact with a corpse resulted in defilement for seven days, required costly purification rituals, and priests were prohibited from all contact with corpses except those of close relatives. Priests could not conduct their official functions while defiled. Because Jews construed "contact with a corpse" broadly—to include touching what a corpse had touched, or inhaling the air exposed to a corpse, or lingering within the shadow of a coffin or grave, the prohibition of defilement required one to maintain at least a six-foot distance from corpses. The priest in the parable might have concluded that the distressed traveler was dead, beyond help, and thus "passed him by on the other side" in compliance with the prohibition of defilement.

Still, other Jewish religious beliefs would weigh against such inaction. The priest could not have been sure that the distressed traveler was dead. In fact, he was not dead. The purity laws were typically trumped by the duty of saving life. Moreover, even if he was dead, Jews were required to bury a *neglected* corpse. If the distressed traveler was dead he would surely fall into this category.

Second, the priest might have feared for his own life. The distressed traveler provided unshakeable evidence that bandits resided in the vicinity. They may well have been lurking in search of more victims. If the priest lingered while caring for the distressed traveler—who might, after all, be dead anyway—he might well be victimized himself.

Third, the priest can observe that the distressed traveler has been stripped of his clothes and was unconscious. Lacking distinctive adornment that might clearly identify him as a fellow Jew and the capability of speech which might clarify matters, the distressed traveler was not automatically seen by the priest as a "neighbor" or tribal member to whom duties might be owed.

In any event, we should not automatically portray the priest in the parable as a thoroughly disreputable moral agent. That the priest "passed by on the other side" does not necessarily translate to moral despicability. On certain formalistic readings of Jewish law, his acts of omissions could be viewed as both morally permissible and prudentially sound. Jesus, of course, was unsympathetic to formalist readings of Jewish law.

WHO IS THE LEVITE?

The second passerby is a Levite, a member of the tribe of Levi who served religious duties and bore political responsibilities for the Israelites, such as accepting tithes from the people. The Levite "came and looked on [the victimized traveler] and passed by on the other side." The Levite may well have observed that the priest had already passed by the victimized traveler. He might have taken his cue, or have been able to rationalize his antecedent inclination not to get involved, from the priest's refusal to render aid. But Levites would not be under purity regulations as stringent as those binding priests. For Levites, the prohibition of defilement concerned only their official activities. Thus, the Levite could have aided the victimized traveler even if the man was already dead. That the Levite "came and looked at him" suggests that the Levite, unlike the priest, came closer to the victimized traveler than six feet, the limit specified by the prohibition of defilement. Might he have been able to determine that the victim was still alive?

In any event, the Levite emulates the omissions of the priest and passes by on the other side of the road. As fear of defilement was not seemingly the primary motive for his decision, we are left with only his fear of being victimized himself—the thieves may still be lurking in search of more prey and may well have been using their first victim as bait—and his (possible) observation of the priest's decision. The Levite may have concluded that the priest was an authority on the interpretation of Jewish law and if the Levite acted differently from the priest he would be implicitly undermining or rejecting the judgment of his institutional superior. Would it not be arrogant for the Levite to assume that the priest was incorrect as to a theological matter or that the priest was insensitive to moral duty? He may well have concluded that, given that the priest had failed to render assistance to the victim, his own initial inclination to pass by rested on firm ground.

Of course, the simplest explanation may be that both the priest and the Levite were morally obtuse. Perhaps the priest, as a member of the temple *aristocracy*, was less than zealous about assuming risks to intervene in the predicament of what appeared to be a dead *peasant*. Perhaps the Levite, not recognizing the victim, felt little or no empathy for his situation and rationalized his disinclination to render aid by citing the example of the priest. Often, the simplest explanation is the most reasonable.

But the simplest explanation is sometimes neither the most charitable nor the most instructive. If we write off the priest and the Levite as merely morally insensitive louts, as two people who failed to fulfill an obvious moral requirement, we miss one of the lessons of the parable: the contrast between a formalistic reading of religious law and a more expansive interpretation that privileges the commandment of love. I submit that the parable is better served by viewing both the priest and the Levite as having plausible, but ultimately unconvincing, reasons for their failure to render aid. While the brief parable does not make clear the deepest motivations and intentions of the priest and the Levite, accepting their actions in the way I have suggested mirrors a contrast that pervades the scripture of the New Testament: interpreting religious law formalistically or interpreting religious law more broadly.

WHO IS THE SAMARITAN?

The surprising hero of the parable is a Samaritan. The choice is surprising because the enmity between Samaritans and Jews was longstanding and profound.

> Jews believed Samaritans to be people of doubtful descent and inadequate theology. They were thought to be descendents of people brought by the Assyrians (and other conquerors) to colonize the land. They were monotheistic, accepted only the Torah, and argued that the true temple was on Mount Gerizim. They obviously shared some convictions with the Sadducees, and in their rejection of the Jerusalem Temple were similar to the Qumran community.[2]

During the time Jesus lived, the enmity between the Jews and Samaritans had deepened because a few years earlier the Samaritans had allegedly desecrated the Jerusalem Temple during Passover by tossing human bones in the temple court. Yet even though he is speaking to a Jewish audience, Jesus selects a Samaritan as the morally superior agent to the Jewish priest and Levite.

This is comparable today to, say, a South Korean religious reformer crafting a story in which a North Korean traveler acts in a morally superior fashion to supposed South Korean exemplars. The choice of hero underscores the theme that a strictly formalistic rendering of religious law is morally inadequate.

The Samaritan accepts the Torah, which suggests that one's "neighbor" is defined by nation and tribe. Moreover, he is traveling in Judea, which makes it likely that the victimized traveler he finds is a Jew. Even though stripped of distinctive dress, unable to speak, and thus not clearly identifiable, the victim, by location alone, is unlikely to be a fellow Samaritan.

The Samaritan may well have observed or deduced the inaction of the priest and the Levite. Assuming proper timing, he either followed them while traveling in the same direction or he passed them while going in the opposite direction. Unlike the Levite, the Samaritan would have no reason to accept the priest's decision to pass by the victim as binding on him. Still, he could have concluded that if Jews thought it acceptable to pass by the (probably) Jewish victim without rendering aid, he was under no moral obligation to assume risks for this stranger.

But the Samaritan does assume risks. As a follower of the Torah, the Samaritan bears some risk of defilement should he touch or come within six feet of a corpse. He also risks the possibility that the predators that beat and robbed the victim might be lying in wait for another victim. Moreover, the Samaritan risks possible retaliation from the victim's family: "For in situations of violence, where revenge was commonly taken, an enemy (even one who helps) could easily become the object of a family's revenge."[3] Most strikingly, the Samaritan assumes these risks on behalf of a stranger, who is not, strictly speaking, a "neighbor," but is, instead, from a tribal perspective an enemy.

What does the Samaritan do for the victim? Whereas the priest "saw" the victim and the Levite "came and looked on" the victim, the Samaritan "came where" the victim was and felt "compassion." The Samaritan did not calculate the risks or weigh competing religious principles, he responded viscerally to the victim's plight. The Samaritan's immediate, intuitive response highlights that Jesus prizes the proper moral dispositions, not merely the appropriate deeds. The Samaritan is not simply doing the morally right act because logic—the rational elaboration of established moral principles and policies—declares that it is the morally right act. The Samaritan does not, thank goodness, anticipate Kantianism. Instead, the Samaritan feels compassion and responds accordingly. Remember, that religious law says "you shall love your neighbor as yourself," it does not merely demand that "you should fulfill your moral duties to your neighbor." People can fulfill their moral duties from a variety of motives that exclude love. To name only a few: people can fulfill moral duty because of their commitments to comply with the conclusions of moral logic; from hope of reciprocated benefit from others; and from belief that fulfilling moral duty will be rewarded in an afterlife. Jesus implies that all such motivations are inadequate. We must *love* our neighbors as we love ourselves. Our actions must flow from the appropriate internal dispositions. This is why the parable does not merely chronicle what the Samaritan did for the victim he comes upon. The parable must note that the Samaritan exuded the proper inner disposition toward this stranger-enemy: he feels "compassion."

Whereas the priest passes the victim by on the other side of the road and the Levite follows suit, the Samaritan pours "oil and wine" on the victim's wounds and binds them up. Commentators have noted the religious imagery: binding wounds is akin to God's actions in saving people; oil and wine are "sacrificial elements in the temple worship."[4] Whereas the priest and the Levite, officials of the temple, pass by the victim, the Samaritan emulates the divine mind-set and exemplifies profoundly the love commandment. More strikingly, he does this at some risk.

> [I]f and when the [victim] regains consciousness, the Samaritan may be insulted for his kindness, because "Oil and wine were forbidden objects if they emanate from a Samaritan." Not only have they come from an unclean Samaritan but the tithe has not been paid on them and by accepting them the wounded man incurs an obligation to pay tithes for them. He has recently been robbed and obviously has no way to pay even his hotel bill . . . the Pharisees [a Jewish sect that stressed strict adherence to the purity laws of the Torah] would have been pleased if the wounded man had shouted, "Begone, Cuthean [sinful idolater], I will have none of your oil or your wine!"[5]

Of course, the Samaritan cannot leave the victim where he has found him. He places the victim on his own donkey and transports him to an inn. We do not know whether the Samaritan rode with the victim on the same animal or whether he led the animal, carrying only the wounded man, to the inn. If the latter, the Samaritan would have voluntarily placed himself in the role of servant in order to facilitate the wounded man's well-being. Moreover, once at the inn, the Samaritan remains overnight and cares for the victim. He has not only rendered immediate assistance, gone out of his way to secure safety for the victim, and delayed his own travel and business commitments, he has also revealed his identity to the innkeeper and perhaps other lodgers.

> The Samaritan, by allowing himself to be identified, runs a grave risk of having the family of the wounded man seek *him* out to take vengeance upon him. After all, who else is there? The group mind of Middle Eastern peasant society makes a totally illogical judgment at this point.

The stranger who involves himself in an accident is often considered partially, if not totally, responsible for the accident. After all, why did he stop?[6]

The Samaritan might have merely dropped the victim off at the inn in the dark of night and fled. He might have even left some money to pay for the victim's lodging and medical care. (Although doing so might have been imprudent: innkeepers were not known for their honesty and generosity.) But the Samaritan remains with the victim and reveals his identity to others. Why? Because loving one's neighbor requires no less. Perhaps the safer path would have been enough for the Samaritan to fulfill his abstract moral duties to strangers, but the riskier course is required for those embodying the inner dispositions presupposed by the love commandment.

But the Samaritan is not finished. He gives two denarii to the innkeeper, promises to return and to pay whatever more extensive amount the lodging and medical care of the wounded man tallies. The Samaritan's commitment is a natural extension of his compassion. At this time and place, people incurring debts that they could not honor were imprisoned. Had the Samaritan not pledged to pay beyond the two denarii, the wounded man would have either not been cared for or after being attended to would have been responsible for a debt he could not pay. Thus, the Samaritan must pledge to stand as surety for the wounded man and must return to the inn sometime after his business commitments are concluded. In sum, the Samaritan has extended himself in several dimensions: he has donated his time; he has endured much inconvenience; he has invested his efforts; he has expended his material resources; and he has exposed himself to risks. He did all this on behalf of a stranger, who if conscious, would have regarded him as an enemy. Through this parable, Jesus eviscerates the prevalent understanding that one's "neighbor" is defined by nation, tribe, or geographical proximity. Moreover, Jesus underscores not merely the range of acts required to fulfill the love commandment but also the inner dispositions that must animate those acts.

Jesus concludes the parable by asking the lawyer a rhetorical question, "Which now of these three, thinkest thou, was a neighbor unto him that fell among thieves?" Of course, the lawyer to answer this question incorrectly would have had to have been morally oblivious. Still, the lawyer does not answer, "The noble Samaritan," or with some such encomium. Instead, he replies, "He that shewed mercy on him." The lawyer seemingly cannot bring himself to praise a Samaritan directly. He declines to personalize his description of the hero of the parable. One wonders whether upon leaving the scene, the lawyer will go and "do likewise" if he is ever in a position to aid a stranger in distress that is labeled an "enemy" by tribal definitions.

MORAL LESSONS

The Parable of the Good Samaritan had secular precursors, at least in regard to the particular situation described. For example, a historian, Diodorus the Sicilian (circa 80–30 BC), explains part of Egyptian law:

> Again, if a man, walking on a road in Egypt, saw a person being killed or, in a word, suffering any kind of violence and did not come to his aid if able to do so, he had to die; and if he was truly prevented from aiding the person because of inability, he was in any case required to lodge information against the bandits and to bring an action against their lawless act; and in case he failed to do this as the law required, it was required that he be scourged with a fixed number of stripes and be deprived of every kind of food for three days.[7]

Although Egyptian law of that time did not and could not prescribe that passersby "love" the victims of wrongful attacks and was unclear on what duties, if any, passersby owed to victims whom they did not actually *see* being killed or suffering violence, the law required passersby who observed unjustified violence to take explicit action and enforced that requirement with strict reprisals for violators. Moreover, the law carved no exceptions based on the national origins of victim or passerby.

Notice that in the Parable of the Good Samaritan, Jesus does not answer the lawyer's second question, "And who is my neighbor?" precisely. Like all parables, this story of morality requires the audience to reflect further. Clearly, the wounded stranger was not antecedently a neighbor of the Samaritan in any of the usual senses of that term. Instead, the Samaritan acted *as if* the wounded man was a neighbor; or he *became* his neighbor through his compassionate deeds; or he *acted as* a neighbor once he understood the wounded man's plight. The parable makes clear that moral duties and love to others is not circumscribed by the parameters typically recognized in Jesus' time: religion, nationality, tribe, or righteousness. The need of others and the opportunity of the moral agent to mollify their predicaments are crucial. Thus, no pre-determined boundary exists that would carefully delineate who is and is not my neighbor.

But how can I "love" strangers? Remember, to perform the proper deeds is not enough to fulfill the commandment; we must love our neighbors. Does it really make sense to think that the Samaritan in the parable could love the wounded stranger merely because the man had been victimized and was in dire need? Perhaps the Samaritan empathized with the victim and acted compassionately to ease his suffering, but could he actually love a person whom he had never met? After all, we have no evidence that the wounded man even recovered consciousness after the Samaritan's ministering.

Perhaps the best understanding is that we should embody a general beneficence toward humanity and an open heart toward individuals. Although we cannot literally love everyone, especially those whom we have never encountered, from the outset, we can demonstrate warmth and good will toward all, and be prepared to love those whose paths cross ours. In any event, we should surely not exclude others antecedently from our beneficence based on artificial barriers such as race, ethnicity, religion, or our evaluations of their moral worth. That the conventional wisdom of our society brands some as "enemies" does not justify their exclusion from our moral concern. At times, we may be called upon to make such people our "neighbors."

The enjoinment to "love thy neighbor as thyself" can be understood as requiring justified self-love and self-respect as a condition precedent to loving neighbors. But, typically, human beings do not need instruction in self-love. We tend to prefer our interests and appreciate our well-being quite naturally. Accordingly, Jesus is probably not urging us to higher degrees of self-regard, but encouraging us to extend our typical concern for self to others in need. Moreover, excessive self-regard amplifies into selfish acquisitiveness, and utter selflessness deflates into subservience. Both self-love and love of neighbors are required for salutary dispositions, choices, and actions. In a sense, a proper understanding of self-love requires exercising the capability of loving neighbors. Instead of perceiving the love of neighbors as an add-on or as subsequent to the proper regard for self, Jesus suggests that the love of self and love of neighbors are mutually sustaining: neither is fully possible without the other. I, no less or more than others, embody intrinsic value, and I genuinely love myself only when I love my neighbors. As such, my moral calculations should include the interests of self but not privilege them above the interests of others. My interests count no less or more than those of every other person affected by my contemplated action.

Jesus also recognizes a distinction between wrongful actions and wrongful omissions. The robbers beat and robbed their victim unjustifiably: they acted wrongly. The priest and the Levite inflicted no further harm, but they did not care enough to attend to the wounded man's suffering: they failed to act rightly. Moreover, the priest and the Levite probably appealed to established religious rules to rationalize their inaction. As always, for Jesus, formalistic interpretations and mechanical application of the results are inadequate to fulfill divine imperatives and to earn "eternal life."

But how much risk and sacrifice are we required to undertake on behalf of our neighbors? Typically, Jesus does not provide a precise answer. Even the level of the Samaritan's own risk and sacrifice are unclear. How likely was it that the bandits who robbed and beat their victim were still in the area waiting for new prey? Was this a common strategy of enterprising thieves in that area during that time? Assuming that the Samaritan was a business traveler, to what extent, if any, were his commercial interests adversely affected by his compassionate deeds? Given his material holdings, how great a monetary sacrifice did he make in paying the innkeeper for the wounded man's lodging and medical care? Even though the wounded man had been robbed, would the Samaritan be reimbursed gratefully by the man's family once those members learned the sequence of events? Or would the family be inclined irrationally to seek revenge against the innocent Samaritan? These are only a few of the questions we need to answer prior to determining precisely how great a sacrifice and risk the compassionate Samaritan voluntarily assumed.

Of course, parables deliberately omit the detailed information on their subjects that would allow the audience to craft fastidious conclusions. Such stories yield a moral trajectory; they do not end with absolute, self-executing imperatives. What it means to "love one's neighbor as oneself" remains contestable. Suppose the Samaritan was required to risk his life more explicitly in order to rescue the wounded man? Would he still be required to undertake the task?

Suppose as the Samaritan approached the wounded man, the thieves, armed and dangerous, popped out of an arid sanctuary and issued an ultimatum, "Traveler, go on your way and you will not be harmed. But try to help the man we just beat and robbed and you, too, will meet his fate!" Would the commandment to love one's neighbor as oneself require the Samaritan to risk his own life in this concrete way in order to aid the victim?

Or suppose that all else in the parable is the same, but in order to pay for the wounded man's lodging and medical care the Samaritan would have to expend most of his material holdings. Moreover, the innkeeper recognizes the wounded man as a person without a family whose members might reimburse the Samaritan, and he demands payment in advance. Also, the Samaritan's own family will suffer significantly because of their patriarch's compassionate efforts on behalf of the wounded man. Under such circumstances, does the commandment to love one's neighbor as oneself require the Samaritan to relinquish most of his finances in order to aid the victim?

I could continue to pose countless hypothetical cases to press the general point: the Parable of the Good Samaritan does not demonstrate precisely the scope and strength of the claim that a "neighbor" has on my effort, time, money, attention, and love. A literal interpretation of the love commandment might well conclude that a neighbor—all those in need whom we might aid?—has *as great* a claim on my effort, time, money, attention, and love as I do. If the notion of "claim" is off-putting—it would sound oddly offensive if my neighbor actually confronted me and claimed to have as strong a title to my effort, time, money, and attention as I do—then we can understand the imperative as placing us under the same duties toward our neighbors as we assume toward ourselves. Even if our neighbors cannot actually claim their due as a matter of right, we are obliged to extend our effort, time, money, attention, and love to them as much as we should to ourselves.

Yet, we must recognize that Jesus was not fond of literal renderings and code-book approaches to morality. While the benefit of parables flows from their vividness and emotional imprint, the morals they convey characteristically lack rigorous formulations. The proper scope of the commandment to "love one's neighbor as oneself" remains a matter of ongoing reflection.

A soul yearning for perfection should not be constrained by antecedently imposed limits: we should not define "neighbor" in ways that include some and preclude others from the outset. Perhaps the commandment is more an ideal toward which to strive than a moral imperative which must be attained: flawed, fallible human beings cannot achieve moral perfection, but in our struggle toward that goal glorious self-transformation occurs. Perhaps by cultivating the proper inner dispositions toward other people, by casting off the limitations imposed by the insularities of nations and tribes, by translating our compassion into salutary deeds, and by developing the appropriate moral habits we can nurture our characters and sculpt our souls in ways that will maximize our chances of arriving at the correct moral solutions to particular cases. Perhaps a well-ordered spirit and a disciplined character are better guides to moral virtue than carefully crafted philosophical principles and policies ... perhaps.

Most important, the parable addresses not only the need of our fellow human beings and our duties to provide succor but the effects of our actions on the people we are becoming.

> [T]he parable addresses its hearers about their own identity. Does a sense of neighbor rooted in the two love commandments—love of God and love of neighbor—define one's being? Such an identity excludes the possibility of asking about the boundaries of neighbor. Boundaries are an important means by which we establish our identities, but an identity growing out of Jesus' sense of being a neighbor obliterates boundaries that close off compassion or that permit racism and attitudes of superiority.[8]

Surely, we should abrogate biased, prejudiced attitudes toward other groups and toward strangers. We should not accept arbitrary, artificial boundaries that carve human beings into "us" and "them." Thus, we should approach others with an open heart, make everyone our "neighbor," or at least act toward them as if they were our neighbor. That part of the love commandment, as illustrated by the parable, may well strike us as compelling.

But does it follow that there are no boundaries as to what we owe our "neighbors"? Even if we accept that no boundaries can define who our neighbors are from the outset, we might well inquire as to how much we owe those whom we make our neighbors. Again, do we owe each neighbor *as much* as we would allot to ourselves? Is such a position possible to translate into action? If so, is such a social practice desirable?

Contemporary social science research casts chilling water on Jesus' enthusiasm for the possibility of widespread human unconditional love. For example, Jonathan Haidt concludes that

> It would be nice to believe that we humans were designed to love everyone unconditionally. Nice, but rather unlikely from an evolutionary perspective. Parochial love—love within groups—amplified by similarity, a sense of shared fate, and the suppression of free riders, may be the most we can accomplish . . . if religion is a group-level adaptation, then it should produce parochial altruism. It should make people exceedingly generous and helpful toward members of their own moral communities, particularly when their reputations will be enhanced. And indeed, religion does exactly this.[9]

PARALLELS IN SECULAR PHILOSOPHY

Attempts to grapple with such issues inundate secular philosophy. The most influential contemporary applied ethicist, Australian Peter Singer, argues that we are morally obligated to do much more for others, even strangers, than conventional practices admit. He begins from an observation from nineteenth-century philosopher Henry Sidgwick that "The good of any one individual is of no more importance, from the point of view (if I may say so) of the Universe than the good of any other."[10] That is, from the vantage point of the cosmos—the external perspective of an indifferent observer or of Nature itself or a deity that values all human creatures equally—the importance of an interest or need does not depend on who embodies it.

Singer's argument, first enunciated in an article called, "Famine, Affluence, and Morality,"[11] can be summarized as follows:

1. Suffering and death resulting from inadequate food, shelter, and medical care are bad events.
2. If it is in our power to prevent something bad from happening, without thereby sacrificing anything of comparable moral importance, we ought, morally, to do it.
3. Millions of human beings are in fact suffering and dying from inadequate food, shelter, and medical care.
4. Millions of human beings in affluent countries have it within their power to prevent much of this suffering and dying without thereby sacrificing anything of comparable moral importance.

Therefore, millions of human beings in affluent countries ought, morally, to prevent those sufferings and deaths.

Singer takes his first premise to be uncontroversial: that suffering and death arising from lacking basic necessities are bad events is unlikely to be contested seriously. He explains his second premise: "By 'without sacrificing anything of comparable moral importance' I mean without causing anything else comparably bad to happen, or doing something that is wrong in itself, or failing to promote some moral good, comparable in significance to the bad thing that we can prevent."[12] Although he is writing in the context of contributing to famine relief, he illustrates his principle by a Good Samaritan–type example: if a person is strolling past a shallow pond and sees a child drowning, who he might rescue easily at only the sacrifice of getting his clothes muddy, he ought, morally, to save the child. In that case, the rescuer would not be sacrificing *anything* morally significant, much less be sacrificing something of *comparable* moral importance.

The force of Singer's "ought" judgment is one of moral obligation: "'I have an obligation to' means no more, and no less, than 'I ought to.'"[13] Thus, on Singer's view, rescuing the child drowning in the pond and contributing to famine relief, under the circumstances described, are moral *imperatives*; they are not supererogatory actions—deeds that are good, go beyond the call of moral requirements, and thus are not wrong not to do.

His argument does not depend on the proximity of human need. Whereas the Good Samaritan of the biblical parable came upon a beaten victim and would otherwise have never known of his need, Singer insists that "it makes no moral difference whether the person I can help is a neighbor's child ten yards from me or a Bengali whose name I shall never know, ten thousand miles away."[14] Human beings today have access to information and communications media unimaginable in biblical times. Singer implicitly reminds us that these technological advances have moral ramifications for the questions "Who is my neighbor?" and "What do I owe my neighbor?" While physical proximity to people in dire need typically means that it is more likely that we will aid them, for Singer it does not follow that we ought to help them instead of others who live farther away. Physical proximity to people in dire need may well result in our being in a clearer position to determine what must be done and to provide immediate aid—reasons that may well impel us toward helping them first. But physical proximity as such bears no special moral significance for Singer.

Moreover, Singer's argument makes no distinction between cases where I am the only person who can supply the required succor and cases where millions are in the same position to help. If I am one of a million bystanders who watch a child drown whom any of us could have easily rescued I am no more or less morally culpable than if I was the only bystander who refused to help. In such cases, moral culpability does not divide among those who are morally deficient and thereby lessen their blame; instead, moral culpability multiplies, and all those who are morally deficient, all other things being equal, bear full moral responsibility for their inaction.

But *how much* are we morally required to sacrifice, in terms of physical risk and monetary disbursements, to alleviate the suffering and deaths of our fellow human beings who are in need? Singer's first answer to this question is severe:

> I and everyone else in similar circumstances ought to give as much as possible, that is, at least up to the point at which by giving more one would begin to cause serious suffering for oneself and one's dependents—perhaps even beyond this point to the point of marginal utility, at which by giving more one would cause oneself and one's dependents as much suffering as one would prevent [to those in need faraway].[15]

Singer recognizes the well-known principle of economics that the same amount of additional money will increase a person's well-being less, the wealthier he or she is: five extra dollars is more significant to a destitute person than to a rich person. Still, Singer struggles with the implications of marginal utility as the standard of moral obligation. He suspects that few if any people in affluent countries would eagerly embrace that standard. Thus, he offers a lower moral standard as a possibility: "we should prevent bad occurrences unless, to do so, we had to sacrifice something morally significant . . . even on this surely undeniable principle a great change in our way of life is required."[16] So his considered view at this point was that the standard of marginal utility remained the most philosophically persuasive principle of distribution, but the more moderate standard—give or risk unless in doing so you must sacrifice something morally significant—would still have revolutionary effects.

In a later rendition, Singer softened even the moderate standard. Fearful that both of his previously offered recommendations might be viewed as too strenuous by almost everyone and that people might conclude that if they cannot fulfill their moral requirements they will not even bother to try, Singer suspects that "public advocacy of [the standard of marginal utility] is undesirable."[17] We will be better off—if our goal is the reduction of absolute poverty—to advocate publicly a reduced standard that more people will embrace even though the best philosophical argument supports a much higher standard. In that vein, while conceding that any such figure will be arbitrary, Singer concludes that 10 percent of one's income is an appropriate amount for those who are relatively affluent.

> [T]hose earning average or above-average incomes in affluent societies, unless they have an unusually large number of dependents or other special needs, ought to give a tenth of their income to reducing absolute poverty.[18]

Singer recognized the radically counterintuitive implications of his position. He was self-consciously a moral reformer—the core of his project was not to validate but to transform our current moral understandings. Where our moral standards and expectations are increased, he believes that our decisions will improve: rigorous moral arguments can augur salutary changes in moral practices.

What is clear is that Singer's answer to the question "Who is my neighbor?" is "everyone."[19] Clearly, Singer renounces tribalism, discrimination based on common religion, race, ethnicity, gender, and the like from the outset. He refuses to carve the universe into friends, acquaintances, and strangers—at least for the purposes of determining whose needs should count in our moral calculus.

His theoretical answer as to how much is owed my neighbors is as much as I have to the point of marginal utility. His practical answer to that question is I owe my needy neighbors aid as long as rendering assistance does not compel me to sacrifice something morally significant; at the very least, if I am relatively affluent I ought to contribute 10 percent of my holdings to help reduce absolute poverty.

As such, Singer's position is a contemporary interpretation of the Parable of the Good Samaritan with a few modest adjustments. If taken literally, the parable of the Good Samaritan could be construed as calling for radical impartiality. To love my neighbor as myself might imply that I should allocate my resources—money, time, and effort—to others in the same way that I think I should allocate them to myself. Thus, in a forced choice situation, where I could distribute, say, a piece of food to another person or consume it myself, if all other factors are equal, then I should figuratively flip a coin to determine the recipient. That is, as between giving the food to the other person or consuming it myself, I should select the recipient randomly because under the conditions specified my "neighbor" has as much claim to the food as I do. Granted, Jesus was always suspicious of strict, code-book understandings of religious and moral law, and Jesus' description of the Good Samaritan's actions does not automatically support the literal interpretation I suggest, but that understanding remains a live possibility.

In any case, Singer's theoretical prescription of giving one's material possessions to stymie world poverty and famine to the point of marginal utility—the level at which by giving more one would cause oneself and one's dependents as much suffering as one would alleviate for the needy—approximates radical impartiality. Moreover, Singer states explicitly that "we cannot, if we accept the principle of equal consideration of interests, say that doing [a particular] act is better . . . because we are *more concerned* about Y than we are about X. What the principle is really saying is that an interest is an interest, whoever's interest it may be."[20]

Unlike the biblical love commandment and the Parable of the Good Samaritan that interprets it, Singer is not counseling universal love. His ethic is grounded in rationality and the principle of equal consideration of interests regardless of the affection one might have for the people who embody them. The biblical imperative is one of deed *and* affection, whereas Singer's ethic is only of deed. That is, Singer does not require that we feel as close emotionally to needy strangers as we do to family and friends. What he concludes—at least when he invokes the standard of marginal utility—is that any difference in affection should not translate into different treatment in terms of allocating our material resources where equal needs are at issue.

RADICAL IMPARTIALITY

Moralists who subscribe to the ideal of radical impartiality can point to a distinguished history for support. In the West, we have the biblical injunction to love thy neighbor as thyself as illustrated in the Parable of the Good Samaritan. This moral ideal was clearly meant to extend self-love to all other human beings, or at least all those with whom one comes into contact. Taken at its most uncompromising, as I have argued, this injunction commands us to manifest the same degree of concern to others that we lavish upon ourselves. Although it is inartfully crafted—as it holds out the possibility that if one is filled with self-hate or ersatz self-love such dispositions are legitimately transferred to others—it offers a powerful moral aspiration. In the eyes of the Supreme Being we are all equal and none of us merits privilege on the basis of identity alone. Instead, human beings all share claims to equal mutual concern based solely on their humanity. To transfer this notion into the language of affection: love for all humanity must be unconditional and unwavering.

But one need not be a fervent subscriber to this strain of Judeo-Christianity to find historical support for impartiality. More than four hundred years prior to the birth of Christ, the Chinese sage Mo Tzu counseled a universal human love that did not distinguish between families, friends, and strangers.

> If men were to regard the states of others as they regard their own, then who would raise up his state to attack the state of another? It would be like attacking his own . . . If men were to regard the families of others as they regard their own, then who would raise up his family to overthrow that of another? It would be like overthrowing his own.[21]

Mo Tzu explicitly advised that we should have as much regard for strangers as for our immediate families, and suggested that until we renounce partiality to immediate families we will be saddled with an incoherent and inferior moral code.

> When we inquire into the cause of these various harms, what do we find has produced them? . . . They come from hating others and trying

to injure them. And when we set out to classify and describe those men who love and benefit others, shall we say that their actions are motivated by partiality or by universality? Surely we must answer, by universality, and it is this universality in their dealings with one another that gives rise to all the great benefits in the world . . . and partiality is the source of all the great harm.[22]

In fact, on Mo Tzu's view, duties among family members could only be understood coherently as particular cases of our duties to humanity.[23] Thus, to differentiate strongly between the degrees of concern we show to intimates and to strangers undercuts the ground of all morality and fragments social life.

Unfortunately, Mo Tzu's arguments are unpersuasive. He typically assumes that only two alternative ethical outlooks are available: either universal benevolence or a partialism that disdains those outside one's immediate circle of concern, which is limited to self, immediate family, and, perhaps, close relatives. For example,

> Because he views his friend in [a partialist way], he will not feed him when he is hungry, clothe him when he is cold, nourish him when he is sick, or bury him when he dies. Such are the words of the partial man, and such are his actions . . . [The universal-minded man] will say, "I have heard that the truly superior man of the world regards his friend the same as himself, and his friend's father the same as his own. Only if he does this can he be considered a truly superior man."[24]

Likewise, Mo Tzu imagines a warrior, strapping on his gear to do battle in a distant land while his family remains in the homeland. To whom should he entrust the care of his family: to a partialist or an impartialist?

> Though one may disapprove of universality himself, he would surely think it best to entrust his family to the universal-minded man. Thus people condemn universality in words but adopt it in practice, and word and deed belie each other.[25]

The contrast, then, is always between an apostle of universal benevolence and a partialist who is, at best, indifferent to the plight of those outside his immediate circle of concern or, more typically, someone bent on harming such people. But partialism need not involve hating people outside one's immediate circle of concern or seeking to harm them. Instead, a robust partialism might embrace general respect for everyone, but special concern for those with whom one is related or intimate. Moreover, if choosing to entrust the care of one's family to an impartialist with a general, undifferentiated, diluted love for everyone and a partialist who is a family friend with special allegiance, one might well select the partialist. Surely, partialism need not be "the source of all the great harm."

Taken at its most uncompromising, the impartiality thesis demands that we assume the perspective of an ideal, detached observer when arriving at moral judgments: I must attach no special weight to my own interests when determining moral action. Moreover, the fact that another person is my spouse, my child, or my intimate friend is morally irrelevant: it provides no moral reason to favor such a person over a complete stranger. An eighteenth-century English philosopher, William Godwin, sums the view up well when he considers whom he should save in a fire, an archbishop or a chambermaid, when he can save only one: "[if the chambermaid is my wife or mother] that would not alter the truth of the proposition [about whom to save] for of what great consequence is it that they are mine? What magic is there in the pronoun 'my' to overturn the decisions of everlasting truth?"[26] We may from a moral viewpoint discriminate between people—Godwin would save the archbishop not the chambermaid—but this may be done only on the basis of *non-relational* characteristics, those that would attract the assent of an ideal, detached observer.

We must understand that the debate about radical impartiality focuses on the level of concrete moral action. All major theories of morality agree that moral rules and principles should apply to everyone alike; that I cannot make myself an exception to the moral law. The debate over radical impartiality centers on the relevant criteria of moral choice under conditions of scarcity such that we cannot all have what we need and what we want.

Crucial to radical impartiality is the vantage point from which it flows. From the standpoint of a God or Nature or an Ideal Observer each of us is equal and none of us has a legitimate claim to privilege based on identity alone. The Parable of the Good Samaritan, along with Godwin, Mo Tzu, and Singer take this God's Eye or cosmic view.

THE PERSONAL MORAL PERSPECTIVE

But human beings making moral choices in our flawed, fallible world also have personal perspectives that seem relevant. As Sidgwick pointed out

> It would be contrary to Common Sense to deny that the distinction between any one individual and any other is real and fundamental, and that consequently "I" am concerned with the quality of my existence as an individual in a sense, fundamentally important, in which I am not concerned with the quality of the existence of other individuals: and this being so, I do not see how it can be proved that this distinction is not to be taken as fundamental in determining the ultimate end of rational action for an individual.[27]

Brushing aside Sidgwick's imperial reference to "Common Sense" (in upper case, no less), his point is telling. Unlike the answer flowing from an Ideal Observer operating from a cosmic perspective, from a personal perspective identity is significant. If the chambermaid is my mother or wife I would surely rescue her to the detriment of an archbishop should I not be able to save both. In doing so, I would not be succumbing to the talismanic power of a pronoun ("my"), but would, instead, be acknowledging that based on our relationship I owe my mother or wife more than I owe a stranger. Should I select randomly and rescue the archbishop, thereby allowing my mother or wife to die, I would be subject to moral disapprobation.

Singer softens what he takes to be the best philosophical standard—give to others to the point of marginal utility—in deference, I believe, to the existence of the personal perspective.

Thus, his practical answer to the question of how much should we give needy strangers is to the point where we do not sacrifice something morally significant; and, at the very least, if I am relatively affluent I ought to contribute 10 percent of my holdings to help reduce absolute poverty.

Of course, practical considerations of limited time, effort, and resources will limit our duties to fulfilling the needs of others, even when those needs are recognized and the others are not distant strangers but known community members. Moreover, special obligations to others we voluntarily contract by dint of our occupations or personal relationships will further limit our capability of fulfilling the needs of others.

Still, radical impartiality has stunningly counterintuitive consequences for family life. Singer ultimately does take into account people with "an unusually large number of dependents or other special needs," which leads to common objections to his general view: What about my family, even if not "unusually large"? Don't I owe them much more than I owe strangers? Should I reduce my spouse and children to the point of marginal utility for the sake of strangers? Don't I owe family members more than I do others even if those other people are needier? Would not contributing even 10 percent of my holdings—Singer's most modest proposal—reduce the well-being of those closest to me?

SHOULD WE BE PARTIAL TO FAMILY AND FRIENDS?

Such questions are addressed by another contemporary secular philosopher, James Rachels. He argues that privileging family members in our moral calculus, even if deeply embedded in conventional moral wisdom, is fatally flawed because it wrongly privileges irrelevant considerations, such as luck, with moral significance:

> Suppose a parent believes that, when faced with a choice between feeding his own children and feeding starving orphans, he should give preference to his own. This is natural enough. But the orphans need the food just as much, and they are no less deserving. It is only their bad

luck that they were not born to affluent parents; and why should luck count, from a moral point of view?[28]

Rachels endorses the view that "universal love is a higher ideal than family loyalty, and that obligations within families can be properly understood only as particular instances of obligations to all mankind."[29] Finally, the conception of morality captures "something deeply important that we should be reluctant to give up. It is useful, for example, in explaining why egoism, racism, and sexism are morally odious, and if we abandon this conception we lose our most natural and persuasive means of combating those doctrines."[30]

Rachels advances a number of insights here. First, he disparages good fortune as morally irrelevant. In a world with radically unequal distribution of resources, a world which praises lavishly the partiality shown by parents to their children and by intimate friends to one another, a child's well-being is wrongly connected to facts beyond the child's control: initial starting position, material circumstances of birth, and the genetic lottery. Second, when he addresses family duties as derived from more general duties to all humans and impartiality as essential to blocking racism and sexism, Rachels is stressing that the entire history of progressive moral thinking is a story of widening our circle of concern. Tribalism is dangerously parochial from a social and moral standpoint. Carving out carefully and narrowly circumscribed loops designating "them" and "us" reflects and fosters misunderstanding and terrorizes deeper moral sentiments. We might expect this from gangs of socially deprived adolescent boys, but not from moral philosophers.

He points out that his ethic leaves room for partiality of affection ("universal love," then, should not be understood literally):

> Love involves, among other things, intimacy and the sharing of experiences. A parent shows his love by listening to the child's jokes, by talking, by being a considerate companion, by praising, and even by scolding when that is needed. Of course these kinds of behaviors also show partiality, since the parent does not do these things for all children.[31]

In that vein, Rachels offers a concession. He implicitly undercuts Godwin's position and concedes that those who advocate no difference between a person's moral requirements toward one's own children and toward other children would appear "morally deranged."[32] Nodding to the strictures of practicality and concluding that the appearance of moral derangement counts against the most radical versions of impartiality, Rachels renders his final verdict in three tiers. First, if a parent is confronted with a choice between providing the basic necessities for one's own children or providing for the like needs of other children, the parent may prefer the interests of his or her own children. So where equal needs are in play, we may permissibly prefer—"perhaps you even ought"[33] to prefer (perhaps!)—to provide for the needs of our children. Second, where the choice is between providing a benefit for our own children or a *slightly* greater benefit for other children, we may prefer fulfilling the interests of our own children. But, third, "if the choice is between some relatively trivial thing for one's own and necessities for other children, preference should be given to helping the others."[34] The overall effect of Rachels' position is that parents may provide the necessities of life for their own children first, but they are not morally justified in providing their own children luxuries while other children lack the necessities of life. Given the number of children who currently lack the necessities of life in our world, the results of accepting Rachels' moral doctrine would be revolutionary.

What constitutes a "luxury" is, of course, contestable. More stringent interpretations would classify almost anything beyond essential food, clothing, and shelter as "luxuries." Thus, even parental funding of his or her child's college education—much less the purchase of cell phones, expensive toys, fancy clothes, and exotic vacations—would count as a luxury. Looser interpretations might accept higher education as a necessity of sorts, but distinguish between the costs acceptable at a state university and the "luxurious" expense of a private institution.

The call to deemphasize partiality to family members resonates in the words of Jesus. The Kingdom of God must be sought above all else. Family, relatives, and friends are of trivial concern by comparison. Jesus goes so far as to say that people must "hate" their family as a prerequisite for being a genuine disciple (Luke 14:26; Matt. 10:37). Although we need not take "hate" literally, the term and context surely advise followers to distance themselves from their families. Jesus' own family relations were strained as evidence exists that his family members rejected his message and that he distanced himself from them (Mark 3:31–34). Jesus was keenly aware that family divisions would dog his message (Luke 12:51–53; Matt. 10:34–46; Mark 13:12). Those who view the historical Jesus as an apocalyptic prophet conclude that Jesus

> [w]asn't teaching about the good society and about how to maintain it. The end was coming soon and the present social order was being called radically into question. What mattered was not, ultimately, the strong family ties and social institutions of this world. What mattered was the new thing that was coming, the future Kingdom. It was impossible to promote this teaching while trying to retain the present social structure.[35]

Those who take the historical Jesus to be a Cynic philosopher would see him as spreading the Cynic creed of radical individuality which rejects the view that family affiliation and affections are required for personal fulfillment. Such interpreters would view Jesus as offering a revolutionary social program somewhat independently of the advent of the Kingdom of God.[36]

PARTIALISM VERSUS IMPARTIALISM AS GENERAL BENEVOLENCE

The appeal to impartialism challenges those who embrace conventional wisdom to sharpen their position. Those aspiring to retain a robust preference for family and friends over the general needs of strangers might revisit the link between differences in affection and differences in material allocation. Either impartialists (a) permit no differences in our affectionate concern for family and our "love" for strangers or (b) they do permit such affectionate differences but conclude that they should not translate into differences in the way we allocate our material resources (or, at the very least, those differences in allocation should be severely limited). I'll call the first impartialist view *universal* or *general benevolence* and the second impartialist view *affectionate difference*.

Who has ever held the universal benevolence position? The answer is not clear, but here are the candidates: Mo Tzu and Jesus. Mo Tzu states the view most clearly, but a strict rendering of the biblical love commandment and the Parable of the Good Samaritan that interprets it makes Jesus a strong possibility. After all, the love commandment is not merely about deeds and the allocation of resources but also relates to the distribution of our affection. The Good Samaritan was not simply acting on some principle of reason that established his moral duty; he was acting from his "compassionate" heart and was responding viscerally to a stranger's (an "enemy's") need.

Although Godwin has an extreme impartialist view, he need not be interpreted as requiring a universal benevolence or an undifferentiated affection; Singer avoids speaking about affections and proudly positions his view as demanded solely by reason; and Rachels understands explicitly the need for parents to lavish more affection on their own children than upon children generally. Thus, they are not candidates for the universal benevolence view.

How might an advocate of conventional wisdom undermine the universal benevolence approach? First, a defender of family partiality might argue that the universal benevolence approach has an impoverished understanding of the value of personal relationships. In a world where people are equally fond of everyone, strangers and family alike, the good news is that the maladies of racism, sexism, religious intolerance, and the excesses of tribalism would vanish. We could well speculate that the overall amount of global happiness would increase. Still, the bad news is that the special joys of intimacy, family affection, and deep love would also evaporate. Radical impartiality of feeling is incompatible with the kind of profound personal relationships that distinguish a robustly meaningful human life. Moreover, we might argue that the sorts of dispositions and virtues—such as honesty, loyalty, caring, patience, empathy, and the like—that comprise the moral enterprise can be learned only from personal relations characterized by partiality of concern.

Although this is a reasonable argument, the universal benevolence approach has a plausible response: Is it so obvious that the overwhelming majority of human beings would choose our present world over a world embracing universal benevolence? The answer may well depend on whom we ask. Certainly those of us who have a reasonably satisfying network of personal relations would agree with the advocates of conventional wisdom; but those of us who suffer from intense, unsatisfied basic needs and who have experienced mainly stormy, frustrating personal relations may dissent. Taken as a world survey, which group predominates?

Second, a defender of family partiality might argue that personal relations have an inherent value and a phenomenology that transcends the requirements of impartial benevolence. Personal relations are not merely different in degree from impersonal relations, they are different in kind: the metaphors of mutual bonds, connectedness, attachments, although faintly capturing the truth, are too effete. Two Sicilian slogans from my youth are helpful in expressing the metaphysical differences between familial and impersonal relationships: *sangu du me sangu* ("blood of my blood"—to indicate the metaphysical links among grandparents, parents, and children) and *nun aviri famigghia e comu essiri un nuddo miscatu cu nenti* ("to be without family is to be a nobody mixed with nothing"). Our families, relatives, and closest friends do not merely interact with us at a distance; instead, they partially constitute who we are: they help define our values, they help sculpt our self-understandings, and they widen our subjectivity beyond the self. If we substitute a tepid universal benevolence for the partiality of intimate relationships, we alter personal identity in dangerous ways. Moreover, the very notion of "love" presupposes partiality. I cannot love everyone even if I am disposed to do so. Love, as opposed to a general benevolence toward all humankind, requires, among other things, participating in common enterprises, sharing information about oneself that is not available to the general public, and spending more time with the beloved than with acquaintances and strangers. Thus, I cannot "love" everyone if for no other reason than I am strictly limited in terms of time, geographic location, and general resources. Brushing aside factors such as my incompatibility with certain personality types, my inability to find numerous other people yearning for intimacy with me, and the like, the phenomenology of love is inherently partial. Accordingly, the imperative of general benevolence inaugurates the doom of interpersonal love.

Again, this is a powerful argument from the standpoint of current social theory and practice, but the prophets of general benevolence have a plausible response. The likes of Mo Tzu and Jesus could argue that the alleged present benefits of family partialism arise only because our present world is fragmented and tribal. In a world characterized by invidious comparisons, ongoing zero-sum contests, and stark distinctions between friends and foes, the consolations of family and intimate relationships seem irresistible; such connections offer refuge from and warmth within a generally hostile environment. But the prophets of general benevolence call upon us to eclipse our present world and transform the planet. In a world where principles of general benevolence were widely embraced, the phenomenology of our needs and satisfactions would change. We would no longer require the comforts of oases from general hostility and estrangement because the overall environment would be one of caring and concern. Although teasing out the specific details of a world we have never known would be overly speculative, the point is that critics of the principle of general benevolence cannot assume present social conditions and the phenomenology of intimate relations as unalterable givens without begging the most important questions at issue (that is, assuming as true that which must be proven as true).

Third, a defender of family partiality might argue that to require people to determine all of their important decisions by impartial consideration of global needs is to destroy the notion of personhood itself. The assumption here is that personhood presupposes partiality in the sense that one's identity and personal integrity must consist in part of projects, aspirations, and life's plans that have unique status in a person's priority of values simply because they are hers.[37]

An interesting question arises. Could a prophet of general benevolence respond that with the proper moral education and socialization the general welfare, at least insofar as it involves satisfying the basic needs of everyone, could in fact become our project, life's plan, and highest aspiration? Is there necessarily an incompatibility between thinking and acting impartially, and one's integrity? Could it not be the case that the reason partialists now suspect that there is such an incompatibility is that as an empirical and contingent matter most people are radical partialists? But is this an inevitable feature of human nature? Or is it a sad commentary on the primitive, parochial level of our moral education and socialization?

John Cottingham, a contemporary English philosopher, would be unconvinced by the questions I have raised on behalf of general benevolence:

> A world in which I accorded everyone at large the same sort of consideration which I accord to myself, my children and my friends would not be "one big happy family"; it would be a world in which affection no longer existed because the sense of "specialness" had been eliminated. It would be a world where much of what gives human life preciousness and significance had disappeared.[38]

One of Cottingham's points is that an ethic of general benevolence transforms each of us into a type of dispassionate, bloodless, conscientious bureaucrat who never displays favoritism when allocating public resources. To partialists, this evenhandedness constitutes a feckless moral ideal because two of the paramount points of the moral enterprise are personal transformation and social nonfungibility.[39]

We return to the questions which haunt advocates of general benevolence: Despite their protestations to the contrary, can they truly accommodate a moral universe where individuality and intimacy remain? Is a universe of impartiality truly a better world on balance than the partialist world that presently dominates our moral thinking?

For their part, Mo Tzu and Jesus could retort that many of the charges hurled by partialism are question-begging. They may charge that partialists, instead of establishing that currently accepted notions are necessary features of human beings, merely presuppose the values of the dominant social order and then simply show how the ideal of general benevolence fails to instantiate those values. If so, then all the partialist has done is show that when judged by partialist standards, the principle of general benevolence will fail. But after all, part of the general benevolence program is to unsettle and transform precisely those partialist values and standards. The advocates of general benevolence may argue that instead of exposing embarrassing implications of general benevolence, all the partialist has done is restate part of the program of general benevolence and register shock. But this response was to be expected from the outset: the entrenched social order is unlikely to welcome a threatening challenger.

Fourth, partialists will insist that the principle of general benevolence is utopian in a pejorative sense. Invoking the "common sense" of Sidgwick, partialists will point out that human beings neither parcel out their affection nor their material goods indiscriminately. We devote much more care, time, and resources to our own plans and projects, and to our own self-development and fulfillment, than we can even begin to conceive of devoting to the needs of humanity generally.

As an empirical matter, partialists are correct. But surely the advocates of general benevolence, such as Mo Tzu and, possibly, Jesus, do not deny this description of current and past practice. The real debate is whether our dominant social practices can and should be transformed. Partialists take the prevalence of common practices as strong (dispositive?) evidence that the ethic of general benevolence is beyond our grasp. Because partialists are also firmly convinced that any concentrated effort to strive for the ethic of general benevolence is accompanied by devastating costs—loss of genuine personal relationships, compromise of the individual's integrity and self-identity—they argue that the quest for this impossible dream is ignoble: we cannot achieve general benevolence and we should not struggle for it.

The advocates of general benevolence ask us to look around this world and see what the dominant practices have wrought. They perceive partialists as overly pessimistic and point out that wide acceptance of general benevolence would not be onerous on any one individual, group, or nation, and would facilitate great overall benefits in the world. Instead of viewing prevalent past and current practices as data for circumscribing what is possible, advocates of general benevolence view them as embodying numerous moral errors that should be repudiated: to limit artificially our social possibilities by accepting the past as dispositive of the future destroys moral progress.

On the level of reason, the debate between the conventional wisdom of partialism and the revolutionary aspirations of general benevolence is inconclusive. Most readers probably find themselves favoring a version of the partialist position, for most of you, by virtue of being in a position to read literature of this type, are not engaged in a brutal struggle for survival. Your probable distance from necessity permits innovative reflection on the terms of social life. But you also have or possess a reasonable chance for a network of relatively satisfying personal relations, and have deeply assimilated dominant social and moral norms. You are the readers to whom partialists can confidently appeal when favorably comparing "our" world with the hypothetical conditions of general benevolence. You appear to have much to lose and relatively little to gain, both materially and emotionally, from a conversion to general benevolence. Furthermore, even if you sympathize with the aspirations of general benevolence, and I speculate that most of you do, you will probably suspect that the burden of persuasion rests with the advocates of general benevolence. That is, no conclusive argument is available on questions such as these: Is human nature inherently and inevitably partialist? Can personhood exist in a world of general benevolence? Can intimacy persist where we do not favor some people in terms of the emotional and spiritual? Therefore, the advocates of general benevolence must convince us to change our minds because our default mind-set registers partialism. Moreover, you are undoubtedly very skeptical about the prospects that the institutions of family and intimate associations can be restructured in a way that preserves their unique values to personal integrity and growth, yet embodies an ethic of general benevolence.

By virtue of enjoying an occupation that permits me to write essays such as this, I am one of you. Advocates of general benevolence focus on the principle of equality, as interpreted from a cosmic vantage point, as definitive of morality. Indeed, Jesus describes relations in the Kingdom of God and invites human beings to prefigure those associations today. In fact, the principle of equality is only one of many principles required for full moral assessment; and the cosmic vantage point is only one interpretive perspective. Accordingly, partialists may well claim that advocates of general benevolence generate disturbing implications only because they wrongly reduce morality to one of its component principles and judge from one interpretive perspective. Although I am not convinced that general benevolence can be proved logically unsound or empirically impossible, neither can general benevolence persuasively alter our default moral theory and practice. Paradoxically, general benevolence might be most successful in an atmosphere of relatively abundant resources where universal benevolence would be less taxing for us all: precisely the atmosphere where general benevolence would be least necessary.

Where general benevolence is most needed, in circumstances of deprivation and scarcity, it may be least persuasive because great numbers of people are preoccupied with a brutal struggle to obtain life's necessities. This paradox suggests another facet of the problem: a serious coordination problem attending general benevolence. Even those who deny the partialist conclusion that our world is preferable to a world of general benevolence must grapple with the fact that an individual's choice is not simply between our world and one of general benevolence; instead, the choice is between our world and acting *as if* we are in a world of general benevolence. Acting as if a world of general benevolence existed does not, in the absence of millions acting likewise, establish the presumed paradise. The pressing question is whether I prefer acting in accord with the partialist norms of our present world or acting in accord with the norms of general benevolence while the vast majority of human beings are acting in accord with the partialist norms of our present world. Accordingly, even someone who is moved by the ideal of general benevolence and who is seduced by its transformative possibilities has a further question to address: Does it make moral and practical sense for me to act on that ideal while millions of other human beings remain partialists?

PARTIALISM VERSUS IMPARTIALISM AS AFFECTIONATE DIFFERENCE

The philosophical impartialism of Singer and Rachels does not require general benevolence of sentiments. Rachels' ethic explicitly allows parents to love their children more than the children of others. He understands that parental love will demonstrate partiality when sharing experiences and nurturing intimacy: parents cannot foster such sharing and nurturing with all children. Moreover, an insipid general benevolence would inadequately provide for children's emotional needs: children need to be regarded as special in a way that general benevolence makes difficult, if not impossible.

Although accepting affectionate differences, Rachels adopts a three-tiered impartialism as described above. The critical feature of Rachels' ethic is that the interests of one's children should not always be paramount when the interests of other children are at issue. When the choice is between benefiting one's children and benefiting other children equally then fulfilling the interests of one's children may (even should) assume priority; when the choice is between benefiting one's children and benefitting other children only slightly more, Rachels' ethic, again, permits privileging the interests of one's children; but if the choice is between bestowing a luxury on one's children or providing necessities for other children, priority should be given to aiding the other children.

The rhetoric trick here is to label the fulfillment of certain interests as "luxuries," a phrase that carries morally pejorative baggage and obscures the real choices most parents face. Because the basic needs of children range beyond the merely material (as Rachels concedes), any reasonable interpretation of where to draw the line between basic needs and luxuries may leave most parents—even those antecedently drawn to impartialism—with precious few material and emotional resources to even consider allocating to the basic needs of strangers. Moreover, the application of Rachels' three-tier ethic is murky: a large chasm exists between what rises only "slightly" above a basic need and what might reasonably be viewed as a "luxury."

Suppose I provide my children a meal that is slightly more costly than the most abstemious entrée available. Would that be permissible under the second tier? Probably, because food is a basic need for both my children and other children. Would funding a typical birthday party for my child qualify? On one hand, it seems part of making my child feel special, but, on the other hand, whether it amounts to a basic need is contestable. Would not contributing that money to famine relief be a better choice under Rachels' ethic? While buying my child a Mercedes Benz automobile strikes us as an obvious luxury, how should we feel about the choice of buying my child a used Chevrolet versus taking that money and contributing to the basic needs of strangers? In our time and place is ownership of a motor vehicle a luxury? Should parents consider funding their child's college education at a state university a luxury? Or does luxury come into play only when they support their child's decision to go to a pricier, more prestigious private institution? Rachels admits that "Clearly, the line between the trivial and the important can be drawn at different places."[40] But I would submit that where we draw that line is critical for understanding our moral obligations under his ethic. The task is especially important for the vast majority of parents who are in a position to confer few "luxuries" of any sort upon their children.

The strength of Rachels' ethic is that he accepts affectionate differences. On his view, we can regard certain people as special: We can enjoy their company more than that of others; mourn their deaths more than the deaths of strangers; revel in their happiness and successes in a way in which we do not rejoice in those of others; spend more time with those whom we see as special and care for them in circumstances and in ways in which we would not look after others. In short, Rachels' ethic distances itself from a radical equality of allocation of emotional and spiritual resources. As a result, Rachels' version of impartialism can accommodate the type of personal relations many of us cherish.

Still, an issue arises as to the relationship of intimacy, in the sense of one's emotional and spiritual allocations, and the distribution of one's material and service goods. That is, while it may be true that Rachels' ethic allows us to see certain people as special, mourn their losses more than those of others, and rejoice in their happiness, may we also distribute material goods and provide aid in sufficient measure to our intimates? Surely, unlike Godwin, Rachels would permit us to rescue the chambermaid who is our mother and not the archbishop; after all, the choice is between equal basic goods. But what if my choice is this: if I save my mother she will survive as she was prior to the incident, but the archbishop will perish; if I save the archbishop he will survive as he was prior to the incident, and my mother will struggle to safety, survive, but remain in a predominantly vegetative state until she perishes twenty years later? The cases no longer involve exactly equal needs. Is saving my mother a "luxury" as she will not die in either case? Should I save the archbishop, who is a stranger, but who will otherwise die?

The key here is to unravel the connection between acting, on emotional and spiritual levels, like someone is your intimate friend and thus special, and often remaining impartial when allocating paramount material and service goods. Is it plausible to act as if someone is your friend, to tell that person that you are friends, yet at the moment of need toggle to a default moral position of impartiality where equal basic needs are not involved? If adherents to Rachels' ethic must embody a moral schizophrenia toward their family and friends, then the general criticism that impartialists cannot truly integrate a coherent understanding of personal relations may persist. That is why drawing the lines among (a) equal basic needs, (b) slight additional benefit to intimates, and (c) luxuries is so crucial.

Singer seems unconcerned about emotional attachments. At its most uncompromising his argument derives its conclusion from impartially considering interests and needs wherever they may exist and to whomever they may belong. For Singer, the moral point of view requires the principle of equal consideration of interests: we must give equal weight in our moral deliberations to the like interests of all those affected by our actions. An interest is an interest, whoever's interest it may be. The principle of equal consideration does not depend on a belief in factual equality, the belief that all people of all interest-bearers are actually equal in relevant physical and mental respects. Instead, the principle depends on the conviction that the most important interests, such as the interests in avoiding unnecessary pain, in developing one's talents, in fulfilling basic needs, in enjoying personal relationships, and in being free to pursue projects, are not affected by factual inequalities. Thus, the moral point of view requires that my own interests cannot, simply because they are my interests, count more than the interests of anyone else. In this fashion, moral reasons are universal—they rise above our own likes and dislikes and ascend to the standpoint of the impartial spectator or ideal observer—which elevates them from the merely relative or subjective.

From the application of the principle of equal consideration, he derives his philosophically preferred position: the standard of marginal utility—relinquish your material holdings to fulfill the basic needs of others up to the point where further donations would render you and yours to the same level of destitution that you seek to ease. His two later renderings—give to the point where you are not thereby sacrificing something morally significant and the 10 percent solution—are made only in deference to the difficulty of persuading people in a thoroughly partialist world to accept a stronger obligation to help those in need than they presently recognize.

Singer's standard of marginal utility does not reflect our biological inclinations, which decidedly favor partialism. Can we retain deeply felt love-bonds but mete out our resources and service goods impartially? Does a type of moral schizophrenia result that undermines personal integrity? Does Singer mistakenly privilege only the cosmic perspective, that of the ideal observer—and thereby betray Sidgwick's "Common Sense" that the personal perspective should not be marginalized?

Of course, Singer retreats from the standard of marginal utility for practical reasons, some of which may be reflected in the rhetorical questions I have just posed. But I would argue that those questions do not merely reflect *practical* difficulties in implementing the standard of marginal utility, but cut to the very core of its *philosophical* acceptability. In that vein, regarding my time, effort, and material holdings as public resources reneges on my self-conception as an individual. Much of life can be viewed as a negotiation between our need for robust individuality and our competing need for intimate community. Each yearning offers great reward but, if amplified, morphs into great disappointment. Thus, my yearning for robust individuality nurtures a feeling of specialness and uniqueness, underwritten by autonomy and freedom; but if I inflate my sense of individuality I may unwittingly invite estrangement, alienation, and hostile isolation. Meanwhile, my yearning for intimate community attaches me to projects, interests, and purposes that widen my subjectivity and connect me to larger concerns, thereby fulfilling my need to share my life and cooperate closely with others; but if I inflate my sense of community I may unwittingly suffocate my individuality, retreat too broadly from autonomy and freedom, and reduce myself to a pathetic drone in the social hive. Singer's standard of marginal utility may well be viewed as distorting the dimension of community to dangerous caricature. If so, a critic might well conclude that a healthy dose of individualism and personal perspective is required to balance communal obligations and to produce a salutary morality. When the cosmic perspective reigns supreme, we are acting as impersonal spectators or detached deities, not as human beings.

Moreover, the standard of marginal utility jeopardizes the principle of personal desert. Typically, we accept that people deserve the holdings that they have justifiably earned through their labors. Some of these holdings, the ranting of libertarians to the contrary notwithstanding, are properly relinquished, usually through taxation, to enterprises facilitating the common good.

But, if in the name of morality, the demands on our sacrifices are pushed to the standard of marginal utility then the principle of desert is under siege. To say that I initially deserve my holdings, but I must, morally, use them to fulfill communal needs up to the point of marginal utility renders my initial claim vacuous. Why not simply appoint a Marquis of Morality who removes the requisite amount from my holdings straightaway? In which case, the notion of initially deserving my holdings evaporates in the name of full disclosure. Of course that would be coercive and involve an identifiable third party, whereas Singer's principle is designed to convince right-thinking people to disgorge their holdings voluntarily. But that seems a minor detail for those antecedently committed to the alleged moral point of view. The acceptance of the standard of marginal utility produces the same effect as would the hypothetical Marquis of Morality. Once a well-intentioned agent voluntarily accepts Singer's standard of marginal utility, he or she is committed to the same results as a person who voluntarily remains in a land ruled by the Marquis of Morality. In both cases, the principle of desert struggles for its existence on life-support. The call "from each according to ability, to each according to need," may resonant in a communist paradise of material abundance, but it rings a sour note under the typical conditions of economic scarcity. Paradoxically, the standard of marginal utility and the Marxist slogan of economic distribution are most convincing under the conditions where they are least needed.

Finally, Singer's methodology is subject to several objections. First, he may be guilty of wrongful reductionism when he derives his concrete moral conclusions from only a few moral principles and observations. Just as libertarians can conclude smugly that all economic redistribution and taxation is theft because they operate only from the moral discourse of negative rights and duties, Singer can conclude that massive redistribution is morally required because he employs only the discourse of equality of interests. Both positions ignore a host of other morally relevant considerations that might alter their conclusions. Second, Singer's analogy between saving a victim in a pond and contributing to famine relief is problematic in that the number of destitute people who are starving is enormous, while the number of people we encounter drowning in ponds whom we could rescue is probably zero or at most a few. If we encountered or knew of countless drowning victims whom we could save—if their number was comparable to the amount of people presently starving—our intuitions about what we owe to such victims might well change. At some point, very early I would think, we would conclude that we had given or risked enough and that it was time for others to assume their fair share of the burden.

But why spend time trying to whipsaw the standard of marginal utility when Singer retreats from that demand and offers two more reasonable alternatives: giving to the point where we are not thereby sacrificing something morally significant and the 10 percent solution? First, Singer continues to cling to the standard of marginal utility as his philosophically preferred position. His later modifications are only pragmatic concessions. Second, and more important, the standard of marginal utility and the approach of general benevolence may well best reflect Jesus' understanding of the love commandment as interpreted by the Parable of the Good Samaritan.

Jesus, like Mo Tzu, privileges the cosmic perspective. Of course, his ideal observer is God. Jesus is unwilling to pay homage to Sidgwick's "Common Sense" and acceptance of the personal perspective as a critical factor in drawing moral conclusions. Moreover, living in a culture and at a time when luxuries were fewer and less splendid than today, Jesus is concerned almost exclusively with matters of the soul. Whether we understand the "Kingdom of God" to mean eternal bliss in the hereafter or the imminent reign of the divine on earth or a state of mind attainable in the present, Jesus advocates that we prefigure the Kingdom of God in our intentions and actions. Whether we conclude that the historical Jesus was precisely as he is depicted in the canonical scriptures or that he was an apocalyptic prophet or a Middle Eastern Cynic philosopher does not alter that message. Whether Jesus was only talking about short-term moral behavior because he was convinced that the reign of the divine on earth was imminent or whether his was a long-term Cynic prescription does not change his radical interpretation of the love commandment. Furthermore, Jesus does not subscribe to what we now take to be bedrock family values. Parents, siblings, spouses, children, and friends have minimal importance when compared to the Kingdom of God. He advised his followers to renounce, among other things, their families (Luke 14:26). Jesus recognized the counterintuitive aspects of his teaching and insisted that his message will divide, not unite, families (Luke 12:51–53).

Thus, Jesus would reject the justifications of partiality to families that I have lodged. Also, in many biblical parables (for example, the Parable of the Laborers in the Vineyard) Jesus distances himself from a conventional understanding of the principle of personal desert. Often in such parables, people will be given more than they deserve, and others who resent that allocation will be scolded for their hardness of heart. (But in such parables people never receive *less* than that to which they are entitled. Does that complicate matters?) Finally, and most strikingly, Jesus takes God to be the genuine owner of everything. Thus, when we give to the poor we are not actually relinquishing what we initially deserved through our labors; instead, we are merely redistributing God's holdings in accord with God's law. In effect, by respecting religious and moral law, we are giving back to God what is God's. From such a perspective, Jesus would rule irrelevant virtually everything I have sketched in my brief for conventional moral and political wisdom.

Although Jesus would not rely on the arguments advanced by Mo Tzu, he would join the Chinese sage in extolling the ethic of universal benevolence. Whether we view Jesus' ethic as a short-term preparation for the Kingdom of God or a long-term solution to human social interactions, his moral perspectives vary radically from the conventional moral wisdom of his time and of ours.

NOTES

1. The section on the interpretation of the parable has been informed by Klyne R. Snodgrass, *Stories with Intent* (Grand Rapids, MI: William B. Eerdmans Publishing Company, 2008); Craig L. Blomberg, *Interpreting the Parables* (Downers Grove, IL: InterVarsity Press, 1990); Richard N. Longenecker (ed.), *The Challenge of Jesus' Parables* (Grand Rapids, MI: William B. Eerdmans Publishing Company, 2000); Kenneth E. Bailey, *Poet & Peasant Through Peasant Eyes* (Grand Rapids, MI: William B. Eerdmans Publishing Company, 2000); J. Duncan M. Derrett, *Law in the New Testament* (London: Darton, Longman and Todd, 1970).
2. Snodgrass, *Stories with Intent*, 345.
3. Sylvia C. Keesmaat, "Strange Neighbors and Risky Care," in Longnecker, *The Challenge of Jesus' Parables*, 281.
4. Derrett, *Law in the New Testament*, 220.
5. Bailey, *Poet & Peasant*, 50–51.
6. Ibid., 52.
7. Diodorus Siculus, *The Library of History*, trans. C. H. Oldfather (Cambridge, MA: Harvard University Press, 1933), book 1, sec. 77, para. 3.
8. Snodgrass, *Stories with Intent*, 357–58.
9. Jonathan Haidt, *The Righteous Mind* (New York: Pantheon Books, 2012), 245, 265.
10. Henry Sidgwick, *The Methods of Ethics* (London: MacMillan and Company, 1874, 7th ed. 1907), 382.
11. Peter Singer, "Famine, Affluence, and Morality," in Peter Singer, *Writings on an Ethical Life* (New York: HarperCollins, 2000), 105–17.
12. Ibid., 107.
13. Ibid., 337, n. 2.
14. Ibid., 107.
15. Ibid., 109.
16. Ibid., 115.
17. Peter Singer, *Practical Ethics* (Cambridge: Cambridge University Press, 2011), 180.
18. Ibid., 181.
19. Singer also famously enlarges his circle of concern to include the interests of nonhuman animals. See, for example, Peter Singer, *Animal Liberation* (New York: Random House, 1975).

20. Peter Singer, "Is Racial Discrimination Arbitrary?" *Philosophia* 8 (1978): 197.
21. Mo Tzu, *Basic Writings*, trans. Burton Watson (New York: Columbia University Press, 1963), 40.
22. Ibid., 39–40.
23. Ibid., 42–43.
24. Ibid., 41.
25. Ibid., 42.
26. William Godwin, "Enquiry Concerning Political Justice" (1798), quoted in Don Locke, *A Fantasy of Reason* (London: Routledge, 1980), 168.
27. Sidgwick, *The Methods of Ethics*, 498.
28. James Rachels, "Morality, Parents, and Children," in James Rachels, *Can Ethics Provide Answers?* (Lanham, MD: Rowman & Littlefield, 1997), 213–33, 215.
29. Ibid., 213.
30. Ibid., 215.
31. Ibid., 223.
32. Ibid., 230.
33. Ibid., 231.
34. Ibid.
35. Bart D. Ehrman, *Jesus: Apocalyptic Prophet of the New Millennium* (New York: Oxford University Press, 1999), 171.
36. See, for example, John Dominic Crossan, *Jesus: A Revolutionary Biography* (San Francisco: HarperSanFrancisco, 1994); *The Historical Jesus: The Life of a Mediterranean Jewish Peasant* (San Francisco: HarperSanFrancisco, 1991); F. Gerald Downing, *Jesus and the Threat of Freedom* (London: SCM Press Ltd., 1987); B. Mack, *A Myth of Innocence* (Philadelphia: Fortress, 1988).
37. See, for example, J. J. C. Smart and Bernard Williams, *Utilitarianism: For and Against* (Cambridge: Cambridge University Press, 1973), 116.
38. John Cottingham, "Ethics and Impartiality," *Philosophical Studies* 43 (1983): 90.
39. See, for example, John Kekes, "Morality and Impartiality," *American Philosophical Quarterly* 18 (1981): 298–99.
40. Rachels, "Morality, Parents, and Children," 231.

TWO

The Prodigal Son: "All That I Have Is Thine"

And he said, A certain man had two sons: And the younger of them said to his father, Father, give me the portion of goods that falleth to me. And he divided unto them his living. And not many days after the younger son gathered all together, and took his journey into a far country, and there wasted his substance with riotous living. And when he had spent all, there arose a mighty famine in that land; and he began to be in want. And he went and joined himself to a citizen of that country; and he sent him into his fields to feed swine. And he would fain have filled his belly with the husks that the swine did eat: and no man gave unto him. And when he came to himself, he said, How many hired servants of my father's have bread enough to spare, and I perish with hunger! I will arise and go to my father, and will say unto him, Father, I have sinned against heaven, and before [against] thee. And I am no more worthy to be called thy son: make me as one of thy hired servants. And he arose, and came to his father. But when he was yet a great way off, his father saw him, and had compassion, and ran, and fell on his neck, and kissed him. And the son said unto him, Father, I have sinned against heaven, and in thy sight, and am no more worthy to be called thy son. But the father said to his servants, Bring forth the best robe, and put it on him; and put a ring on his hand, and shoes on his feet: And bring hither the fatted calf and kill it; and let us eat, and be merry: For this my son was dead, and is alive again; he was lost, and is found. And they began to be merry. Now his elder son was in the field: and as he came and drew nigh to the house, he heard music and dancing. And he called one of the servants, and asked what these things meant. And he said unto him, Thy brother is come; and thy father hath killed the fatted calf, because he hath received him safe and sound. And he was angry, and would not go in: therefore came his father out, and intreated him. And he answering said to his father, Lo, these many years do I serve thee, neither transgressed I at any time thy commandment: and yet thou never gavest me a kid, that I might make merry with my friends: But as soon as this thy son was come, which hath devoured thy living with harlots, thou hast killed for him thy fatted calf. And he said unto him, Son, thou art ever with me, and all that I have is thine. It was meet that we should make merry, and be glad: for this thy brother was dead, and is alive again; and was lost, and is found.

(Luke 15:11–32)

INTERPRETATION OF THE PARABLE

The younger of two sons asks his father for his inheritance.[1] This may well have been taken as tantamount to wishing his father dead. At least, the request is unorthodox and signals a fractured relationship. Moreover, upon receiving the money, the younger son leaves his family and strikes out on his own in a distant land. In so doing, he abrogates his share of the future responsibility to care for his aging father.

In accord with Jewish religious law, as between two brothers inheriting an estate, the older would receive two-thirds of the property and assume primary responsibility for caring for aging parents. The younger brother might receive the remainder, but not in the instant case. The prodigal son of the parable would not be likely to receive land, but perhaps a portion of the monetary equivalent. In any event, he would not have received authority to sell any family land while his father was alive. Some commentators conclude that the younger son would have received the monetary equivalent of two-ninths or less of the family estate.[2] That the father was willing to grant his younger son's precipitous request anticipates the father's later effusive generosity and love.

> In light of the implications of the request, it is all the more remarkable that the father concurs. In the Middle Eastern milieu the father is expected to explode and discipline the boy for the cruel implications of his demand. It is difficult to imagine a more dramatic illustration of the quality of love, which grants freedom even to reject the lover, than that given in this opening scene.[3]

The prodigal son, then, begins with several moral deficiencies. His request demonstrates conclusively that he undervalues his relationship with his father; that he is unconcerned about his future responsibility to help care for his aging father; that he is avaricious and is overly concerned with material accumulation; and that he yearns to cast aside highly respected agricultural work and to leave his family, underscoring his feckless values and broken relationships. That the younger son did not consult with his older brother prior to lodging his inheritance claim shows additional disrespect for family relations. Most important, leaving the family land signals a significant change of identity; the prodigal son seeks to distance himself from his family and his past, and to remake his self-image.

His conduct after receiving the early inheritance only compounds his depravity: he squanders his money with "riotous living." A reader might be tempted to end analyzing the parable at this point and conclude that the moral of the story is transparent: young and ignorant is a poor combination to attain worldly or spiritual success; young, ignorant, with money guarantees worldly and spiritual failure.

But there is much more to learn. The prodigal son scampers off to a "far country," presumably inhabited by Gentiles. He exhausts his money foolishly on "riotous living," the nature of which our imaginations can speculate. Then a great famine strikes the land—to ancient minds perhaps symbolic of divine retribution—and the prodigal son becomes a field hand who cares for the swine owned by a citizen (undoubtedly a Gentile) of the forsaken country. The prodigal son is reduced to collaborating in his own shame. To an ancient Jew, few labors would have been considered more despicable than caring for swine. The Old Testament stigmatized swine as unclean; eating and even touching swine were proscribed.

Formerly a privileged offspring of a respected patriarch, the prodigal son is reduced to lusting after "the husks that the swine did eat" and to desperation as "no man gave unto him." Moreover, he has wasted the family's property among Gentiles. The prodigal son has relinquished his manhood, and shamed himself and his family.

At some point, we fantasize that every young person will be struck by an epiphany, a transforming experience where ignorance is supplanted by enlightenment, where degradation is redeemed by goodness, and where shame is banished by aspiration. Unfortunately, such salutary episodes elude too many of our youth. But this is a parable with a purpose. The prodigal son "came to himself" and decides to go home and throw himself on his father's tender mercies.

To what does "came to himself" translate? Does the prodigal son simply evaluate the situation, understand that his options have evaporated, regret his infelicitous handling of his money, and decide to pursue his only genuine possibility? If so, then the prodigal son is not remorseful for his sins, but regrets only that he squandered his funds unwisely and now strives to make the best of his deplorable situation.

Or does "came to himself" signify that the prodigal son now actualizes the better angels of his nature? He now realizes the goodness that has always lain within him, but that only now does it arise from his deprivation: having nothing left to lose, the prodigal senses a newly won freedom from the bondage of material possessions and comes to terms with his "true self."

Or does "came to himself" dispense with the baggage of finding one's true self and connote, instead, the prodigal son's sincere repentance? After all, he vows that he will confess his sins against both heaven and his father. But which sins? Is he repenting only his foolishness in wasting his money which has led to his shame of family and self? Or is he thoroughly remorseful for having asked prematurely for his inheritance and all that that request signified about his values and relationships?

Despite the confidence of some commentators in one or another, these conclusions are all plausible but contestable. The prodigal, however, does recognize that his past actions disqualify him from calling himself his father's son. He will ask only to become a hired servant.

> As a "hired servant" he will be a free man with his own income living independently in the local village. His social status will not be inferior to that of his father and his brother. He can maintain his pride and his independence. But there is more. If the prodigal becomes a hired servant, he may be able to pay back what he has lost.[4]

On this reading, the prodigal son wants to redeem himself in the only way available to him under the circumstances. Perhaps the timing of the prodigal's remorse is less important than its fact. While the prodigal may well have been fully remorseful at the moment he "came to himself," he had certainly attained that state after luxuriating in his father's bountiful welcome upon his return home. The only difference is whether he achieved full remorse independently or whether his partial repentance blossomed into full remorse upon his father's gracious acceptance of his return. The point of the parable disappears if we suppose that the prodigal son acted only strategically when he "came to himself" and that he remained only a rational calculator of his interests upon his return.

So the prodigal son decides to return. While still a "great far off," his father spots him and runs to him. In fact, a dignified patriarch with flowing robes would almost certainly not run after anything. Such action was considered beneath such a man. Of course, the father in our parable is not an ordinary man. That he would run, once again, highlights his uncommon love of and generosity toward his son.

Prior to his son's return, would the father have known about the young man's plight? Would he have been awaiting his son's return? Not likely. His son had traveled to a "far country," and communication, if any, would have been difficult and slow. Moreover, the prodigal would not have been anxious to broadcast his escapades and their results prior to coming "to himself." Also, we have no reason to think the prodigal had allies or foes in the far country that might have transmitted word to the father. Of course, the father may have anticipated that his younger son would receive an infelicitous reception and craft an ignoble result in the far country. The patriarch would undoubtedly understand keenly that a young, ignorant man with money would curry worldly and spiritual failure. More strikingly, that the father saw the prodigal while he was still a "great far off" symbolizes the patriarch's ongoing concern and vigilant aspiration that his wayward son would return. If and when that moment occurred—if he who was lost could be found—the father would be well prepared.

The father's unconditional love of his son, again, resonates: he "fell on his neck and kissed him." He does not issue recriminations; he does not scold his son for his malfeasance; and he does not seek explanations. When his son blurts out, "Father, I have sinned against heaven, and in thy sight, and am no more worthy to be called thy son," the father does not respond directly to the assertion. Instead, he instructs servants to fetch a robe, ring, and shoes, and prepare a feast. By his words and actions, the father demonstrates his forgiveness of and visceral reconciliation with his son.

For his part, if he was not fully remorseful upon undertaking his return home, the prodigal is now totally cognizant that his underlying sin "against heaven" and his father was his fracturing of their relationship. The son did not and could not have carved away at his father's love for him. His father's love was unconditional and thus even if it was unrequited it would persist. But through his earlier actions, the prodigal had destroyed or revealed the already-decrepit state of their relationship. Unlike love which can be merely one-sided but nevertheless genuine, relationships by definition require more than one participating party. A person cannot maintain an unrequited relationship.

To assume at this point in the parable that the father has forgiven his son is natural. But we might question whether forgiveness is the appropriate description. To forgive another person presupposes, among other things, that one person recognizes that another person has wronged him. In virtually any other case, that understanding would fit our story crisply. But does the patriarch in the story conform to that rubric? As an embodiment of unconditional love, an exceptionally high bar for human beings to attain, did he acknowledge that his son's earlier actions had wronged him? If so, why did he condone those actions? After all, the father could have refused his son's unorthodox request and sought immediately to repair their relationship through conventional channels. Is it possible that the father's unconditional love blinded him to his son's moral deficiencies and prevented him from denying anything to his son? Was the father, in effect, an unwitting collaborator in or an enabler of his son's weak moral will? If so, perhaps the father, despite prevalent cultural understandings at the time, never perceived that his son had wronged him and never conceptualized a transgression to be forgiven. In that vein, we should appreciate that the father's unconditional love for his son already transcended the cultural norms of his day, and a person can be insulted only if he takes another person's actions to be insulting.

That the father's kiss and embrace of his son symbolize reconciliation is beyond dispute; it takes at least two parties to reconcile and repair a relationship. That the father's words and actions constitute forgiveness is less clear. Maybe the father separated the son's wrongful actions from the son's person ("hate the sin, love the sinner"). Perhaps the father granted his son's request as a last resort to facilitate a future reconciliation. That is, anticipating that his son, upon receiving his inheritance, would react foolishly, the father was convinced that only by permitting his son's folly and waiting for his son to come to his senses, would the two men ever repair their relationship. Such strategy would be beyond risky. What if the son got lucky and parlayed his inheritance into a fortune? Or what if the son was extremely unfortunate, consorted with an unsavory crowd, and was murdered for his money?

In any event, we can safely conclude that either the father had recognized that his son had wronged him and all was now forgiven or the father never acknowledged that his son had wronged him so there was nothing lingering to forgive. Notice that in either case the prodigal son has no reason to offer to become one of his father's hired servants, and he does not. That the father is prepared to accept him fully and reinstate complete family privileges is transparent from the father's actions and from his instructions to his servants to gather a robe, ring, and shoes for the returning prodigal and to prepare a feast. The father's unconditional love, reflecting God's limitless grace and expansive compassion for human beings, transcends contractual boundaries. Forgiveness and reconciliation resist the constraints of arms-length bargaining.

Notice also that the father had not undertaken to find his son in the "far country" or to influence his conduct after the disposition of his estate. The prodigal son remained a free man responsible for his deeds. If a person is to be transformed and redeemed, he or she must not be subject to external compulsions. Salvation requires a level of awareness and contrition. In the instant case, the prodigal must reach out to his father.

The father's dash to meet his prodigal son and his conjuring of a feast may signal the need for his son to repair relations with his community. Surely the wider community would have taken the son's request for an early inheritance as insulting and presumptuous. By doing the extraordinary and rushing out to meet his returning son, the father sends a message to his society: I bear only joy at my son's return. By having his servants slay the fatted calf and prepare a feast, the father invites some members of the community to participate in that joy. We must assume that people outside the immediate family attended the celebration as this was customary when a calf was slaughtered. The prodigal son's fractured relations with his community must also be repaired. In any case, I cannot overemphasize that the father's reactions to the return of his son, like his embodiment of unconditional love, are not typical of patriarchs of his time and place. He may well represent the divine spirit tending to the fallibilities of the human flock.

In all of this the stress is on personal transformation and redemption: "For this my son was dead, and is alive again; he was lost, and is found." Once the prodigal son leaves his father's home and the wider community he was in effect morally and spiritually dead. Stunningly, he "came to himself" and was reborn. Nurtured by the unconditional love and graciousness of his father, we must conclude that the prodigal son will now maximize what has hitherto lain dormant within him. He will grow into a worthy member of family and community, who evinces high moral and spiritual values. The son has always had the potential to attain this end but for whatever reasons needed to undergo a certain painful process in order to actualize his highest attributes.

But what are we to conclude about the elder son? Although he was not consulted by his younger brother prior to the initial request for an early inheritance, he, too, received his share: "And he divided unto *them* his living." The older son has remained within the family and wider community and it may seem that his relationships are intact. But first impressions, like destitute relatives and sales overtures from telemarketers, are not always what they seem.

First, the older son had an obligation to broker peace between his father and the younger son. He either ignored that obligation or failed miserably in his efforts. Instead, he accepts his share of the early inheritance. Second, his reaction to the feast demonstrates the frailty of his family relations. The older son resents the attention lavished on his younger brother, is angry at his father for his generosity to the prodigal, and refuses to participate in the feast. In fact, the older son would have been expected not only to attend the feast but to discharge certain ceremonial duties. Third, when his father pleads with the older son to share in the festivities—an entreaty that should have been unnecessary—the older son is churlish. He complains that he was never given even a measly baby goat to celebrate with his friends, yet the father now has the prized fatted calf slain to celebrate the return of a son who has squandered his money with "harlots." (How does the older son know this? Is he only projecting his own subconscious desires?) One is tempted to interject, "Poor, baby, you already have the bulk of your father's estate but still think it appropriate to whine about not being given a goat to share among your friends for no reason other than to make merry. Ever think there might be an asymmetry between the animating causes of your hypothetical celebration and the instant case?" The older son does not recognize that his father, under conventional understandings, might well have rebuked him severely for not attending the feast and for not discharging his family duties. Fourth, the older son reveals the spirit in which he has contributed in the past to the family: "these many years do I *serve* thee." He has regarded his relationship with his father as one of servant to master. He has neither recognized nor accepted his father's unconditional love. Fifth, the older son has a formalistic, narrow understanding of morality. He claims never to have transgressed a commandment and he assumes that doing no harm is equivalent to moral goodness. In short, he recognizes the stringency of negative moral duties, which require us to refrain from certain actions, but ignores the importance of positive moral duties, which require us to perform certain actions. To conclude that the older son is insecure, obsessed with his place in the family hierarchy, self-absorbed, and even mean-spirited is undeniable.

Indeed, the older son is obtuse and radically misunderstands the nature of unconditional love. Such love is not finite, not a commodity to be divided among its claimants like so many slices of a delicious pie. When allotting desserts, supply often cannot fulfill demand. But the economics of unconditional love are different. Unlike a coveted pie, where unconditional love resides, its supply can always fulfill demand: the father does not love the older son less because he now exuberantly welcomes back the prodigal son. The father loves both of his sons equally and unconditionally; he makes that clear to the resentful young man: "Son, thou art ever with me, and all that I have is thine." Moreover, the father makes clear to his older son what should have been stunningly obvious to him all along: "It was meet that we should make merry, and be glad: for this thy brother was dead, and is alive again; and was lost, and is found." The family celebrates exuberantly when one of its own is transformed and redeemed; what was fractured has been healed. Will the older son "come to himself," repair his own broken familial relationships, and bask in his father's grace and generosity? The parable ends without suggesting the answer. What is most important is that the older son has been invited to join the congregation of those rejoicing. Whether he will participate with a full heart and open mind remains a pressing question. We can only hope that he will "come to himself."

The two sons bear resemblances: "One is lawless without the law, and the other lawless within the law. Both rebel. Both break the father's heart. Both end up in a far country, one physically, the other spiritually. The same unexpected love is demonstrated in humiliation to each. For both this love is crucial if servants are to become sons."[5] In both cases, we wonder how such an evidently special father could have sired and raised such ungrateful and insensitive scions. Both sons are lost in the sense that their family relations are inadequate: the older son feels like a servant, while the younger son, prior to his return, valued his father's material goods more than he treasured his father.

The Parable of the prodigal son glistens with numerous lessons: sinners can and should repent their transgressions and seek personal transformation and redemption; participants and third parties should facilitate and rejoice in the redemption of others; where unconditional love resides, forgiveness of transgressions is warmly available when penitents are willing to embrace it; just as the historical Jesus associated with undesirables such as tax collectors (who typically collaborated with Roman oppressors and skimmed profits from overcharging their compatriots), lepers (in violation of purity laws), and prostitutes, we, too, should not simply write off those who are stigmatized as incorrigible; and to be a full member of family and community requires much more than the proper bloodline and geographic position—a proper understanding of salutary relationships is required as is the appropriate disposition of heart and soul.

Still, questions linger. From a divine perspective, the notion of unconditional love may resonate. But can human beings genuinely love others unconditionally? If so, what is the object of such a love? If human beings can love others unconditionally is such affection limited to parent-child relationships? Can spouses love each other unconditionally? If so, is such a love desirable?

THE PARADOXES OF AGAPIC LOVE

In the parable, the father's love of his sons seems to be agapic.[6] If a person loves another person agapically, then the beloved person's characteristics, properties, and actions are irrelevant to the lover's affection. The beloved person's perceived value as determined by individuating attributes would simply not be the ground or object of the love. On this conception, the lover loves the beloved person unconditionally. The love would be unwavering: even if the beloved person is ungrateful, even if the beloved person does not love in return, even if the lover has perceived the beloved person's personal qualities inaccurately, the lover would still love the beloved person. As such, agapic love aspires to surmount all obstacles and persist through all vicissitudes. Regardless of how the character of the beloved person changes, the lover's amorous regard remains constant. The lover desires the best for the beloved even if acting on those desires results in her self-denial. Instead, agapic love creates value in the beloved person: by dint of his love, the father bestows value upon the prodigal son and offers the same to the older brother.

However, agapic love is more easily described than experienced. The genesis of the concept is biblical. God presumably loves all of God's creations agapically. Even if some human beings stray from the moral law repeatedly in the vilest fashions, God loves the sinner while despising her sins. God's act of creation and ongoing affection bestow value upon us. Beyond resolute divine affection, parents often seemingly love their children agapically. Despite the disappointing actions or unworthy character development of their offspring, many parents remain thoroughly loving.

Characteristically, Jesus demonstrates that agape overrides religious custom. Accused by the Pharisees of violating the religious prohibition of working on the sabbath, Jesus replied, "What man shall there be among you, that shall have one sheep, and if it fall into a pit on the sabbath day, will he not lay hold on it and lift it out? How much then is a man better than a sheep? Wherefore it is lawful to do well on the Sabbath days" (Matt. 12:10–12; Mark 3:2–4; John 9:14–16).

Still, the paradox of agapic love is undeniable: on the one hand, the object of agapic love is supposedly a distinct individual, not merely a set of properties. The father in the parable loves *the prodigal son* and *the older brother*; he does not love everyone or, as far as we know, anyone else agapically. But, on the other hand, if a person's properties are irrelevant how can we distinguish one person from another? Stripped of all constitutive and accidental properties, what remains of a person? And if we are all the same once we are divested of our individuating properties, then why love *this* person instead of *that* person? How is the prodigal son genuinely the object of his father's love if none of the sons' properties are relevant to the father's love?

This paradox arises even in the case of God, who presumably loves all of God's human creations equally regardless of their individuating properties or moral worth. God's love is not discriminatory or partial. God may love human beings not for their individuating characteristics, but for their participation in a general humanity. Thus, Neera Kapur Badhwar observes that

> Agape can, consistently be unconditional in the sense of being independent of the individual's *personal* nature and worth—of that which distinguishes him from other persons—but not of his *human* nature and worth—of that which distinguishes him from non-humans. Agape also, in other words, must be of the individual for what he is, even though only qua *human being*, and not qua *person* . . . But what is the evidence for this common humanity, this equal potential for worth or virtue that we all, supposedly, share? There seems to be no *empirical* evidence . . . the only way to sustain belief in a universal potential for goodness is by means of a transcendental metaphysics of the person (in the religious version, the idea of man as created in the image of God).[7]

However, according to religious doctrine, that God agapically loves the spark of the divine embodied by every human being is unlikely. That would transform an agapic love into an egocentric self-love: God would love that aspect of every human being that reflects God's own image. Again, we must ask: Exactly what is it that God loves agapically?

Some thinkers argue that agapic love excludes all self-love and all desire to obtain something for the lover. Thus, Anders Nygren argues that

> God does not love in order to obtain any advantage thereby, but quite simply because it is His nature to love—with a love that seeks, not to get, but to give. This means, in other words, that no teleological explanation or motivation of His love can be entertained . . . God does not love that which is already worthy of love, but on the contrary, that which in itself has no worth acquires worth just by becoming the object of God's love. Agape has nothing to do with the kind of love that depends on the recognition of a valuable quality in its object; Agape does not recognize value, but creates it.[8]

On this view, agapic love has no external grounds, but, instead, flows from the internal nature of the lover. Moreover, the agapic lover seeks nothing from the bestowal of love. Finally, God is not responding to the common humanity of human beings—their potential for worth, value, or virtue—or to the spark of the divine they presumably embody. Instead, God's agapic love is selfless, spontaneous, unmotivated by factors external to God's nature, indifferent to the value or potential for value of God's beloved creatures, and independent of desire and longing.

Although acute in several respects, Nygren's portrayal deepens the mystery of agapic love. If God *must* love agapically because of God's basic nature, does that suggest that God's love is not freely bestowed? If God's love is utterly unmotivated by any external considerations, must that imply that God's love is independent from all desire?

For example, why cannot God freely bestow agapic love upon human beings because he desires to create value thereby? Why cannot God have other-directed desires such that God wishes to elevate human beings—enhance their worth and value—through God's love? On such a view, God's agapic love is motivated, but by reasons still internal to God's nature. That is, God would not be recognizing or responding to the antecedent, external condition of human beings, but God would be choosing to enhance the value of God's own creations.

Oddly, although Nygren emphatically concludes that God's agapic love is spontaneous and unmotivated, he later describes agape as the initiator of fellowship with God:

> In the relations between God and man the initiative in establishing the fellowship lies with Divine Agape . . . all the other ways by which man seeks to enter into fellowship with God are futile. This is above all true of the righteous man's way of meritorious conduct, but it is no less true of the sinner's way of repentance and amendment . . . God must Himself come to meet man and offer him His fellowship. There is thus no way for man to come to God, but only a way for God to come to man: the way of Divine forgiveness, Divine love.[9]

I will not consider at this time whether Nygren has described accurately the *only* way that human beings can attain fellowship with God. But he has identified a possible internal motivation of God's agapic love: to offer fellowship to human beings. Presumably, God desires that human beings accept this fellowship, and God is pleased (or satisfied or fulfilled or gratified) when they do. If so, Nygren's previous explanation of agapic love—as completely free from desire, seeking no end, and indifferent to the potentials of the beloved—must be adjusted.

Perhaps we can conclude that God's agapic love flows from God's desire to elevate the worth of his human creations—either by offering fellowship or bestowing value directly by means of love; that God further desires that human beings will make the most of God's love; that God benefits in some way when that occurs, either by being gratified or pleased or the like; that whatever benefits God garners from extending love are not God's prime reasons for loving; that God's love toward all human beings remains unconditional, even if his offer of fellowship is repudiated by some individuals; that while God's love is not motivated by external factors, we can identify possible internal motivations; and that God's agapic love is thus bestowed for the sake of human beings.

Such an understanding of agapic love drains some of its mystery while remaining faithful to its widely accepted basic contours. That God benefits in some way when human beings accept God's offer of love does not imply that God's love is egocentric, acquisitive, or fundamentally selfish. On the contrary, a God lacking other-directed desires would be a strange being. (Perhaps such a God would be akin to an Epicurean deity utterly indifferent to and unaware of the external world.) That God aspires to the mutual good of fellowship with his human creations does not dilute the glory of agape, but, instead, enhances our understanding of the phenomenon. Moreover, "selfishness" connotes ignoring the interests of others when one ought not to do so—a notion completely inappropriate in this context. That a moral agent, divine or human, gains fulfillment or gratification from advancing the interests of others counts in the agent's favor; it is not a factor that degrades the quality of the action or the actor. Would it not be bizarre to aid other people in important ways yet remain utterly indifferent to the success of your deeds? Morally deficient people typically lack other-directed desires, while those of us who embody and act on such desires are more likely to fulfill our moral obligations.

Moreover, my revised understanding of agape retains the basic dimensions of the phenomenon: unconditionality, constancy, creation of value in the beloved, arising from the nature of the lover, not directed to only those deemed antecedently deserving, not derived from the perceived antecedent worth of the beloved, and not motivated by acquisitive, egocentric concerns. By stripping the concept of agape of its more mysterious elements, we render this type of love more accessible and compelling.

If we understand the Christian notion of agapic love in this way, it strays from the dominant understanding of Jesus' time. Conventional Jewish wisdom of Jesus' day was that God loved righteous worshippers but did not love the unrighteous, the sinner, or the heathen. As always,

Jesus' radical message conflicts with standard rule-book interpretations of religious and moral law. Just as Jesus consorted freely with prostitutes, tax collectors, and those deemed unclean—in opposition to the received wisdom of his culture—his interpretation of the love commandment, both in terms of divine and neighborly relations, rings a revolutionary chord.

PARENTAL AGAPE

But how, if at all, does agape relate to human affection? Nygren believes that human agape arises from divine agape. First, he sketches human agape:

> Agape-love is directed to the neighbor himself, with no further thought in mind and no sidelong glances at anything else . . . When my neighbor happens to be also my enemy, obviously no reason for my loving him can be found in his own character or conduct . . . unless love for one's neighbor is directed to the neighbor alone, unless it is concerned exclusively with him and has literally no other end in view . . . then it has no right to the name of neighborly love.[10]

Nygren concludes that the efficient cause of such love must be God's loving nature.

> God is not the end, the ultimate object, but the starting point and permanent basis of neighborly love . . . It is not as the "Prime, Unmoved Mover" that God sets love in motion, but He is Himself involved in its motion. Being Himself Agape, He brings forth Agape. It is not as being loved, but as loving, that God sets love in motion . . . Since God is Agape, everyone who is loved by Him and has been gripped and mastered by His love cannot but pass on this love to his neighbor. In this way God's love passes over directly into the Christian's love for his neighbor.[11]

Thus, on this view, God's love empowers people to love even their seemingly unlovable neighbors. The object of such love must be the spark of the divine that even our enemy embodies.

Of course, this view leaves unexplained how someone who has not self-consciously embraced God's love could nevertheless love agapically. Although God supposedly loves all his human creatures equally, that not all of us are "gripped and mastered" by that love is clear. Many (most?) human beings easily resist the call to "pass on this love" to neighbors. Thus, those who do respond positively to God's love and who do pass on that love even to "enemies" must bring something to the love relationship with God that others do not.

The most likely place to begin our inquiry into human agape is with parental love. I would argue that if parental love can be agapic, it need not be viewed as the simple passage of God's love from parents to children. Given that even nonbelievers and otherwise disreputable parents have the possibility of bestowing such love, we cannot persuasively account for the phenomenon by invoking Nygren's view of why some human beings can love their supposed enemies.

But the paradoxes of agapic love, again, arise in the case of parents. If some parents love their children agapically, then the children's constitutive attributes, character development, choices, and deeds, are irrelevant to sustaining that love. What, then, is the basis of and what is the object of such a love?

I would argue that if parental agapic love is possible—and I think that it is—such affection bears both similarities to and differences from divine apagic love. For example, if parents love their children agapically, unlike God, they can still differentiate them from all others whom they do not love agapically: Angelo and Vittoria are *my* children; I helped create them; we are in the world together, we share one flesh; in a certain metaphysical sense, we are not fully separate and distinct. Such parents begin with affectionate feelings toward their offspring. These feelings reflect their sense of agency in the act of procreation, their visceral acceptance of the parent-child bond, and their place in an ongoing generational chain that widens their subjectivity. Such feelings and the phenomena that underwrite them *cause* parents to believe that their children are inherently and objectively valuable independently of their children's choices, deeds, and future development. Thus, in parental agapic love, at least one property of the beloved does seem relevant: "that this is my child" distinguishes the person whom the parents love agapically from the numerous other human beings that the parents do not love unconditionally. This enduring *relational* property, then, belies the tradition that insists that agapic love is *completely* devoid of attention to the properties of the beloved.

Yet, it is true that such parental love is neither completely selfless nor independent of desire. Here Sidgwick's "Common Sense" is validated: we are concerned with the quality of our existence as individuals in a sense that is fundamental and different from our concern with the quality of the existence of other individuals. If I am correct, the metaphysical connection that some parents recognize with their children extends that "Common Sense" preference from self to progeny. Moreover, the phenomenon of parental agapic love is thereby not experienced as merely a bestowal from self to "other." Again, parents and children with the requisite metaphysical connections are not fully separate and distinct. Understood in this fashion, parental agapic love cannot be selfless. Nor is such love free of desire: the procreative process typically originates in desire, and the yearning to deepen metaphysical bonds often continues as children grow. Because the parent-child bond in such cases precludes the members from being fully united and fully distinct, agapic love is also underwritten partly from other-directed desires.

Obviously, not all parents embody the feelings described for their children or bestow the agapic love depicted. I am trying to capture the phenomenology of parental agapic love as it occurs in our world. I do insist that parental agapic love does sometimes happen. To what extent and how frequently is contestable. Consider a case that I will present as a hypothetical but which I am certain has actually occurred: Parents conceive, bear, and raise their child to young adulthood. To other people, the child embodies little if any social value. He is rude, obtuse, rebellious, surly, and a sociopath. Draw the details as starkly as you prefer. Yet his parents, although heartbroken by his choices and actions, love their child agapically. Finally, the child decides to perform the ultimate treachery. He loads a shotgun and murders his father in front of his mother. He then turns to his mother and prepares to shoot her. With her final gasp, the mother whispers, "I love you," to her despicable son. With the mother's death agapic love expires.

My understanding of parental agapic love in our world can help explicate the Parable of the Prodigal Son. The father's metaphysical connection to both his sons animates his agapic love for both: "All that I have is thine." Both of his sons acted imprudently, selfishly, and, most importantly, in utter ignorance of their father's love for them. Or, perhaps, worse: they may have been aware of their father's affection for them but, nevertheless, declined the invitation to reciprocate. Had either son, at any point, have chosen to slay their father we must assume that the patriarch's final words to his murderer would have been, "I love you."

Taken at the human level instead of the allegorical divine level, the father in the Parable of the Prodigal Son loves both of his sons unconditionally. From the earlier discussion, I take this to be a bestowal of affection often found in our world today. Although elements of the parable would have been viewed suspiciously from the vantage point of dominant parental practice during Jesus' time, in our own time it may conjure warm memories of parents whose love overlooked our shortcomings and transgressions for the sake of the family unit. The reality of agapic parental love must be heeded. Taken at the divine level, the parable reminds us that repentance and forgiveness remain genuine possibilities; that God loves us unconditionally and seeks our fellowship; and that a resolute will and open heart ensure that personal transformation is always possible.

Of course, the parable may well be best understood as an allegory of God's love for God's human creations. Surely, Jesus was uninterested in sentimentalizing family relations in his world. Thus, the historical Jesus might well be completely indifferent to my analysis of contemporary parental agapic love. In fact, Jesus might regard parental agapic love as an obstacle to the universal benevolence that captured his interpretation of the love commandment: to the extent that parents love their children agapically they are less likely to allocate their resources impartially and more likely to circumscribe their circle of concern. Thus, my analysis of parental agapic love should be taken as a way to understand a worldly phenomenon, not automatically as the message Jesus intended to send by way of the Parable of the Prodigal Son.

AGAPE AND ABSTRACTION

To dismiss agapic love as hopelessly abstract and ethereal—as I was tempted to do earlier—is too facile. Jesus' instruction in the Parable of the Good Samaritan is that our neighbor is anyone we meet who is in need (or anyone who is in need, whether we meet them or not); loving our neighbor requires us to fulfill those needs if possible; and loving our neighbor requires more than the appropriate actions—it requires that we act from the proper dispositions of compassion. To regard our neighbors appropriately, then, requires an unconditional affection toward them that spurs us to fulfill their needs. Such love is not grounded in their merit, past service to us, or our hope for reciprocal benefit. Instead, Jesus insists we must love our neighbor agapically and concretely.

The question arises as to whether such love is possible. Perhaps a few people, totally devoted to service to others might approximate this ideal, but is the ideal of agapic love unreasonable for the overwhelming majority of people? Yes, a few exemplars such as Mother Teresa might stand as contemporary illustrations of the lessons of the Parable of the Good Samaritan, but can this ethic be universalized? The rest of us have families to raise, careers to foster, and responsibilities to discharge.

The radically egalitarian ethic of Jesus, however, paid little attention to careers, explicitly distanced people from their families, and took our highest responsibility to be nurturing our souls and those of our neighbors. When we bestow agapic love upon our neighbors we reflect an image of God's unconditional love for us. By surrendering to God's love, we open our hearts to higher purposes. In loving our neighbors agapically we recognize their inherent dignity and make them subjects of our concern, regardless of their personal deserts and other entitlements. We are in the world together as equal participants in the stream of life. Moreover, although agapic love is often depicted as affection that is utterly distinct from attention to the beloved's properties, a more precise rendering is recommended. God's agapic love is directed toward his human creations, and, thus, the property of "being a human creation of God" is implicated in divine agapic love. Human agapic love of neighbors also attends to a general property in the beloved: the image of God, the spark of the divine that every human being presumably embodies. Our regard for our neighbor is grounded in one unalterable, universal property of human beings, not in special attributes or traits that distinguish individuals. As such, each neighbor's well-being is equally important. Jesus did not enjoin human beings to love everything agapically, but only to love God and to love our neighbors unconditionally. As such, human agapic love is not truly a bestowal of value upon others after deliberation; instead, it acknowledges the value in others that God has already bestowed.

In the words of Soren Kierkegaard:

> Your neighbor is every man, for on the basis of distinctions he is not your neighbor, nor on the basis of likeness to you as being different from other men. He is your neighbor on the basis of equality with you before God: but this equality absolutely every man has, and he has it absolutely.[12]

Because agapic love of our neighbors is neither preferential nor personal, it cannot serve as the basis or the starting point of erotic love or friendship love, both of which are inherently preferential and personal. An issue arises as to whether agapic love of neighbors is genuinely the love of a person. Stripped of all constitutive attributes, relationships, past deeds, deserts, other entitlements, and the like, what remains of the concrete individual? When we love our neighbor unconditionally, do we truly love her as a unique person? Surely, if we love agapically we do not love our neighbor because of her identity, but, still, we must focus on the concrete individual to determine the nature and extent of her needs and which of her needs we ought to fulfill. Each of our neighbors will be different in these regards, at least to some extent. That is, to structure the acts appropriate to express our unconditional love for our neighbors we must attend closely to their individuating characteristics and circumstances. Given that agapic love of neighbors requires both the proper affection and the appropriate deeds, the concrete individual does not disappear. Unconditional love cannot require identical treatment of all neighbors, for so doing would ignore the fact that our neighbors do not always share the same needs; agape must focus, instead, on equal consideration of different needs. Accordingly, unconditional love of neighbors does not imply fungibility—that one neighbor is indistinguishable from and replaceable by another. I may well love all my children equally and unconditionally, but it hardly follows that I view them as indistinguishable from or replaceable by each other.

Although most of us can identify, at best, only a few practitioners of widespread unconditional love in our world, the enjoinment to love our neighbor agapically is not merely an abstract, contentless slogan. To approximate the ideal requires great sacrifice—relinquishing the pursuit of most of the values and prizes that the world cherishes, including robust family relations, individual status, and career possibilities—but that should not surprise anyone who attends to Jesus' moral message: we are to prefigure now the more genuine values and prizes of the impending Kingdom of God.

EROTIC AGAPE

Another category of lovers must be assessed in terms of apagic love: sexual or erotic lovers, who must confront an even thicker paradox of agapic love. Is such a love based on the constancy of the lover's nature and not at all on the beloved person's nature? Must such a love be grounded in illusion or philosophical error? Is the lover simply infatuated with the idea of being in love?

Moreover, that we should *want* to be loved unconditionally by our spouse is unclear. Although such a love provides much consolation—after all, no matter what we do and how we act we will still bask in love—but provides little incentive for personal growth. Why strive mightily to realize our idealized possibilities when doing so presumably does not matter to our lover? Granted, we may have other reasons to actualize our highest potentials. But, typically, we would believe that some motivation to do so should arise from our love relationship. We do not have to be committed apostles of an abstract Platonic theory of love to suppose that erotic love should elevate us and spur our growth.

We might conclude charitably that even though agapic love is not hostage to whether the beloved person realizes her ideal possibilities, the lover still cares whether the beloved person grows because doing so will enhance the beloved person's well-being. On this reading, regardless of whether the beloved person attains his highest potentials or whether he descends to the dark side of his nature, the lover will still love the beloved person; but the lover can still urge the beloved person toward self-improvement because, as always, she desires the best for the person she loves. Moreover, apart from the other reasons given, the beloved might strive to realize her ideal possibilities not in order to entice her lover to love her more (as that is by stipulation impossible), but instead as a way of expressing her reciprocal love. Even if love is unconditional, it will be better for my lover if I realize my ideal possibilities.

Still, in agapic love that occurs outside a divine or parental context, the basis and ground of the affection is murky. Does the lover really love the beloved person as a concrete individual? Or does the lover exude agape simply as a symptom of an oppressed psyche or lack of self-esteem? We can imagine a critic bursting upon the scene, discrediting agape in sexual contexts, and braying that erotic love is merely an obsession with a person in all of his or her particularity, not an unwavering, seemingly ungrounded commitment to another.

Again, agapic love in erotic contexts confronts a major problem not faced by divine and less frequently by parental agapic love: whether agape arises from the *deficiencies*, instead of the abundant generosity and grace, in the nature of the lover. For example, to love agapically in erotic contexts may betray a woeful misunderstanding of the importance of mutuality and reciprocity in spousal relationships. An erotic love that is one-sided or overly beneficial for one of the parties calls into question whether the lover has a sufficient sense of self-worth. As numerous feminists have pointed out for decades, women who have been systematically oppressed by patriarchal inequality often embody overly submissive psyches that permit further exploitation within the confines of heterosexual love and intimacy. The need to connect to the value represented by the man when one's own value is difficult or impossible to establish can result in an unconditional love that is unrequited. In such cases, the agapic love in play does issue from the lover's nature and does bestow additional value upon the beloved person, but it is also a response to an oppressive environment. Rather than arising from the woman's bountiful generosity and affection, such an agapic love springs desperately from the lover's damaged soul and struggles mightily to connect to a generic value. Whether consciously or subconsciously, the lover in such situations is motivated by her destitute situation, and her love is underwritten by her need to construct self-love however artificially. As such, the love is classically unconditional in certain respects—it bestows additional value on the beloved person; it persists despite the lack of reciprocation; it is creative and not directed only to deserving individuals—but in other respects strays from classical agape—it does desire, whether consciously or not, to obtain something for the lover; it does arise from desire and longing; it is not completely indifferent to the antecedent value of the beloved person, at least when that person is understood generically.

Without mutuality and reciprocity, love, whether agapic or not, becomes self-defeating. As Barbara Hilkert Andolsen comments,

> A person must be concerned for his/her own integrity as well as the other's good. Human beings can fail to establish life-enhancing relationships by erring in the direction of excessive self-surrender as well as excessive selfishness. One can completely lose oneself in the other and to do so is just as wrong as to remain totally self-centered.[13]

An agapic erotic love such that the lover unconditionally loves the beloved person without mutuality and reciprocity raises the threatening specter of the dark side of community: the individuality of such a lover may be extinguished because of an overly obsequious devotion to the beloved person.

But put aside the one-sided unconditional love that I have sketched. What should we say about requited unconditional love in erotic contexts? Is it possible? Is it desirable?

Suppose we filter out all distorting considerations of patriarchal oppression, individual exploitation, radically unequal sexual bargaining power, and the like. Suppose further that the two lovers we are examining are relatively equal in all relevant respects such as social, economic, and political status. Whether we imagine them as heterosexual or homosexual lovers is not critical to the illustration. What is crucial, however, is that the parties claim to love each other unconditionally.

That human, sexual love could arise without desire and longing, and that it could exclude all self-love is difficult to comprehend. As already noted, even parental agapic love is not free from such elements. Moreover, to love someone erotically without regard for their individuating characteristics, those constitutive attributes that make the person who he or she is, re-invokes the problem of identifying the object of the love. Unlike divine and parental agapic contexts, we cannot here summon the relationship of creator to creation as part of the explanation. Once we strip others of individuating attributes, we may have no reason to single out Gina rather than Maria as the object of our affections.

We might conclude that if I have feelings or sense an emotional connection to Gina, while I am indifferent to Maria, then I will believe that Gina is inherently and objectively valuable. That is, my feelings for Gina will generate my belief that she is special and worthy to be the object of my love in ways that others are not. But, still, on this account I would be responding to my perception of Gina's special value. The source of that perception—whether it arises from feelings themselves caused by a yet to be explained process or whether it springs from my initial assessment that Gina embodies special excellences worthy of being loved—is of little importance. The mere fact that I am responding to Gina's perceived individual value seems to disqualify my love from being agapic.

Even if I am incorrect about this, the process by which feelings of love are generated apart from all beliefs about the beloved person's attributes is murky. While we can understand how erotic love, once in place, can cause new beliefs about the objective value of the beloved person, the more difficult task is to explain coherently how erotic love initially flows from feelings or emotions independently of perceptions of the beloved person's excellences. I conclude that genuine agapic love in erotic contexts is impossible, at least in the initial stages of a relationship.

If my conclusion is wrong, I would still argue that such a love, even if possible, is not desirable. To love another or to be loved erotically without concern for one's individuating attributes calls into question whether we are loved or love a genuine person. We can describe a person, roughly, as composed of current excellences, neutral characteristics, annoying traits, vices, a fixed history, and a set of idealized possibilities. To love someone independently of these components, to love agapically in that sense, is to love only a figment of one's imagination (or a more general property shared by all human beings or a specific, enduring relational property such as "this is my child" or "this is my creation"). Even to love someone only for the characteristics they presently embody is to ignore her idealized possibilities, to deny her a future by freezing your conception of her in the present. To love erotically a person must include an assessment and appreciation of her attributes, a project that responds, in part, to the person's perceived value.

If agapic love is possible in erotic contexts, I would think that it occurs much later in a successful relationship. After years of a successful union, two people may well conclude that they could not even conceive of being with anyone else. They may at that point continue to love each other regardless of how each changes; although even here they might observe limits. To continue to love the beloved other even though she has contracted Alzheimer's disease is one thing — perhaps love persists in deference to the joint identity that has been forged and out of respect for the shared past and enduring commitment. To continue to love the beloved after she has voluntarily decided to become a mass murderer of innocent people is quite another.

Again, because agapic love of our neighbors is neither preferential nor personal, it cannot serve as the basis or the starting point of erotic unconditional love or friendship love, both of which are inherently preferential and personal. Agapic love of children is preferential and personal but involves bonds of blood and rearing (in the case of biological parents) or selection and rearing (in the case of adoptive parents) as well as the absence of the eroticism characteristic of romantic love. Thus, agapic love of children cannot serve as a model for erotic unconditional love. Accordingly, where erotic agape resides, it is the homage love pays to metaphysical bonds and shared histories nurtured over time.

The Parable of the Prodigal Son offers us a glimpse of the unconditional love God presumably bestows upon human beings. Moreover, the story energizes our efforts to repent our transgressions, forgive those who have repented, and rejoice in the positive transformation of the human spirit. The parable reminds us that we have the power to change: where there is life there is hope. Finally, the tale can be interpreted on the human level as a glorious example of parental agape, a narrative of a parent whose affection for his son overwhelmed all resistance and recognized no limits. The deeper challenge will be to extend unconditional love to mere acquaintances, strangers, and even enemies where enduring, intimate relational properties are absent.

NOTES

1. The section on the interpretation of the parable has been informed by Klyne R. Snodgrass, *Stories with Intent* (Grand Rapids, MI: William B. Eerdmans Publishing Company, 2008); Craig L. Blomberg, *Interpreting the Parables* (Downers Grove, IL: InterVarsity Press, 1990); Richard N. Longenecker (ed.), *The Challenge of Jesus' Parables* (Grand Rapids, MI: William B. Eerdmans Publishing Company, 2000); Kenneth E.

Bailey, *Poet & Peasant Through Peasant Eyes* (Grand Rapids, MI: William B. Eerdmans Publishing Company, 2000).
   2. Snodgrass, *Stories with Intent*, 131; compare with Bailey, *Poet & Peasant*, 164–69.
   3. Bailey, ibid., 165.
   4. Ibid., 177.
   5. Ibid., 203.
   6. The section on agape has been informed by Neera Kapur Badhwar, "Friends as Ends in Themselves," in Clifford Williams, ed., *On Love and Friendship* (Boston: Jones and Bartlett Publishers, 1995); Anders Nygren, "Agape and Eros," in Clifford Williams, ed., *On Love and Friendship* (Boston: Jones and Bartlett Publishers, 1995); Barbara Hilkert Andolsen, "Agape in Feminist Ethics," in Clifford Williams, ed., *On Love and Friendship* (Boston: Jones and Bartlett Publishers, 1995); Robert C. Solomon, *The Passions* (New York: Anchor Press, 1976); *Love: Emotion Myth, and Metaphor* (New York: Anchor Press, 1981); *About Love: Reinventing Romance for Our Times* (New York: Simon & Shuster, 1988); Robert Nozick, "Love's Bond" in *The Examined Life: Philosophical Meditations* (New York: Simon & Shuster, 1989), Irving Singer, *The Nature of Love, Volume 3: The Modern World* (Chicago: University of Chicago Press, 1989); Gene Outka, *Agape* (New Haven: Yale University Press, 1972); Soren Kierkegaard, *Works of Love*, trans. Howard and Edna Hong (New York: Harper and Brothers, 1962).
   7. Badhwar, "Friends as Ends," 210, 213.
   8. Nygren, "Apage and Eros," 137, 131.
   9. Ibid., 132–33.
   10. Ibid., 145–46.
   11. Ibid., 146.
   12. Kierkegaard, *Works of Love*, 72.
   13. Andolsen, "Agape in Feminist Ethics," 170–71.

THREE

The Laborers in the Vineyard: "Whatsoever Is Right, That Shall Ye Receive"

For the kingdom of heaven is like unto a man that is an householder, which went out early in the morning to hire laborers into his vineyard. And when he had agreed with the laborers for a penny [a denarius — the standard daily wage of a day laborer] a day, he sent them into his vineyard. And he went out about the third hour [9 a.m.], and saw others standing idle in the marketplace, And he said unto them; Go ye also into the vineyard, and whatsoever is right I will give you. And they went their way. Again he went out about the sixth [noon] and ninth [3 p.m.] hour, and did likewise. And about the eleventh [5 p.m.] he went out, and found others standing idle, and saith unto them, Why stand ye here all the day idle? They say unto him, Because no man hath hired us. He saith unto them, Go ye also into the vineyard; and whatsoever is right, that shall ye receive. So when even [6 p.m.] was come, the lord of the vineyard saith unto his steward, Call the laborers, and give them their hire, beginning from the last to the first. And when they came that were hired about the eleventh hour, they received every man a penny. But when the first came, they supposed that they should have received more, and they likewise received every man a penny. And when they had received it, they murmured against the goodman of the house, Saying, These last have wrought but one hour, and thou hast made them equal unto us, which have borne the burden and heat of the day. But he answered one of them, and said, Friend, I do thee no wrong; didst not thou agree with me for a penny? Take that thine is, and go thy way: I will give unto this last, even as unto thee. Is it not lawful for me to do what I will with mine own? Is thine eye evil because I am good? So the last shall be first, and the first last: for many be called, but few chosen. (Matt. 20:1–16)

INTERPRETATION OF THE PARABLE

The historical Jesus was a moral transformer.[1] He began from but sought to refashion significantly the conventions of Jewish law that formed his cultural context. The story of the laborers in the vineyard is designed explicitly to help explain the anticipated "kingdom of heaven." Nevertheless, the parable contains critical moral lessons for everyday human behavior.

The owner of a vineyard hires workers for his vineyard. He goes to the marketplace five different times to contract for more laborers. Clearly, his hiring practices are puzzling and inefficient. Would he not have known how many workers he would need and for how many hours they must work? Moreover, as the workers in question are day laborers—hired without an extended contract and dischargeable at will—their supply would be ample and demand for their services would be uneven. Thus, they would be eager to be hired. Of course, parables are designed to teach lessons and not to document historical events. As part of their charm, all moral fables include mystifying details.

The typical workday for vineyard laborers would be twelve hours, from about 6 a.m. to 6 p.m. The five work shifts in the parable break down as follows:

Table 3.1. The Workers' Pay Scale

Crew Name	Hours Worked	Pay Received
The first hired ("the stalwarts")	12	Denarius
The second hired ("the backups")	9	Denarius
The third hired ("the nooners")	6	Denarius
The fourth hired ("the penultimates")	3	Denarius
The fifth hired ("the fortunate sons")	1	Denarius

At first blush, the case by the stalwarts is compelling: they worked a full day and received the same pay as those who worked only one hour. Moreover, they worked during the hardest period of blistering heat. In contrast, the fortunate sons labored only one hour in the cool of early evening. The implicit allegation of the stalwarts is that the vineyard owner's allocation of wages is unfair as it violates the principle of "equal pay for equal work."

However, the vineyard owner has a plausible response: the stalwarts received precisely the amount that they had agreed to work for; what I pay other workers should not be their concern; that I have chosen to be generous to those who were hired later is my prerogative. The implicit defense of the vineyard owner centers on the principle of "freedom of contract": employers and employees are at liberty to agree voluntarily to the term of wage-labor contracts, and they are morally responsible for fulfilling the conditions to which they have agreed. Beyond that, they have no further duties to one another regarding their employment relations.

But could the stalwarts allege that they have been exploited? Had they known from the outset that the vineyard owner was capable of paying a full day's wage for only one hour of work they would have driven a tougher bargain for their full day's work; or they might have slunk back into the labor crowd at the marketplace, dallied in the shade until 5 p.m., then emerged enthusiastic to work when the vineyard owner appeared at that time.

The vineyard owner might respond that the stalwarts are unbecomingly envious of those to whom he has chosen to be generous. Assume that a denarius is by the standards of time and place considered a fair day's wage for a full day's work. That the stalwarts, who were hardly in a strong bargaining position, accepted the standard terms is unremarkable. They were not exploited unless all workers in such an economic system are exploited—in which case the claim that a certain group of workers was exploited is merely commonplace. That the vineyard owner has chosen to treat the fortunate sons generously, and to a lesser extent the other groups, in no way disadvantages the stalwarts.

For example, suppose the vineyard owner followed the principle of equal pay for equal work. He paid the stalwarts their agreed-upon wage, while paying the backups, the nooners, the penultimates, and the fortunate sons a proportionate wage (in this case 3/4, 1/2, 1/4, and 1/12, respectively, of the wages received by the stalwarts). All workers left the vineyard satisfied that they had received pay commensurate with the services they had rendered. The next week, however, during a festive holiday, the vineyard owner decided to bestow gifts widely. He conferred no gifts upon the stalwarts, but recognizing the greater need of the other members of the other groups, he gave them money. Moreover, the amount of the gifts to the members of the other groups brought each man to the precise level he would have received had he worked a full day in the vineyard the previous week. That is, at the end of the holiday, each person who worked for the vineyard owner during the previous week received a total of one denarius in a combination of wage-gift.

Given such a scenario, what complaint could the stalwarts reasonably lodge? By definition, they had no entitlement to claim they had been denied their due because the vineyard owner had not bestowed gifts upon them. No one has an entitlement to a "gift." If so, the vineyard owner can plausibly conclude that what happened at his workplace was parallel to the hypothetical example. Thus, the stalwarts have no persuasive claim that they have been denied their due merely because the owner had decided to bestow gifts at the end of the workday to members of the other groups.

Of course, the stalwarts might rejoin that the two cases are not parallel. To whom the vineyard owner bestows gifts is of no concern to the stalwarts, but the vineyard owner's violation of the principle of equal pay for equal work directly affects them. At the vineyard, the owner was not bestowing gifts; he was presumably compensating labor. His words to the latecomers are instructive: "whatsoever is right I will give you," "whatsoever is right, that shall ye receive." The stalwarts might well contest that what the vineyard owner paid the four groups of latecomers was "right" given conventional understandings of the day. In sum, the owner's payments to the fortunate sons and the other latecomers were connected to the services they had expended on his behalf; they were not gifts as such. Moreover, suppose the vineyard owner was following his own general practice of compensation: regardless of the time at which he hires day laborers, he pays them one denarius at the end of their work. If this practice was known, the stalwarts could have bargained for a contingency clause in their employment contract: "We agree to work twelve hours for a wage of one denarius. However, if other laborers on that same day work fewer than twelve hours but receive one denarius for their services, then our wages will be increased in proportion to the greater number of hours that we worked." Thus, in the instant case, if such a contingency clause were in place, the stalwarts would have received twelve denarii each for their services; the backups would have received nine denarii each for their services, and so on down the employment line.

Of course, the prospective employer could have rejected the contingency clause and refused to hire the stalwarts. In the context of the employment conditions of the time and place at issue, that result would have been likely. Or the prospective employer might have replied, "I will hire you for twelve hours of labor at a compensation of one denarius each. The terms under which I hire other workers, if any, is not your concern. Take it or leave it." If the stalwarts accepted those terms they would have waived their privilege to complain formally about the vineyard owner's subsequent compensation to the latecomers.

Prior to continuing this discussion further, I must concede that many, probably most, interpreters would resist my entire analysis. Instead, they would argue that the Parable of the Laborers in the Vineyard has nothing to do with human economics and matters of labor compensation. Some interpreters conclude that the parable is explicitly designed to transcend mundane human calculations of desert and fairness: God's grace of salvation is a gift that is not subject to human expectations.[2] If God decrees that "the last shall be first, and the first last," so be it. If God's will is mysterious in that "many be called, but few chosen," that merely underscores the limitation of human understanding. On this interpretation, that the actions of the vineyard owner, who represents divine agency, cannot be justified under the principle of equal pay for equal work is irrelevant. God's will and generosity are simply not subject to the same principles that guide human interactions.

Other interpreters would agree that the Parable of the Laborers in the Vineyard has nothing to do with human economics and matters of labor compensation. But they perceive the point of the parable as undermining the hubris, envy, and arrogance of Jesus' disciples.[3] As the disciples began to understand themselves as special—Jesus' closest confidants and first chosen ministers—their self-importance amplified. On this view, the parable is structured to deflate the pretensions of preening acolytes. Under the looming Kingdom of God: "the last shall be first, and the first last." Thus, the apostles had better get their minds and souls in order.

Still other interpreters insist that the point of the parable is to defend Jesus' associations with and acceptances of sinners.[4] While conventional Jewish wisdom believed that such associations served to condone or enable moral transgressions, Jesus sought sinners out in hope of facilitating their redemption and personal transformation. On this understanding, once again, the Parable of the Laborers in the Vineyard has nothing to do with human economics and matters of labor compensation. Instead, the vineyard owner represents divine generosity and Jesus' proclivity for advancing the interests of those perceived to be "the last" in society.

These and other interpretations of the parable embody much merit. As always, I am trying to glean practical moral lessons from the biblical parables. I do not aspire to demonstrate the only or even necessarily the best overall way to understand the stories as such. I do aim at arriving at the best way to understand the parables in order to extract principles for leading a good human life and for moral guidance.

So we return to my analysis. One moral lesson is the conflict between two different notions of justice—proportionate reward and contractual fulfillment—and the conflict between contractual fulfillment and generosity. The stalwarts define justice and expect compensation in accord with proportionate reward: those who worked twelve hours deserve higher wages than those who worked one, three, six, and nine hours, respectively. The vineyard owner defines justice in terms of contractual fulfillment—satisfying the terms of a voluntarily agreed-upon labor contract. Having fulfilled his obligations under the labor contract, the vineyard owner insists he has been fair to the stalwarts and his treatment of the four groups of latecomers flows from his generosity, a discretionary function of his will to which no one has an antecedent entitlement.

> For having toiled all day long, [the stalwarts] naturally expect some kind of bonus. As they see it, natural justice requires a proportional system of recompense. But the landowner insists on fulfilling the exact terms of their contract, that was to pay them what he considered "just" . . . a full day's wage. So when the grumblers accuse the owner of unfairness, the only injustice in the situation is their own selfishness. Hence the appropriateness of the owner's challenge. . . . "Is [thine] eye evil because I am good?" The [stalwarts] have received their just reward. But they show themselves to be estranged from the larger graciousness of the one who had engaged their services. Therefore the landowner's words imply dismissal: ["Take that thine is, and go thy way"].[5]

However, conflicting understandings of justice are not so neatly resolved. The stalwarts' claim of proportionate reward as a paramount principle of justice resonates in the contemporary law of the United States. If a group of say, women, is found to be paid less for rendering the same services for which men are paid more, the disadvantaged group often has a claim of discriminatory treatment even where members of both groups contracted independently with their employer for the wages they receive. If the employer responds to the women—"Is your eye evil because I chose to be generous with men?"—and dismisses their allegation with a curt, "Take what is yours by contract, then take a hike," his remarks would be judged insufficient and insensitive.

Of course, one important difference between these two cases is the claims of discrimination lodged by women, along with those levied by certain racial, ethnic, and religious minorities, receive special scrutiny under our legal system. Such consideration is a remedial response to decades of past demonstrable disenfranchisement suffered by these groups. In the case of the parable of the vineyard workers, we must assume that the laborers are Jewish men, all of whom are peasants. Clearly, the stalwarts could not allege that they were discriminated against based on their gender, religion, ethnicity, or race.

Still, the underlying allegation in both cases is violation of a paramount principle of justice: proportionate reward as embodied in the slogan "equal pay for equal work." What differs in the two cases is the underlying cause of that violation. In the hypothetical case offered, the employer violates the principle based on the gender of the workers; in the parable, the vineyard owner violates the principle based on whim masquerading as generosity (at least when viewed from the vantage point of the stalwarts). My point is that the stalwarts' charge that the vineyard owner has been unfair because he transgressed the principle of proportionate reward cannot be summarily dismissed as "selfishness" and inability to perceive the goodness of the vineyard owner's "generosity." The stalwarts' cause should survive a motion for summary judgment in the court of morality. Whether that cause is ultimately persuasive is another matter.

However, by the time they were paid, the stalwarts should not have been surprised that they received no bonus. As the vineyard owner's steward paid each crew in turn, beginning with the fortunate sons, the stalwarts would have known that each shift received the same amount and that the employer was not following a principle of proportionate reward. No worker received less than he was promised, but—assuming one denarius was the standard wage for a day's labor in vineyards—four of the crews received more than they deserved.

Perhaps the vineyard owner reasoned that any payment less than the standard wage would be insufficient to meet a worker's subsistence requirements. Thus, the owner's generosity would be grounded in his perception of the workers' needs, not on the basis of what they merited by their efforts. If the vineyard owner represents divine agency—after all, the parable begins by claiming to describe the "kingdom of heaven"— then one point of the story is to demonstrate that the divine will is not limited by human calculations of justice grounded in the principle of personal desert. No one will receive less than he or she deserves, but some may well receive more than they deserve. Such inequality, according to the lesson of the parable, should not engender envy or resentment.

> The parable breaks any chain of logic connecting reward, work, and human perceptions of what is right. God's judging is not regulated by human perceptions of justice, and lurking behind that statement is a whole theology of mercy . . . *just as no one should begrudge a good man who goes beyond justice and gives to the poor, so no one should begrudge God's goodness and mercy as if God's rewards were limited to strict calculation.* Implicit is the assumption that God's judgment will be contrary to human expectations . . . Jealousy and all thoughts of ranking or privilege must be jettisoned.[6]

Like the Parable of the Prodigal Son, in the Parable of the Laborers in the Vineyard, resentment and claims of injustice arise from differential reward grounded in generosity. Unlike the generosity demonstrated in the Parable of the Prodigal Son, the generosity flowing in the Parable of the Laborers in the Vineyard does not center on moral transgressions, repentance, and personal transformation. Instead, the generosity revealed in that parable focuses on transcending strict calculations of justice based on personal desert and centers on sensitivity to human need.

But if a crucial lesson of the parable is the insufficiency of this world's values for the coming Kingdom of God, should we not prefigure that Kingdom by working to transform the values of our world now? That is, rather than viewing the parable as merely illustrating that God's will is not subject to human expectations and human calculations of justice, should we not labor zealously to bring human expectations and calculations of justice in line with the divine will to the extent that is possible? If so, then the point of the parable is not simply to supply information about the impending Kingdom of God, but to encourage human beings to transform their values right now.

MORAL LESSONS

In that vein, we should address several specific moral lessons that derive from the general instruction about the insufficiency of this world's present value system. First, the parable cautions human beings against making invidious comparisons and seeking superiority over others. When judging our station, worth, and honor by comparing ourselves with others, determining what we deserve in relation to them, and becoming indignant when others seemingly receive more than they merit, we err grievously. The slogan "the last shall be first, and the first last," underscores the imprudence of seeking superiority over others as the road to personal fulfillment. At its core, the Kingdom of God is an intimate community, not a gaggle of isolated individuals vying for supremacy in zero-sum contests.

Second, where each receives what he or she was promised and all receive equally based on need, no moral deficiency occurs even where some receive more than they deserve based on the duration of their work. This is a radically egalitarian message not currently part of the dominant understanding of our world. The result in the parable of the vineyard workers *does* seem unfair when analyzed by our conventional notion of distributive justice. (That is why my youthful complaint to my fifth-grade teacher bore currency. What I failed to understand then was that the incongruity between the moral of the parable and our dominant notion of distributive justice was one of the points of the story: we should transform our dominant notion of distributive justice, or, at least, deflate its importance in our moral calculations.)

Third, the notion of fairness, or what is appropriate overall, is a broader moral conception than the notion of personal desert based on effort and production. In the Kingdom of God, no one will be treated unfairly. That is, no one will be disadvantaged by the generosity of the sovereign. All will be given what they were promised; even though, based on their need and on divine generosity, some may receive more than they deserve when judged on their effort and production, no one will be disadvantaged by such action. In the parable, the stalwarts were not disadvantaged by the vineyard owner's generosity to the other four crews. Evaluated by the number of hours worked, the four crews of latecomers received more than they deserved. But this allocation neither came at the expense of the stalwarts (they did not receive less than they were promised in order to pay the other four crews) nor did it place the stalwarts in a worse position than they had expected to be in at the close of the workday (their legitimate expectations were not frustrated by the vineyard owner's generosity to the other four crews of workers).

Fourth, the sovereign of the Kingdom of God is not limited by contractual arrangements and the existing notion of distributive justice. The divine will is at liberty to be gracious, and the stalwarts might well be faulted for objecting to that liberty. The cumulative extent of the vineyard owner's largesse is unclear. To determine that figure we must multiply the total number of unworked hours for which he paid by the total number of workers. The total number of unworked labor for which the owner paid is eleven hours for each fortunate son, nine hours for each of the penultimates, six hours for each nooner, and three hours for each backup. We do not know how many workers defined each of the four categories so we cannot arrive at a precise calculation.

The value of twelve hours of labor can be set at one denarius. If we stipulate arbitrarily that each category of workers included, say, ten men, the total number of unworked labor hours for which the vineyard owner paid would be 290 (10 × 11 plus 10 × 9 plus 10 × 6 plus 10 × 3), the equivalent of just over 24 denarii or 24 days of labor of one worker. The extent to which this would constitute a genuine sacrifice would be measured by the vineyard owner's holdings. To conclude that the owner could easily afford this sum is reasonable. In any event, what holds true for God should hold true for human beings: in allocating resources, we should not be limited by the obligations of our contractual arrangements and the existing notion of distributive justice prevalent in our society.

As always, the lessons of this parable require further reflection. We must examine more deeply claims of distributive justice based on proportionate reward ("equal pay for equal work") and based on contractual fulfillment (strict adherence to terms of an agreement).

THE NOTION OF DESERT

As do several other biblical parables, the story of the laborers in the vineyard raises the issue of distributing rewards in accordance with the principle of desert. In all such cases, Jesus' conclusions are not constrained by the principle of allocating goods on the basis of strict justice—people receiving precisely what they deserve as determined by their past deeds. For example, the Parable of the Laborers in the Vineyard is typically understood as being grounded in two moral axioms: people should not receive less than they deserve; but some people will receive more than they deserve because of the generosity and bestowal of grace of the agent doing the distributing. Of course, at the transcendent level that agent is God, but these axioms can also be implemented at the human level. Applying these two axioms produces another moral principle:

where no one has received less than he or she deserves any resentment or envy or jealously directed at those who have received more than they deserve is misplaced and demonstrates a deficiency of character. Instead, everyone should rejoice in that no one has been short-changed and some have been especially fortunate. The moral axioms at issue preclude the appropriateness of invidious comparison among people. That others received more than I did should be irrelevant where I have received my due.

Although the foregoing may strike readers as eminently reasonable, the foundational moral issues are less than clear. Often, to what my "due" amounts depends on what others in similar situations under like circumstances receive. For example, on the mundane level of family relations, suppose two children receive certain benefits from their parents—benefits that can plausibly be viewed as what they are due; but the third sibling is always given more. Is it not natural for the two children to conclude that their parents favor the third sibling and to experience discomfort as a result? Under the stipulations of the hypothetical, they cannot legitimately complain that they have received less than they precisely deserved, but may they nevertheless plausibly allege unfairness? May they understandably charge that their parents are "playing a favorite" in a fashion that undermines their self-esteem? Or do their misgivings flow merely from the four horsemen of unworthy character: frustration, envy, anger, and self-pity?

To begin to unravel the answers to such questions, we must clarify the notion of desert. I will focus only on the concept of *personal* desert. Accordingly, I will not discuss other locutions and questions of desert such as "Do beautiful artistic pieces deserve attention?" or "Do useful, valuable material objects deserve care?"

A few general principles underwrite the principle of moral desert:[7] (a) If people deserve something they do so on the basis of some prior performance or by virtue of some possessed characteristic; (b) If someone deserves something, then that is a good reason for giving that something to him or her but not always a sufficient or conclusive reason; (c) The nature of the something to be distributed—whether it is a prize, reward, blame, punishment, praise, or the like—will determine, at least partially, the nature of the basis that warrants the person's claim of deserving that something.

Typically, for someone to claim to deserve something he or she must point to some prior performance that might warrant the claim: the person must have done something in the past. We deserve something in virtue of prior acts for which we are responsible. In some cases, though, we may justifiably claim to deserve something based on our possession of a relevant characteristic and not on a prior performance.[8] For example, I deserve equal consideration of certain of my interests, along with those of other human beings, based only on my possession of humanness. However, a person who lacks both a relevant past performance and a relevant characteristic has no legitimate claim based on desert. For example, we cannot justifiably claim that we deserve to win the New York State Lottery or that we deserve our natural talents. In the case of the lottery, merely purchasing a ticket and wishing on our lucky stars that we might win are past performances that are not enough to support a justified claim of desert. In the case of natural talents, we possess them due only to the genetic lottery; we did nothing, we were nothing, prior to our birth.

Claims of desert are typically, although not always, connected to the results of voluntary actions over which we have major control. The notion of desert is often invoked to treat human beings appropriately given that they are responsible for their actions. Having no control over the amount and type of natural talents we possess or over who wins the New York State Lottery, we can assert no credible claim of desert in either case. To conclude that a person deserves something furnishes a reason, but not always a conclusive consideration, that he ought to receive it.

Claims of desert must be distinguished from claims of entitlement, another principle of justice. Consider the following example: The Buffalo Bills play the Miami Dolphins for the right to enter the Super Bowl. The Bills prove conclusively that they are the better team and also that they exerted the most effort on this particular Sunday. However, because of a stunning series of lucky breaks, fortuitous decisions by the game officials, and cooperation of the weather, the Dolphins win the contest, 21–20. To claim that the Bills *deserved* to win—Should not the better team that tries harder be declared the more deserving?—is reasonable. But even if the Bills are unanimously deemed the more deserving team, they are neither *entitled* to play in the Super Bowl nor do they have a *right* to play in the Super Bowl. The Dolphins, the less deserving squad, is entitled and has a right to compete in the Super Bowl. By the same token, the winner of the New York State Lottery did not deserve to win but is entitled to the prize.

To summarize the distinction between the two claims of distributive justice: (d) Someone is *entitled* to a prize if and only if he or she has fulfilled the qualifying conditions specified by the rules determining who receives that prize; (e) Someone *deserves* to win a prize if and only if he or she demonstrated to a higher degree than all other competitors the skill and effort set forth as the basis of the competition.

Accordingly, one may be entitled to something but not deserve it, and one may deserve something but not be entitled to it. For example, children may work steadfastly to support their elderly, disabled parents and observers may well conclude that the children deserve a reward for their effort, commitment, and contribution, but there may simply not be a reward for which they qualify and thus none to which they are entitled. Having been legally designated in a will, Jones may be entitled to a huge inheritance that observers might accurately conclude Jones does not deserve based on their examination of Jones's life. Desert and entitlement, then, are two distinct claims of justice that sometimes conflict when others determine what one *ought* to receive. Although they deserved to win the crucial game, the disappointed Bills cannot legitimately claim they are entitled or have a right to compete in the Super Bowl. The right to compete in the Super Bowl is conferred on that team that fulfills the relevant qualifying condition—winning the preceding playoff game—and not necessarily on the team that deserved to win that game. Thus, (f) If someone deserves something it does not follow that he or she has a right to that something; and (g) If someone is entitled to something, then he or she has a right to that something.

Again, a person may deserve something although not be able to lodge a justified claim to it either because there is no prize or award to be claimed or, even if there is such a prize or award, because he or she has not fulfilled the qualifying conditions to receive it.

Consider the following: (h) Mary deserves praise; (i) Mary deserves blame; (j) Mary is entitled to praise, and (k) Mary is entitled to blame. Under the appropriate conditions, the first three attributions make sense. But the fourth is problematic. While a person may deserve either praise or blame (or reward or punishment), the claim that a person is entitled to blame (or punishment) rings hollow. Entitlement is a consideration of justice that applies only to things that people desire or ought to desire. In contrast, desert is a consideration of justice that sometimes applies—in the cases of punishment and blame—to things that people typically do not desire. In that vein, to claim that someone has a right to praise or reward is compelling under the appropriate circumstances, but to claim that someone has a right to blame or punishment is odd. Accordingly, the notion of rights is tightly connected to the concept of entitlement but not to the concept of desert. In that vein, the notion of personal desert is mainly or entirely pre-institutional; it is a natural moral notion that is not conceptually tied to political institutions, social structures, and legal rules. The notion of entitlement is mainly or entirely institutional; it is an institutional notion that is logically linked to political institutions, social structures, and legal rules.

This distinction, though, is far from ironclad. Several desert claims do presuppose a sociopolitical context because of the nature of the treatment or object at stake. For example, to say that Mary deserves a Pulitzer Prize, Vito deserves the Medal of Honor, and John deserves a long stretch in prison are all legitimate assertions under the appropriate circumstances, and they all presuppose the existence of different social, military, and legal institutions. Still, claims of desert, unlike those of entitlement, do not arise merely by fulfilling the conditions specified in an institutional system of political or legal rules. Mary, Vito, and John may have satisfied the conditions laid down for their respective treatments, but doing so is not the basis of their desert claims. That there are such things as the Pulitzer Prize, the Medal of Honor, and imprisonment is a function of institutional arrangements. But desert claims, unlike entitlement claims, related to these awards and treatments must be grounded on bases other than satisfying the qualifying conditions specified for them. The basis of desert, then, remains certain qualities that Mary, Vito, and John embodied and how those qualities animated their respective actions.

Numerous bases have been offered in support of claims of desert. For example, a person may lodge a claim of desert based on moral worth; on success in contributing to society; on general productivity; on effort expended in seeking to contribute to society or to general productivity; or on the possession of relevant characteristics. Of course, these considerations do not always coalesce easily. Who deserves the prize—the person who made the most effort or the person who demonstrated the most skill and produced more? The nature of the object at stake and a series of value judgments will typically determine the appropriate basis of the desert claim. For example, if a scarce medical resource can be administered to only one of two equally needy patients, one of the possible recipients might be more deserving of the resource based on her superior contributions to society. Of course, that she ought, all things considered, to receive the resource based only on the fact that she is more deserving is another matter. In other contexts, claims of desert based on greater societal productivity are irrelevant. For example, a renowned, stunningly productive citizen is not allowed to vote more times in a national election than an ordinary person.

Controversy swirls around the question whether need is a legitimate basis for desert claims. We might see need as the type of personal characteristic that grounds desert claims to, say, medical treatment or allocation of food. But need is less a personal characteristic and more a (hopefully) temporary condition or situation. A person is needy not because of his or her inherent personal attributes but because of a series of describable choices, causes, and events. In fact, we are all antecedently needy until our biological, psychological, and material desires are satisfied to one degree or another. But what of a person whose needs flow from an extraordinary run of misfortune, none of which is due to her misdeeds or shortcomings? To conclude that she deserves a break or some good fortune is not misplaced. We would be assuming that nonculpable people should not be subject to a disproportionate amount of bad luck. We hope that luck would finally even out or at least occasionally smile on those it had unduly assaulted. Such a desert claim would underscore the disparity between a person's blameless performance and massive misfortune. Having not deserved relentless battering from lady luck, the person now deserves a squaring of accounts. Of course, such a claim appears platitudinous. Having no control over the whims of fortune, we are casting only a hope into the wind.

Suppose you had one delicious slice of pepperoni pizza to bestow and two possible recipients. Both were strangers who were equal in all respects—contributions, effort, productivity, and the like. However, one had been the constant victim of bad luck, while the other was unremarkable in that regard. Would you conclude that the nonculpable victim deserved the food more than the other person and you now had a chance to reverse the cycle of misfortune, at least to a small extent? Although the two possible recipients are equally needy in terms of food, they are unequally needy in terms of reversing past outrageous fortune. Neither is entitled nor do they have a right to the slice, but a review of past circumstances might well impel you to decide in favor of the unfortunate pilgrim. Still, the case is not clear cut. If the two famished people are equal in respect to contributions, effort, and productivity, then more credit might be given to the person who battled through more adverse circumstances; perhaps effort is not equal after all. Or perhaps the more unfortunate of the two was blessed with greater (undeserved) innate talents that permitted her to equal the production of her more fortunate but less naturally gifted colleague. If so, attributions of desert are more ambiguous. In any event, appeals to need are better severed from appeals to desert. The two types of appeals often constitute conflicting claims to just distribution of social goods. However, innocent suffering and bad luck can affect a person's desert claims in indirect ways.

Moral desert arises from voluntary choices, deep intentions, sincere efforts, and cultivated character. But from a human perspective the idea of rewarding or punishing the internal origins of moral desert is highly problematic. Lacking unambiguous access to motivations, intentions, and past socialization, human evaluators cannot easily separate what someone genuinely deserves from what someone acquired by luck.

For example, John Rawls argues that none of us deserves our innate talents and initial social position.[9] After all, none of us can point to any prior performance or antecedent characteristic by virtue of which a legitimate claim of desert for those things could bloom. Rawls concludes that we do not deserve those rewards and prizes that flow from such undeserved qualities. He suggests that the major bases for desert claims—effort, productivity, contribution, and even moral worth—greatly depend on undeserved innate talents and initial social position. Even our willingness to make an effort and fulfill one of the major bases of desert depends largely on our initial starting position, social circumstances, and innate talents. Rawls tacitly accepts the principle that we deserve something if and only if we deserve the characteristics by which we obtain that something. (The principle would hold for all desert claims other than those based on possessing relevant characteristics, some of which would not be deserved.)

However, even if *willingness* to work is a character trait that a person embodies because of the luck of the genetic lottery, *actual* work and effort may still underwrite a genuine claim of desert. The mere possession of desirable character traits flowing from the genetic lottery such as high intelligence, willingness to work, physical strength, natural wit, and the like do not produce genuine desert claims. Lacking the animation provided by effort, such desirable characteristics produce little or nothing. Possessing desirable characteristics as innate gifts is one thing, but exercising those characteristics is quite another. Manifesting and exercising desirable character traits require concentrated effort that vivifies legitimate desert claims. To treat people as they deserve is to respond to them as autonomous, free beings responsible for their actions. Doing so also heightens our understanding that by crafting our actions in certain ways, we can strongly influence how others will respond to us. When others treat us as we deserve they are responding to us according to our deeds, commensurately to what we have earned.

Of course, even if a person does not deserve something it does not follow that he ought not to receive it or even that he is not entitled to it; it follows only that the notion of desert cannot provide him with any claim to it. Rawls highlights the problem that while a person may well deserve certain things, it is typically impossible to calculate what she genuinely deserves, and this epistemological problem renders the notion of desert a feckless practical guide to the distribution of social goods. To calculate what accomplishments, exertions of effort, notable deeds, and the like flow from characteristics that a person deserves or has earned and what arises from undeserved initial social position and innate talents is virtually impossible.

Happily, God presumably discerns infallibly the inner intentions, motivations, and cogitations of human beings. All the hoary problems infecting human judgments regarding just deserts can be brushed aside. Are human beings genuinely free? Can we deserve certain treatment even though we do not deserve our initial starting position, social circumstances, and innate talents? How can we separate the effects of innocent suffering, bad luck, and the like from the results of our actions for which we are fully responsible? How do the different bases of desert interrelate when calculating a person's overall moral desert?

In any case, judgments about desert presuppose that human beings possess free will and are responsible for their choices and actions. As existentialists are fond of reminding us, experience is the greatest "proof" that human beings have freedom. We cannot deny our freedom once we experience the anguish of choice, profoundly sense we could have done otherwise than we did, and, at times, break entrenched habits and patterns by apparent acts of will. Although neuroscience may insist that my decisions and choices are conjured in my brain prior to my consciousness of them, my felt experiences persist. Even if science repeats that my mind is subject to the typical material pattern of causes and effects, even if all events are determined by prior chains of causes and effects, we cling to a thin reed: causation need not be compulsion. My choices are neither random nor coerced. If freedom requires making choices and acting on the basis of reasons that are not causes, then rationally establishing freedom is gravely problematic. But our experiences scream out and win the day: How could we live and act under the self-conscious view that we are unfree? How would we experience the world? If we are antecedently constructed to experience and thus believe that we are free, what rational evidence could change our manner of living other than in a purely academic way? Even if we are convinced by the evidence against human free will, we must heed Jean-Paul Sartre's slogan, "We are condemned to be free," and paraphrase it: "We are condemned to live *as if* we were free." Sartre insists that we are radically free and fully responsible. His rallying cry of "No Excuses" amplifies that theme. As a matter of theory, Sartre may well be incorrect, but as a function of practice—how we must live our lives—his program resonates deeply. We are biologically constructed to live as if we are free. No other practical alternative is available.

Accordingly, we must *assume* that human beings are autonomous, responsible, free moral agents responsible for their actions, and that God can correctly answer all of these questions and everything else. The conundrums of the principle of desert may well be unsolvable by human beings, but surely God is uniquely placed to make infallibly correct determinations, however mysterious to us.

FREEDOM OF CONTRACT

In the Parable of the Laborers in the Vineyard, the stalwarts and the owner of the vineyard had agreed orally to a standard contract of that time and place. The stalwarts would labor for twelve hours and receive a denarius for their service. The other sets of workers, agreed to work nine, six, three hours and one hour, respectively, for "whatsoever is right." The terms of payment were vague, but the various sets of workers either trusted the vineyard owner to be fair or they simply had no alternative or both. We must conclude that they assumed that their wages would be proportionate to the hours they worked. Certainly, none of these workers could have reasonably expected to receive a full-day's wage, the amount the vineyard owner doled out to them at the end of the day.

From a contemporary standpoint, the stalwarts and the vineyard owner were exercising freedom of contract: they had agreed voluntarily to a wage-labor exchange. Freedom of contract presumably honors and encourages the exercise of individual liberty and autonomy, thereby recognizing the inherent dignity and worth of the bargainers; facilitates efficient allocation of resources, as market forces, particularly the supply of workers and the demand for labor, determines wage-labor exchanges; and thereby promotes economic growth.

But the principle of freedom of contract is not absolute. Numerous voluntary agreements will not be enforced by modern courts.[10] For example, contracts to perform illegal acts, such as embezzlement or prostitution, under state or federal criminal law are not enforceable. More important, the doctrine of unconscionability allows courts to refuse to enforce contracts on grounds of unfair surprise, disparity of bargaining power, and procedural or substantive unfairness. Procedural unconscionability includes the presence of duress, fraud, undue influence, failure to comply with the duty to disclose, obscure terms, vastly unequal bargaining power in adhesion contracts, and the like.[11] Substantive unconscionability includes the presence of contractual terms that are strikingly immoral (for example, the sale of a baby) that contravene public policy (for example, contracts that include penalties of physical punishment for breach or delay) or that unjustifiably subvert a party's purposes for contracting (for example, radically one-sided contracts).

We must assume that the contract forged by the stalwarts and the vineyard owner in the parable would be a permissible, enforceable wage-labor contract given the standards of the time and place. The elements of procedural and substantive unconscionability are absent. No illegal or immoral acts are in play. One might argue that the vast disparity in bargaining power between the vineyard owner and day laborers suggests that the agreed-upon wage was meager and thus exploitive. But the lessons of the parable work best when we brush this aside. Moreover, to make such a claim about an ancient economic transaction from contemporary standards reeks of anachronism.

Assuming the general propriety of the contract, the *entitlements* of the parties vest. The vineyard owner is entitled to twelve hours of labor from each stalwart, who is in turn entitled to receive a denarius at the end of the workday. The notion of desert fades into the background. We need not and should not make assessments of what the vineyard owner and stalwarts deserve. Upon consummating their contract, each party has vested rights and duties based on the entitlements flowing from their agreement. From the standpoint of distributive justice, the murkier, more contestable judgment as to what they deserve becomes unnecessary.

PROPORTIONATE REWARD

The principle of equal pay for equal work often conflicts with freedom of contract. This notion of proportionate reward is grounded in a straightforward claim of personal desert: if two people work equally—as judged by productivity and amount of time expended—they deserve to receive the same wage, all other relevant things being equal. The desert claim is based on effort, time, and results. Under such circumstances, any inequality in pay must be justified by a relevant difference between the two workers. Some examples of permissible differences that could justify unequal pay for two workers who labored the same number of hours: one worker might earn a higher salary based on seniority, years worked on the job; one worker might have produced more in a reward system based on merit; or one worker might earn more to offset a previous distributive injustice he or she endured. From a contemporary standpoint, however, differential pay based on group characteristics such as gender, race, religion, or ethnicity is impermissible. In such cases, unequal pay for equal work is redolent with the stench of discrimination, prejudice, and bias.

Thus, the entitlements flowing from freedom of contract and the desert-based claims grounding the principle of proportionate reward may conflict. To argue that freedom of contract permits differential pay for similar work—after all, the workers agreed to the terms of their respective contracts without fraud or duress—will be unsuccessful in many cases, especially those wherein previously disenfranchised groups receive lower pay in the absence of justifying relevant differences.

The claim of the stalwarts in the parable must be viewed as a claim grounded in desert: We worked eleven, nine, six, and three hours more, respectively, than the other groups of workers, yet we received the same wage. The stalwarts received precisely that to which they were *entitled*, but they feel short-changed in terms of what they *deserved*: they expended more effort, as judged by hours labored; they did so under more trying conditions—under the piercing sun; and they produced more through their efforts. Accordingly, even though they deserved more than the other groups, they received the same wage. They are alleging that they should receive more pay than the other groups because they worked longer hours and produced more than those groups. The stalwarts' claim is that the vineyard owner was paying the various groups equally for unequal work. While the *entitlements* of the stalwarts are defined by their wage-labor contract with the vineyard owner, what they *deserve* must take into account the comparative effort, time expended, and productivity of the different groups of laborers. To judge the stalwarts as merely casting an "evil eye" on the beneficence of the vineyard owner may well be harsh. On the contrary, they do seem to have a plausible, prima facie claim that they have not been treated in accord with the principle of desert.

If my analysis rings true, then the standard interpretation of the parable must be adjusted. Again, the typical analysis concludes that people should not receive less than they deserve; but some people will receive more than they deserve because of the generosity and bestowal of grace of the agent doing the distributing. These two axioms produce another moral principle: where no one has received less than he or she deserves, any resentment or envy or jealously directed at those who have received more than they deserve is misplaced and demonstrates a deficiency of character. Instead, everyone should rejoice in that no one has been short-changed and some have been especially fortunate. The adjustment I offer is that the parable more precisely stands for the following propositions:

People should not receive less than that to which they are *entitled*. But some people will receive more than they *deserve* because of the generosity of the distributing agent. Where no one has received less than he or she is *entitled* to, any resentment toward those who received more than they *deserved* is misplaced and demonstrates a deficiency of character. Instead, everyone should rejoice in that no one has been short changed in terms of their entitlements and some have been especially fortunate.

Now imagine that each group of workers in the parable agreed to a wage-labor contract with the vineyard owner. The facts of the agreement involving the stalwarts remain the same. Three hours later, the vineyard owner offers the backups a denarius each for nine hours work; they would, presumably, be pleased to accept the terms as they would receive a standard full-day's pay for three-fourths of a day's labor. Later, the vineyard owner returns and offers the nooners, penultimates, and fortunate sons a denarius each for six hours, three hours, and one hour of labor, respectively. Presumably, each set of workers would be increasingly thrilled to accept the terms as they would be earning a full day's pay for a fraction of a day's labor. Under the hypothetical, each set of workers has vested entitlements upon formally agreeing to the terms offered by the vineyard owner. At the end of the workday, when the vineyard owner presents each worker with one denarius, all entitlements under the respective contracts have been fulfillment. No worker would have a legitimate complaint that the wage he had received was insufficient with regard to his *entitlements*.

Of course, the stalwarts could lodge a plausible complaint based on the principle of *desert*: in the absence of justifying differences among the various groups of workers, the principle of desert implies that those who worked longer hours, thereby expending more effort and producing more, should receive higher wages than the other groups of workers. That is, the principle of desert supports allocation based on proportionate reward.

Still, under the hypothetical, the principle of desert provides only a reason, and not automatically decisive evidence, for morally appropriate conclusions. The vineyard owner could point out that the differential contracts were not grounded in discrimination or prejudice against disenfranchised groups; on the contrary, the workers in one group were indistinguishable from those in the other groups in terms of gender, religion, ethnicity, and the like. Moreover, no group was exploited in that even the stalwarts received what was taken to be a fair wage for a full day's labor. Thus, in this case, distributive justice is served where entitlements are fulfilled precisely.

Claims grounded in the principle of desert seem more abstract here and should not trump entitlement requirements. One might retort that had the stalwarts known in advance that the other groups would be receiving the same wage as they were offered even though working fewer hours, they would have refused the owner's offer and bargained for a higher wage. But advocates of the vineyard owner could rebut this charge, citing two considerations: first, when the owner initially approached the stalwarts he was unaware that he would be returning to contract for more workers—hence, he could not have made the stalwarts aware of what he himself did not know at the time; second, the owner offered the stalwarts the standard agreement for day laborers—he had not sought to short-change them given established labor practices of the day and place. Moreover, the stalwarts would have been unlikely to refuse to work given that their alternative would be idleness.

The situation in the parable, however, is different from my hypothetical. There no group of workers has set entitlements other than the stalwarts. The other groups have agreed to work for nine hours, six hours, three hours, and one hour, respectively, for "whatsoever is right." While they undoubtedly assumed that they would receive wages proportionate to their hours worked, they ended up receiving a standard full day's pay. The parable includes no evidence that, say, the backups objected that they had been short-changed because the fortunate sons, who had labored eight fewer hours, received the same wage as they had. We must assume that all members of groups other than the stalwarts were overjoyed at receiving higher wages than they had expected.

But a problem emerges. The last four groups of workers lacked fixed entitlements because they labored without a clear contract. By offering to pay "whatsoever is right," the owner explicitly allows wider moral considerations—than those arising from the principle of entitlement—to come into play. Thus, the stalwarts might well have argued that proportionate reward underwritten by the principle of personal desert should determine economic distribution.

Unlike the case of the previously considered hypothetical, in the parable the principle of entitlement should not clearly control moral conclusions for two reasons: first, among the various groups of workers, only the stalwarts have fixed entitlements; and, second, by invoking the phrase "whatsoever is right," the vineyard owner has invited wider moral assessment.

To demean the character of the stalwarts by asking accusatorily "Is thine eye evil because I am good?" seems harsh. The stalwarts are not envious of gifts that the vineyard owner has bestowed generously and independently of wage-labor agreements. Instead, a charitable interpretation would conclude that the stalwarts question the vineyard owner's allocations in the context of a series of wage-labor agreements *wherein the owner had tacitly accepted the relevancy of moral considerations beyond strict entitlements*. Of course, the vineyard owner might have offered moral considerations that could have justified his policy of disproportionate reward. For example, perhaps the members of the other groups were needier than the members of the stalwarts; perhaps they had fewer opportunities to be employed, and the like. But in the absence of such moral considerations, the vineyard owner's icy rebuke of the stalwarts seems excessive.

Again, my analysis understands the parable only at the level of human economics. Those who insist plausibly that we should analyze the story only in terms of Jesus' need to soften the growing pretensions of the apostles or of Jesus' efforts to defend his associations with and acceptance of sinners or of Jesus' message that God's grace of salvation is a gift that is not subject to human expectations will be unmoved.

Nevertheless, I offer my analysis from the assumption that the parables are also designed to provide moral lessons for leading a good human life. To the extent possible, the parables are invoked to guide human beings in their efforts to prefigure the Kingdom of God—in whatever form we understand that Kingdom—by our actions today in our world. As always, Jesus' prescriptions in the Parable of the Laborers in the Vineyard transcend the conventional wisdom of his time and place. As ever, Jesus forces us to reassess the received opinion of our time and place.

NOTES

1. The section on the interpretation of the parable has been informed by Klyne R. Snodgrass, *Stories with Intent* (Grand Rapids, MI: William B. Eerdmans Publishing Company, 2008); Craig L. Blomberg, *Interpreting the Parables* (Downers Grove, IL: InterVarsity Press, 1990); Richard N. Longenecker (ed.), *The Challenge of Jesus' Parables* (Grand Rapids, MI: William B. Eerdmans Publishing Company, 2000).

2. See, for example, Snodgrass, *Stories with Intent*, 370–71.

3. Ibid.

4. Ibid., 374.

5. Michael P. Knowles, "Everyone Who Hears These Words of Mine," in Longenecker, *The Challenge of Jesus' Parables*, 300–301.

6. Snodgrass, *Stories with Intent*, 377.

7. This chapter has been informed by Joel Feinberg, *Doing and Deserving* (Princeton: Princeton University Press, 1970); John Kleinig, "The Concept of Desert," *The Philosophical Quarterly* 8, no. 1 (1971); David Miller, *Social Justice* (Oxford: Oxford University Press, 1976); Julian Lamont, "The Concept of Desert in Distributive Justice," *The Philosophical Quarterly* 44, no. 174 (1994); Brian Barry, *Political Argument* (London: Routledge & Kegan Paul, 1965); George Sher, "Effort, Ability, and Personal Desert," *Philosophy and Public Affairs* 8, no. 361 (1979); Fred Feldman, "Desert: Reconsideration of Some Received Wisdom," *Mind* 104, no. 413 (1995); John Rawls, *A Theory of Justice* (Cambridge, MA: Harvard University Press, 1971); Robert Nozick, *Anarchy, State, and Utopia* (New York: Basic Books, 1974); Michael A. Slote, "Desert, Consent and Justice," *Philosophy and Public Affairs* 2, no. 323 (1973); Alan Zaitchik, "On Deserving to Deserve," *Philosophy and Public Affairs* 6: 370 (1977).

8. Feldman, "Desert," 418.

9. Rawls, *Theory of Justice*, 311–13.

10. See, for example, *United States Nursing Corp. v. Saint Joseph Medical Ctr.*, 39 F.3d 790, 792 (7th Cir. 1994).

11. Robert A. Hillman, "Debunking Some Myths About Unconscionability," 67 *Cornell Law Review* 1 (1981).

FOUR

The Unforgiving Servant: "Shouldest Not Thou Also Have Had Compassion?"

Therefore is the kingdom of heaven likened unto a certain king, which would take account of his servants. And when he had begun to reckon, one was brought unto him, which owed him ten thousand talents [an absurdly astronomical amount]. But forasmuch as he had not to pay, his lord commanded him to be sold, and his wife, and children, and all that he had, and payment to be made. The servant therefore fell down, and worshipped him, saying Lord, have patience with me, and I will pay thee all. Then the lord of that servant was moved with compassion, and loosed him, and forgave him the debt. But the same servant went out, and found one of his fellow servants, which owed him an hundred pence [100 denarii]: and he laid hands on him, and took him by the throat, saying, Pay me that thou owest. And his fellow servant fell down at his feet, and besought him, saying, Have patience with me, and I will pay thee all. And he would not: but went and cast him into prison, till he should pay the debt. So when his fellow servants saw what was done, they were very sorry, and came and told unto their lord all that was done. Then his lord, after that he had called him, said unto him, O thou wicked servant, I forgave thee all that debt, because thou desiredst me: Shouldest not thou also have had compassion on thy fellow servant, even as I had pity on thee? And his lord was wroth, and delivered him to the tormentors till he should pay all that was due unto him. So likewise shall my heavenly Father do also unto you, if ye from your hearts forgive not every one his brother their trespasses.

(Matt. 18:23–35)

INTERPRETATION OF THE PARABLE

The servant of a king ran up a debt of ten thousand talents.[1] In the place and at the time of the parable that would be such an astronomical amount as to be impossible to repay.

> A "talent" is a measurement of weight of gold, silver, or copper. It varied between approximately 60 and 90 pounds. Ten thousand talents would be about 204 metric tons. Depending on which metal was used, a talent was the equivalent of about 6000 denarii, which would make the first servant's debt 60,000,000 denarii, and at one denarius a day . . . would require a day laborer over 164,000 years to repay! The annual salary of Herod the Great was reportedly 900 talents . . . The price of a slave usually ranged from about 500 to 2000 denarii.[2]

The fantastic amount of the debt undoubtedly illustrates the expansiveness of the king's forgiveness. At first, once the servant could not repay the debt, the king orders a fire sale: the entire family would be sold into slavery—fetching at most two thousand denarii per person—and the family's holdings would be liquidated. The servant, literally, flings himself on the mercy of the king, pledges repayment over time (which under the circumstances could never have occurred), and "worships" the king. Moved by the servant's entreaties and suddenly pitying his dire financial condition, the king forgives the entire debt. In an amazing alteration of fate, the servant has gone from a debtor who has saddled himself with an obligation that is impossible to fulfill to a potential slave to a financially free person. Had the parable ended at this point we might well conclude that perfecting the art of "worshipping" superiors and begging for forgiveness of our transgressions were the secrets to success in the Kingdom of God. We are told that the king "would take account of his servants." This suggests that he is seeking settlement of all monies owed him and we should assume that all those who sought forgiveness and "worshipped" him met a happy fate similar to the resolution enjoyed by this first debtor-servant.

But there is more to the story. The forgiven servant seeks out one of his colleagues who owes him a hundred denarii. He, literally, tries to squeeze the money out of his fellow servant, choking him while demanding payment. The debtor falls before the forgiven servant's feet and pledges repayment while requesting a time extension. Either because the forgiven servant embodied no compassion or because his colleague's performance was less convincing than his own earlier efforts with the king, the forgiven servant has his colleague thrown into a debtor's prison. The forgiven servant had not absorbed the lessons of his encounter with the king.

Fellow servants observe all of this, sympathize with their imprisoned comrade, and inform the king. The lord summons the forgiven servant and points out the obvious: while the king had responded compassionately to the forgiven servant's dire predicament once he had pled his case, the forgiven servant was obdurate and pitiless when placed in the same situation regarding his debtor-colleague. The king then withdraws his forgiveness and delivers the man to "tormentors" until the day that servant can pay his debt in full—which is never.

The lessons of the parable are clear: God's forgiveness, analogously to that of the king in the first scene of the parable, is boundless; those who have been forgiven and who have benefited from compassion (and grace) have a special duty to forgive the transgressions of their fellow man; and those who fail to forgive the transgressions of their fellow man will incur a terrifying destiny. In sum, forgiveness and compassion are the hallmark characteristics of the Kingdom of God. Crucial to these lessons is that forgiveness encompasses both material and spiritual realms. Forgiving material debts in response to the dire need of others is often wise use of money; forgiving the spiritual and nonmaterial transgressions of others is often wise use of compassion.

The paramount philosophical issues arising from the parable revolve around the notions of forgiveness and mercy.

THE CONCEPT OF FORGIVENESS

The paramount questions surrounding the concept of forgiveness are these: What is involved when one person forgives another? What is the relationship between wrongdoers and their transgressions? Is forgiving others a moral duty or a supererogatory act? Must the transgressing party repent his wrongful deed in order to earn forgiveness? What sort of attitude is required in order for one person to forgive another? What is the relationship between retributive justice and forgiveness? Does forgiving wrongdoing condone past and encourage future transgressions? Why should we forgive wrongdoers, and why is forgiveness important? What is the difference, if any, between forgiving a wrongdoer and forgetting his wrong? Is Jesus' view of forgiveness unique in some respects?[3]

Let's begin by describing the elements of forgiveness. In order for one person to forgive another we must identify a wrong that has been committed by the latter of which the former is aware. If no wrong has been committed then there is nothing to forgive. Moreover, if a wrong has been committed but the victim is unaware of that act, then she is not in a position to forgive. Furthermore, if a wrong has been committed and the victim is aware of the wrong, but she does not know the identity of the wrongdoer, then she cannot forgive the wrongdoer. Bear in mind also that not all misdeeds are legal wrongs punishable by the judiciary nor are all moral wrongs grave and significant. A moral wrong as simple and relatively minor as speaking ill of a friend to another person is a misdeed subject to possible forgiveness. For purposes of simplification, I will designate the wrongdoer as "Thayer" and the wronged party as "Vanzetti." Thus, our *first element: Thayer wronged Vanzetti and Vanzetti acknowledges that Thayer wronged him.*

However, sometimes people transgress against others under circumstances where they are not fully responsible for their acts. That is, the transgressor has a legitimate excuse or justification for his act. An excuse would mitigate or erase the transgressor's moral culpability for the act. Perhaps the transgressor was subject to an irresistible impulse, or was coerced into acting by an external force, or was deceived into thinking that the act was actually permissible, or was otherwise not responsible for what he did. A justification would demonstrate that the act was not in fact a wrong because the agent performed it because of a public necessity, in deference to a higher duty, in self-defense, or the like. If the transgressor acted with justification, then he committed no wrong that is subject to forgiveness; if he acted with a legitimate excuse, then he may not be morally culpable for the act and, again, he is not subject to forgiveness. Thus, our *second element: Thayer is fully responsible and morally culpable for his action and Vanzetti acknowledges these facts.*

If a transgressor is to be forgiven the only person in a position to forgive is the person who was wronged, her agents, and, perhaps, those uncommonly close to her who were also wronged to some extent. This is the case at least where we are discussing interpersonal forgiveness. In cases of judicial forgiveness, we can view the decision makers as the legal agents of the victim or, probably better, we can consider such instances legal forgiveness independent of the victim. Surely, a judge might forgive a miscreant under circumstances where the victim of the wrongdoer's transgression remains obdurate and vice versa. Moreover, after coming to understand the relevant facts, the public at large may feel sympathy for the wrongdoer, but unaffected third parties are not in a position to forgive the wrongdoer. Thus, our *third element: Only Vanzetti, his explicitly empowered agents, and, perhaps, those uncommonly close to Vanzetti who were also wronged to some extent by Thayer are in a position to forgive Thayer.*

In order to forgive, the victim does not accept or condone the past wrong, or encourage future wrongs. Instead, the victim continues to acknowledge that the transgressor is fully responsible for his wrongful action. What forgiveness requires is that the victim surrenders all negative feelings and attitudes toward the transgressor that arose from the wrongdoing. Forgiveness, then, is a function of how the victim regards the transgressor. Thus, our *fourth element: In order to forgive Thayer, Vanzetti must relinquish his negative feelings and attitudes toward Thayer that arose from Thayer's wrongdoing.*

But how can the victim attain such a state? How can the victim retain his conviction that he has been wronged and that the perpetrator is fully responsible for that wrong yet relinquish his negative feelings of the perpetrator that sprang from that event? It would seem that the victim must distinguish the wrongful deed from the value of the fully responsible agent who performed it. That is, the victim cannot *define* the perpetrator by the wrongful deed at issue. The victim must perceive the perpetrator as more and better than the wrongful deed that gave rise to the understandably negative attitudes toward the perpetrator that the victim initially embodied. In effect, the victim must distance the perpetrator from his wrongful action, or perhaps more precisely, the victim must evaluate the perpetrator from a wider, more charitable perspective. At first blush, the victim judges the perpetrator only by the instant wrong he has committed; in order to forgive the perpetrator, the victim must either separate the perpetrator from the wrongful deed or assess the perpetrator from a broader, more sympathetic vantage point. Thus, our *fifth element: In order to forgive Thayer, Vanzetti must distinguish the wrongful deed from the value of the fully responsible person, Thayer, who performed it.*

This is easier stated than achieved. What could lead the victim to separate so neatly the wrongful deed from the value of the fully responsible perpetrator who performed it? After all, evaluating the perpetrator from a wider perspective may well result in learning about a host of other, even more horrifying, misdeeds that the person has wreaked upon other victims. One possibility is that the perpetrator sincerely repents his wrongdoing. Under such circumstances, the perpetrator distances himself from his wrongful deed. He invites the victim to no longer define him by his wrongdoing and to judge his value as higher than he had demonstrated by his mischief. Here the victim does not need to *create* a distance between the perpetrator and the wrongful deed but merely *recognize* the distance that the perpetrator himself has forged through his repentance.

Suppose a perpetrator of a wrong has sincerely repented. Does this imply that the victim of that wrong is obligated to forgive the perpetrator? From the vantage point of conventional moral wisdom, the answer is "no." Forgiving the perpetrator would be a supererogatory act on the part of the victim, not the discharge of a moral duty. The question, however, is more difficult to answer from the vantage point of Jesus. For example, Jesus instructs his disciples, "Take heed to yourselves: If thy brother trespass against thee, rebuke him; and if he repent, forgive him. And if he trespass against thee seven times in a day, and seven times in a day turn again to thee, saying, I repent; thou shalt forgive him" (Luke 17:3–4); and when the apostle Peter inquired, "How oft shall my brother sin against me, and I forgive him? Till seven times?" Jesus answered, "I say not unto thee, Until seven times: but, Until seventy times seven" (Matt. 18:21–22). In the Parable of the Unforgiving Servant: "And his lord was wroth, and delivered him to the tormentors till he should pay all that was due unto him. So likewise shall my heavenly Father do also unto you, if ye from your hearts forgive not every one his brother their trespasses" (Matt. 18:34–35).

The force of such passages appears to hold that a perpetrator's repentance is a sufficient condition for the victim's forgiveness. Moreover, the passages from Matthew do not seem to require repentance on the part of the perpetrator; the victim must forgive even trespassers who are recidivists. On this interpretation, a perpetrator's repentance triggers a moral duty on the part of the victim to forgive; here forgiveness is not a supererogatory act. Moreover, these passages hold open the possibility that even if the perpetrator does not repent and continues to transgress against the same victim that victim *must* forgive. In effect, even where the perpetrator has not distanced himself from his misdeed, the victim must somehow *create* that distance between the agent and his wrongful act.

Nicholas Wolterstorff resists such an interpretation. He is concerned that understanding a perpetrator's repentance as sufficient condition for the victim's forgiveness would imply that such a transgressor would have a vested right to be forgiven once he repented. Thus, a victim who refused to forgive would have wronged the repentant perpetrator. This is unacceptable for Wolterstorff so he offers two possible alternative interpretations of the biblical passages.

One possibility is that Jesus' words set forth an ideal toward which to strive, one that goes beyond the requirements of moral duty and retributive justice:

> One possibility is that Jesus is setting before them a better way to go, a way that goes beyond what duty and justice require, a way in tune with the ways of our Father in heaven, the way of supererogatory love.[4]

I find this possibility unpersuasive for two reasons. First, the language of the biblical passages is not aspirational. Jesus informs his disciples that they *shall* forgive those trespassers who repent. If Jesus was setting forth a series of supererogatory suggestions we would expect the term "should" instead of "must" and "shall." Second, Jesus is not "setting before them a better way" in the sense of offering them an alternative moral wisdom that they might emulate. Instead, Jesus appears to be informing them of *the* proper way to act in the world. His words are neither equivocal nor wavering.

The second possibility that Wolterstorff offers is that the duty to forgive does not vest a right in the repentant perpetrator but, instead, vests a right in third parties: Jesus and God the Father. Thus, a victim who refused to forgive a repentant transgressor would not be wronging the transgressor but would be wronging God.

> The other possibility is that he is declaring that they have an obligation toward Jesus and our Father in heaven to forgive the repentant wrongdoer. This would be a so-called third-party duty; they have a duty *toward* Jesus and the Father *with respect to* their fellows to forgive them. Correlative to this third-party duty would be a third-party right: Jesus

and the Father have a right against them with respect to their fellows, to forgive their fellows. If they did not forgive the brother who has wronged them and is repentant, they wrong not the brother but Jesus and the Father.[5]

In my view, this is by far the stronger of the possibilities that Wolterstorff presents for at least two reasons. First, the language of the Parable of the Unforgiving Servant suggests that God takes special umbrage at those who refuse to forgive their trespassing neighbors. Without being blasphemous, God apparently takes the refusal to forgive personally—as if God has also been wronged by the refusal. Second, this interpretation permits what I take to be the gist of Jesus' position on forgiveness: where there is repentance there is no option, we must forgive. As is typical, Jesus' view goes beyond the conventional moral wisdom of his day as well as that of our time.

I would, however, add to Wolterstorff's second possibility. Why does God take the refusal to forgive a repentant wrongdoer so personally? I suspect that not only does God sense that God's rights have been infringed but also that the repentant wrongdoer has also in some sense been short-changed. I would offer the following: once the wrongdoer repents he *deserves* to be forgiven by the victim of the wrong, but he is not *entitled* to be forgiven. That is, the repentant wrongdoer lacks a vested right to be forgiven; he is not in a position to claim that he must be forgiven because he possesses such a right. Thus, a victim who refuses to forgive the repentant wrongdoer has not violated his rights. But the repentant wrongdoer *deserves* to be forgiven because he has distanced himself from his misdeed. Claims based on desert do not always vest a right, and this is one such case. The desert claim in this case provides a moral reason why the victim should forgive the repentant wrongdoer. Such reasons are not automatically conclusive, but where, as here, there are no countervailing moral reasons, then they should determine moral action. In refusing to forgive, the victim would be unjustifiably giving the repentant less than he deserved. Accordingly, God's ire is twice raised: one of his human creatures is receiving less than he deserves and God's third-party rights have been infringed. In this fashion, we can preserve our intuition that the repentant wrongdoer is not in a position to demand forgiveness as his right yet underscore Jesus' conviction that forgiveness in such cases is mandatory. Thus, our *sixth element: From the standpoint of human conventional moral wisdom, Thayer's sincere repentance is one way that he can distance himself from his wrongful action. Under such circumstances, from the standpoint of conventional morality, Vanzetti's forgiveness is not morally required but is recommended as a supererogatory act. From the standpoint of Jesus' revolutionary moral message, Thayer's sincere repentance creates an obligation such that Vanzetti must forgive Thayer. Should Vanzetti refuse to forgive Thayer under such circumstances he would have failed to discharge his moral duty in that he would have given Thayer less than he deserved and he would have infringed on God's third-party rights.*

But suppose that the perpetrator of a wrong does not repent and thus does not distance himself from his transgression. Is it possible for the victim to create unilaterally a distance between the wrongdoer and his wrong? If so, under what circumstances would such a creation of distance occur?

One set of possibilities would be wrongdoings that seem out of character. Here the victim might conclude that the misdeed does not reflect the overall worth of the perpetrator because the wrongful action is aberrational. For example, if a person has an otherwise acceptable record of past behavior and the instant wrong is a first offense. If so, the first offense may well be judged as out of character for the perpetrator. Under such circumstances, the victim might create unilaterally a distance between the wrongful deed and the value of the perpetrator. Even in the absence of the perpetrator's repentance, the victim may decide to forgive the transgressor even though the victim continues to recognize that the transgressor is fully responsible for wronging her. But why would the perpetrator not repent in such a case? At the extreme, he might have died prior to having the chance to repent. Forgiving the dead for their transgressions remains possible. Even if the perpetrator has not died, he might not repent because he mistakenly believes that his act was permissible. Here he would remain fully responsible for the wrong and also responsible for his mistaken belief. Moreover, another case occurs where the perpetrator does repent his wrong but the victim is unaware of that fact and thus cannot take it into account. Another possibility is that the perpetrator lives under the fatuous code of never regretting any of his acts and never apologizing for them. Following this stringent principle rigidly, the perpetrator does not consider repentance a live option.

Another example of wrongdoings that seem out of character is the perpetrator who has enjoyed a salutary relationship with the victim and whose current wrong seems minor by comparison to the past benefits of the relationship. Even in the absence of repentance, the victim may well create unilaterally a distance between the instant wrong and the overall character of the perpetrator and forgive the misdeed.

Beyond wrongdoings that seem out of character, other possibilities for forgiving in the absence of repentance can be advanced. For example, suppose I am having difficulties in an intimate relationship that has hitherto brought me great joy. I have a well-intentioned but somewhat inept friend who is greatly concerned for my well-being. She tries to intercede in my problem and facilitate reconciliation between my lover and me. However, by officiously intermeddling in my affairs she makes the problem worse. She wrongs me by insinuating herself into my situation without my permission and by making an unpleasant situation much worse. She would remain fully responsible for her wrongful deed—her worthy intentions are neither excuses nor justifications for her actions. Still, even in the absence of repentance, I may well forgive her because her actions were well intentioned although poorly executed.

Yet another case for forgiving in the absence of repentance centers on the suffering of the perpetrator. If the transgressor has already suffered significantly, perhaps even disproportionately to the gravity of the wrong, then the victim may choose to forgive. For example, suppose a prominent person commits a wrong that becomes highly publicized. As a result, the transgressor suffers a host of humiliations including loss of reputation, fading business opportunities, family dissolution, and the like. As the victim of that wrong, I might well conclude that the transgressor has suffered sufficiently and forgive him even in the absence of repentance.

Does forgiving unrepentant transgressors unjustifiably condone wrongdoing? I think not. Remember, by creating a distance between the agent and his wrongful act, the victim can still deplore the wrong but reconcile with the wrongdoer. Remember that in all the cases of the victim unilaterally creating distance between the wrongdoer and his deed that I have presented, the perpetrator remains fully responsible for his action, which remains a wrong.

However, I do not want to oversell the notion that victims can create unilaterally a distance between wrongdoers and their misdeeds. Clearly, that will depend on the gravity of the misdeed, the antecedent character of the transgressor, what happens after the offense, and how the transgressor conducts himself in the aftermath. That the transgressor has the opportunity to repent his wrong but fails to do so cannot, all other things being equal, count in favor of forgiveness.

Moreover, the neat separation of agents from their acts can be dangerous. Just as in the case of agapic love, when we begin stripping people of their choices, actions, and deeds they begin to fade away as concrete individuals and appear more as abstract exemplars of humanity.

To forgive the person requires, among other things, that enough constitutive attributes remain that we can distinguish among individuals. These remarks are intended as cautions to those who are tempted to forgive as a matter of course.

But is this not what Jesus requires? Does Jesus not insist that we forgive others who trespass against us and that we do so even if they do so repeatedly? Does Jesus not hold that repentance is a sufficient but not a necessary condition of forgiveness?

Whether Jesus requires that the perpetrator of an offense repent his wrongdoing in order to gain the forgiveness of his victim is unclear. If Jesus' moral message is that we should forgive only repentant sinners, then his teaching in this regard only underscores Jewish tradition. If Jesus teaches that we should forgive even unrepentant sinners—that we can create unilaterally the distance between sinner and sin that is necessary for forgiveness—then his approach is characteristically novel. Moreover, understanding Jesus this way coheres neatly with numerous other aspects of his moral message: bestowing generosity and grace even where those gifts are not strictly deserved; prefiguring the ideals of the Kingdom of God now; and forgiving the trespasses and debts of other people just as we hope that God will forgive our moral shortcomings.

But we should not take this observation too far because to do so would make the act of repentance insignificant. Jesus also implores us to repent our sins as a step toward personal transformation. To be forgiven automatically creates a disincentive for perpetrators of offenses to distance themselves from their sins as a prelude to invigorating their hearts and souls. In fact, just as in the Parable of the Prodigal Son, Jesus rejoices in the personal transformation of repentant sinners more effusively than he does in the presence of even the steadfast rectitude of the morally upright: "I say unto you, that likewise joy shall be in heaven over one sinner that repenteth, more than ninety and nine just persons, which need no repentance" (Luke 15:7); "They that are whole have no need of the physician, but they that are sick: I came not to call the righteous, but sinners to repentance" (Mark 2:17).

The most reasonable conclusion to draw is that repenting our sins is paramount, both to begin to repair our relationship with the person whom we have wronged and also to begin our internal transformation. That is, perpetrators of wrongs should do for their part the work required to distance themselves from their misdeeds. But on at least some occasions, injured parties should create unilaterally the distance between sin and sinner required for genuine forgiveness. To do so as a matter of course would nullify much of the incentive to repent and could even encourage more wrongdoing, but to do so on appropriate occasions brings glory to a host of concerns critical to Jesus' moral message. At times, even where the perpetrator of a wrong against us does not repent his misdeed, we should forgive him even while recognizing the severity of his wrong. Knowing when to render such forgiveness, like most of Jesus' moral teaching, requires practical moral wisdom and is not susceptible to adjudication by applying bright-line rules or formalist reasoning.

Thus, although some biblical passages may suggest such a stance, we should not conclude that Jesus requires human beings to always forgive their trespassers even in the absence of repentance. While I do accept that Jesus holds the strong view that repentance by a perpetrator of a wrong is a sufficient condition for forgiveness, I do not conclude that Jesus held the even stronger view that victims must always forgive as such. After all, Christian theology is clear that even God typically requires repentance of sins. While God may bestow grace and confer more upon some human beings than they deserve or to which they are entitled, God presumably does not do this as a matter of course. Moreover, if Jesus required all victims to forgive automatically their trespassers, repentance would in effect be irrelevant for forgiveness—just an interesting sidebar to the required story.

Thus, our *seventh element: Even if Thayer does not repent his wrongful deed, Vanzetti can create unilaterally a distance between Thayer and his wrong such that Vanzetti can forgive Thayer. Some relevant circumstances that may energize that unilateral creation: the instant wrong is the perpetrator's first offense; the perpetrator's wrong was grounded in good intentions; the perpetrator and the victim enjoyed a prior salutary relationship; or the perpetrator suffered sufficiently in the aftermath of his wrong. Should Vanzetti forgive Thayer on the basis of Vanzetti's unilateral creation of distance between Thayer and Thayer's wrong, then Vanzetti's forgiveness is a supererogatory act. Jesus' revolutionary moral message seems to confirm this analysis generally but suggests that sometimes morality requires that victims forgive those who wrong them even in the absence of repentance.*

What is the metaphysical result of forgiving a wrongdoer? Where the transgressor repents and the victim forgives, we can talk in terms of reconciliation. Neither party views the other as alien or estranged. Each has made an effort to mend the rupture between them. Even if they did not enjoy a prior relationship, once the instant misdeed established them as victim and transgressor they were involved with each other. At that point, hard feelings ensued: the victim, understandably, joined the transgressor to his wrongdoing and judged the transgressor negatively. Once the transgressor repents and the victim forgives, the victim relinquishes his hard feelings toward the perpetrator and the transgressor separates herself from her wrongful deed. This opens the way for reconciliation and renewal.

The Parable of the Prodigal Son provides a classic example: the father forgives the wrong that his younger son has inflicted upon him; recognizes that his son has repented; refuses to judge his son based on his worst moments; and immediately offers reconciliation and renewal of their relationship. Of course, from the narrative, the father did not relinquish retributive feelings toward his son because the father never gives evidence that he bore such sentiments. Either the father never fully recognized his son's actions as wrongs or he acknowledged his son's actions as wrongs but refused from the start to harbor retributive emotions toward his son.

But what occurs when the victim unilaterally creates the distance between the transgressor and her misdeed? Here the transgressor has not separated herself from her misdeed. How can reconciliation and renewal take place unilaterally? A relationship requires at least two parties. Where the transgressor refuses to repent her wrongful act, to talk of reconciliation and renewal is misplaced. To be more precise, I would think that the victim's forgiveness in the absence of repentance is an offer of reconciliation that can occur only if the transgressor reciprocates in kind. Even in the absence of the transgressor's repentance, the victim has relinquished his hard feelings, but that is insufficient for reconciliation. The transgressor must bring something to the table.

Some reasons why the victim might be inclined to forgive transgressors are epistemological: Human beings are flawed, fallible creatures; we all err at times; we cannot know fully the background socialization of transgressors; we cannot arrive at fully accurate judgments about the characters of other people; and we rarely are fully aware of the social circumstances other people endure. A principle of charity suggests that judging other people by their worst moments and by their most immoral acts is unwise. Instead, a wider assessment is recommended, and the opportunity to atone for one's worst moments should be offered.

Thus, our *eighth element: Should Vanzetti forgive a repentant Thayer, the metaphysical result is reconciliation and renewal. Should Vanzetti forgive an unrepentant Thayer, the metaphysical result is an offer of reconciliation and renewal from Vanzetti to Thayer. To accept that offer, Thayer must distance himself from his wrongful act or otherwise reach out to Vanzetti.*

What is the relationship between forgiveness and punishment? Is forgiveness compatible with fully exacting the requirements of retributive justice? Or does forgiveness imply the waiving of all punishment?

Forgiveness is personal between the transgressor and the victim (or her agents or, perhaps, those especially close to her) and involves the victim's positive change of *feelings* toward the transgressor. Punishment is typically a legal notion whereby rightful authorities exact deprivation on the transgressor for a host of purposes: retribution, restitution, deterrence, rehabilitation, or incarceration. Retributive punishment implies depriving the transgressor of his freedom and many of his privileges in order to balance moral scales: the transgressor deserves to be retributively punished because he is responsible for wrongdoing. Restitution implies forcing the transgressor to make his victim whole by restoring, to the extent possible, the *status quo ante* through monetary compensation. Deterrence implies depriving the transgressor of his freedom and many of his privileges in order to deter him or others from committing similar offenses. Rehabilitation implies depriving the transgressor of his freedom and many of his privileges in order to reform him. Incarceration implies depriving the transgressor of his freedom in order to protect society from his possible mayhem in the future.

Should the victim forgive the transgressor, she relinquishes her retributive feelings and her fantasies of vengeance. That is, the victim surrenders all thoughts of retaliation along with her harsh evaluation of the transgressor. The victim may, however, still conclude that institutional punishment of the (convicted) transgressor is appropriate on grounds of deterrence, rehabilitation, or incarceration. Moreover, forgiveness is compatible with seeking and accepting restitution from the transgressor. Indeed, making restitution is one way that a transgressor can facilitate the process of reconciliation and renewal.

Consider the following scenario: a perpetrator transgresses against a victim. After the perpetrator repents his wrong, the victim forgives him. She pleads with the legal authorities to forego punishing the perpetrator because she is convinced that he poses no future danger to others. The court, nevertheless, sentences the convicted perpetrator and cites retributive grounds.

That the court has retributively punished the offender does not vitiate the victim's forgiveness of that offender. The victim's forgiveness is personal and involves her surrendering feelings of revenge and retribution. That the rightful authorities decide to punish the offender does not alter the victim's state of mind toward her transgressor.

One might argue that once the offender has served his sentence, once he has "paid his debt to society," then his wrong is expunged and there is nothing for the victim to forgive. In my judgment, that view is mistaken. Yes, the offender should now be allowed to rejoin society and enjoy freedom, but the victim's feelings toward the offender are still at issue. For example, suppose a negligent or reckless driver of a motor vehicle seriously injures a pedestrian. The victim was not targeted by the motorist; the harm was accidental. But the reckless driver is still culpable for his wrong, and the victim, we will suppose, is paralyzed by his malfeasance. The driver sincerely repents his actions, pleads guilty, and is sentenced to a significant term in prison. He serves his time as a model prisoner and is eventually released.

Does it follow that the moral universe is now balanced and there is nothing for the victim to forgive? Hardly. In such a case, the *status quo ante* is impossible to restore. The victim has been and remains paralyzed. That the reckless driver has been retributively punished registers no effects on the victim's condition. She could have, of course, forgiven the transgressor at the time he repented and pled guilty, but suppose that she did not. Her career as an Olympic skier was ruined and she harbors ill will toward an obtuse motorist who was texting while driving at a high speed. Once the offender serves his sentence and is released, her feelings may or may not change. But the point is that forgiveness is still an option. That the convicted motorist has served his sentence does not imply that his wrongdoing has been expunged and that there is no wrong that might be forgiven.

This is in fact the case even in those situations where restitution does seem to restore the *status quo ante*. Suppose a reckless motorist slams into your parked car which is occupied by you and your small child. Miraculously, although your vehicle is severely damaged, you and the child suffer no significant injuries. Neither you nor the reckless driver has car insurance, but he makes full restitution, and your car is returned to its former condition. Does it follow that forgiveness is impossible because restitution has expunged the reckless driver's wrong? No.

You have still suffered great fear at the time of the collision, terror at the thought of the injuries that might have occurred, and major inconvenience during the period when your car was being repaired. The reckless driver's restitution cannot alter those facts. You may or may not decide to forgive his recklessness, but the point is that the possibility of forgiveness is not eliminated by his act of restitution—restitution does not expunge the wrong in the sense that there is nothing remaining that might be forgiven.

Jesus has an important addition to this analysis. Let's imagine a recidivist wrongdoer who never repents his deeds. In fact, he consistently reaffirms his connection to his transgressions. After every offense, even after those for which he is apprehended by the authorities, he brays, "I am proud of my mischief. These acts are true to my character. I apologize for nothing. I hope to increase my mayhem in the future. I've got to be me." In other words, by refusing to recant his actions and by pledging more of the same if possible, he utterly refuses to distance himself from his wrongdoing. Let's also assume that the typical ways that victims can unilaterally distance perpetrators from their wrongs are unavailable in this case. That is, the victim is not the subject of the perpetrator's first offense; the perpetrator's wrong was not grounded in good intentions; the perpetrator and the victim did not enjoy a prior salutary relationship; and the perpetrator cannot reasonably be judged as having suffered sufficiently in the aftermath of his wrong. Under these circumstances, it does not seem that the victim can forgive his transgressor because the required distance between the offender and his wrongful deed has not been established by the offender and cannot be created by the victim.

What would Jesus say? Even where forgiveness, as in the case above is not possible, the victim must still love his offender and advance his good. For example, "For if ye love them which love you, what thank have ye? For sinners also love those that love them. And if ye do good to them which do good to you, what thank have ye? For sinners also do even the same. . . . But love ye your enemies, and do good, and lend, hoping for nothing again; and your reward shall be great" (Luke 6:32–35); "Ye have heard that it hath been said, An eye for an eye, and a tooth for a tooth: But I say unto you, That ye resist not evil. . . . Love your enemies, bless them that curse you, do good to them that hate you, and pray for them which despitefully use you, and persecute you" (Matt. 5:38–39, 44).

This means, in part, relinquishing retributive feelings and banishing vengeful attitudes. Victims are enjoined to advance the good of even their offenders who remain "enemies." While it is easy to love those who love us and to benefit those who benefit us, the genuine test of our humanity is our response to those who transgress against us. We should not respond to transgressors precisely as they have treated us or even with the proportionate punishment that they deserve. Instead, we should aspire to a taxing ideal: loving those who have injured us. Perhaps the victim can also forget about the transgression, at least in time. Still, these approaches do not rise to the level of forgiveness because the required distance between offender and offense has not been established or created.

Is it humanly possible to love our unrepentant "enemy," seek to advance his good, and, perhaps, forget about his transgressions? Let's return to the hypothetical case I sketched. The recidivist offender, apparently lacking all redeeming social value, who, after being convicted of a major crime, snarls churlishly and sputters that he desires only to inflict more mayhem in the future. Can the mother of the young man, who was the murder victim of this lowlife, genuinely love the murderer, forego feelings of revenge, and seek his good? Although she probably will never forget what the murderer has done and cannot forgive him in the fullest philosophical sense of that term, I must admit that some victims—in this case, the mother of the victim—can achieve Jesus' ideal.

I say this because I was once an attorney in New York City and witnessed precisely such an event on a few occasions. Obviously, this does not occur as a matter of course, but only rarely. But I have seen and heard victims and their parents profess love for those who have grievously transgressed against them; they seemingly surrendered all thoughts of vengeance. Moreover, some of these paragons have tried to advance the good of these offenders after their convictions. Obviously, such a response is wildly counterintuitive, radically at variance with conventional moral wisdom, and fiercely at odds with human instincts. That some victims and their parents acted in such a manner can be explained only by their embrace of Jesus' revolutionary moral message.

We might wonder at the object of love in such cases. Is it the recidivist offender, in all his brutish ignobility? Is it some aura of humanity in which the offender shares by virtue of being a member of the human species? Is it love of Jesus, as a sort of third-party beneficiary?

In any event, our *ninth and final element: Should Vanzetti forgive Thayer, he would abandon his retributive feelings and his fantasies of vengeance. Vanzetti would surrender all thoughts of retaliation along with his harsh evaluation of Thayer. However, Vanzetti may still conclude that institutional punishment of the (convicted) Thayer is appropriate on grounds of deterrence, rehabilitation, or incarceration. Moreover, Vanzetti's forgiveness is compatible with his seeking and accepting restitution from Thayer. In fact, Thayer's restitution is one way that he can facilitate the process of reconciliation and renewal with Vanzetti. Moreover, neither Thayer's repentance, nor his punishment by rightful authorities, nor his restitution expunges his wrongdoing such that there is nothing remaining for Vanzetti to forgive. Finally, Jesus' revolutionary moral message enjoins victims to relinquish their retributive feelings and banish their vengeful attitudes even where forgiveness is not philosophically possible because the required distance between offender and offense is absent. Victims should aspire to the ideal of loving those "enemies" who have injured them and of enhancing their good.*

Perhaps we should not oversell the virtues of forgiveness. We should, at least, mention the dangers of forgiveness too easily bestowed. When victims forgive perpetrators of wrongs too facilely, they may increase the possibility of serial transgressions. If we are all free moral agents, responsible for our actions, then we must also accept the consequences of our mistakes. To be forgiven automatically may encourage wrongdoers to continue or amplify their wayward approach to life. For example, family members who continually forgive a spouse's or parent's abuse or aggressive actions may be unwitting collaborators in or unsuspecting enablers of future escalations of that violence. Moreover, just as we have epistemological problems in determining the mind-sets of perpetrators of wrongs, we have similar problems when assessing the sincerity of their repentance. Surely, the chronicle of wrongdoing is replete with fraudulent expressions of remorse by perpetrators who understand well that victims and legal authorities welcome such demonstrations. To reward such false repentance with forgiveness brings no honor to either victim or perpetrator. We might insist on a type of moral symmetry: if we lack epistemological certitude about the intentions and motives of perpetrators of wrongs such that we are in a poor position to judge them, so too, we lack certitude regarding the sincerity of their expressions of repentance and are thus in a poor position to forgive them. Finally, those who forgive too easily might suffer from a lack of self-esteem; because of intense guilt or feelings of inferiority, they may on some level think they deserve to be transgressed against. Accordingly, to conclude that some instances of forgiving are appropriate and some are inappropriate is reasonable.

From another vantage point, it may seem that those who forgive others arrogate to themselves the positions of judge and moral superior. Despite Jesus' injunction to avoid judging others (Matt. 7:1), forgiving others presupposes that the victim has judged that a perpetrator has wronged him or her and the perpetrator is fully responsible for that transgression. The victim has judged that something bad has happened that might be forgiven. The victim, one might well argue, then places himself or herself in a position of moral superiority: although the victim initially harbors resentment and, probably, thoughts of retaliation, the victim will forego those sentiments in the interests of magnanimity. In effect, the victim has turned the tables on the perpetrator in that the perpetrator may well sense that the victim believes that the act of forgiveness places the perpetrator in the victim's debt. Behind the apparent purity of the victim's motives may lay a repressed resentment and subtle moral retaliation that is masked by high-minded rhetoric. Perhaps victims who forgive do so in service of their own empowerment: they assume the role of divine judge and generously bestow forgiveness upon their moral subordinates. The act of forgiveness, then, may at least sometimes be laced with moral condescension; to forgive another person may be a way to elevate oneself and to underscore that person's moral inferiority. This is especially true in cases where the quality of the perpetrator's act is somewhat contestable or where the perpetrator's responsibility for that act is ambiguous.

A truly stellar individual, such as the father in the Parable of the Prodigal Son, who does not respond to supposed slights with resentment and negative judgments, lacks the prerequisites of forgiveness. In that parable, I would argue that the father, a paragon of unconditional love, does not truly forgive his wayward son because he never judged that his son had wronged him. Lacking negative sentiments toward his son, the father could not relinquish them in order to forgive.

My point is not that all acts of forgiveness mask mendacious motives, but only that not all acts of forgiveness are morally pure. Assuming we had full access to the inner spirits of other people, we would need to evaluate fully the motives and intentions of forgiving people to assess the moral quality of their acts; the act of forgiveness as such is not morally self-ratifying. As Jesus taught, inner motives and intentions are critical to moral assessment. Of course, that places us, again, in the role of judge, a position that Jesus instructs us to avoid. The deeper conceptual problem, then, is this: Is Jesus' injunction to avoid judging others compatible with his imperative to forgive the transgressions and shortcomings of others? How can we forgive others without judging the quality of their actions and motivations?

If Jesus is enjoining human beings to forgive in the same fashion as God forgives us, then we might point out that the judgments of God have advantages that those of human beings lack, one of which is epistemological infallibility.

THE CONCEPT OF MERCY

The main questions surrounding the concept of mercy are the following: Does dispensing mercy conflict with the demands of retributive justice? Must merciful actions arise only from praiseworthy motives and reasons? Is mercy an imperfect duty such that moral agents have full discretion as to when, to whom, and for what reasons they bestow mercy upon others? Can a person who is vulnerable to rightful authority claim merciful treatment as a matter of right? What are the differences between institutional and personal mercy? What grounds decisions that mercy is appropriate in a particular situation? How is mercy different from forgiveness?[6]

Let's begin by describing the elements of mercy. To act mercifully is to refrain voluntarily from using one's power or to use that power to a lesser extent against another who is vulnerable to that power. In such instances, the merciful agents would be acting against existing reasons to act in ways that would cause or refrain from alleviating the vulnerable person's suffering.

Whereas forgiveness centers on the victim relinquishing certain kinds of negative feelings toward the perpetrator of an offense against her, mercy focuses on certain types of actions. Often when one forgives the perpetrator of an offense against her there is no action available to her other than an expression of her feelings (and even that expression may be unavailable in cases such as forgiving someone who is dead).

One may *feel* mercifully toward another person but if that sentiment does not result in action it may remain obscure. Moreover, one can act mercifully toward another person from unpraiseworthy motives. To attain the virtue of mercy a person must embody the relevant praiseworthy dispositions to act mercifully on a sufficient number of occasions. Finally, one can act mercifully toward another without forgiving him. That is, one could refrain voluntarily from using one's power to its fullest extent against another person who is vulnerable to that power without possessing the requisite state of mind and desire for reconciliation that characterize forgiveness. On other occasions, however, forgiveness is a way of demonstrating mercy. When a victim of a wrong relinquishes retributive emotions toward the perpetrator of the transgression, offers personal reconciliation, and distinguishes the transgression from the transgressor, his action is merciful if he also refrains from using his power over the transgressor to its fullest extent. This is especially so in cases where the transgressor has not repented his misdeed.

In legal contexts, merciful acts occur when one party is vulnerable to the legal power of another party; the vulnerable party is susceptible to suffering or other detriment as a result of the legal power of the party in the superior position; the party with the power advantage recognizes the vulnerable party's situation and refuses voluntarily to exercise his or her legal power or does not wield it to the typical extent; and as a result, the suffering or other detriment of the vulnerable party is softened. In such contexts, mercy implores us to accept less than what justice requires. In judicial contexts, mercy alleviates suffering that is legally deserved or which authorities are otherwise entitled to exact.

Merciful acts, however, need not arise from praiseworthy motives. For example, in *The Merchant of Venice*, Shylock might have been merciful to Antonio because he thought so acting would be sound long-term business strategy. Perhaps, Shylock could have bestowed mercy on Antonio because Shylock was convinced that his reputation would be enhanced by doing so and his usury business would thereby benefit or because he concluded that Antonio would thereafter forego rendering interest-free loans that interfered with Shylock's business. If so, calling Shylock's waiving of the penalty provision of his bond with Antonio an act of mercy would be appropriate even though his motivation would be purely self-interested. But I do not think that every reason of self-interest will do. In the narrative of the play, Shylock does not enforce the penalty provision of the bond, but he does so only because his own life is in jeopardy. To call Shylock's actions merciful under such circumstances sounds a sour note, especially because judge Portia (disguised as Balthasar) had already instructed us that mercy cannot be coerced but must flow "as the gentle rain from heaven."[7] While her suggestion that mercy springs only from praiseworthy motives is incorrect, her intuition that "coerced mercy" is problematic, perhaps even an oxymoron, is persuasive.[8] I would argue that a necessary condition of merciful action is that it be voluntary. Shylock's coerced relinquishment of the penalty provision is not voluntary, whereas mercy dispensed for some non-praiseworthy reasons, such as Shylock's waiving of the penalty provision for reasons of self-interest in the hypothetical I sketched above, is voluntary.

For purposes of simplification, I will designate the potentially merciful person as "Shylock" and the vulnerable party as "Antonio." Thus, our *first element: Shylock is merciful to Antonio if and only if Antonio is vulnerable to Shylock's power; Shylock has reason to use his power to its fullest extent against Antonio; Shylock recognizes Antonio's vulnerability; but Shylock voluntarily refrains from doing so. In a legal context, judge Shylock's power would result from Antonio's conviction for wrongdoing, and judge Shylock's mercy would involve his voluntarily exacting less punishment upon Antonio that the demands of retributive justice would decree. In both personal and judicial contexts, Shylock's motives for being merciful need not be praiseworthy, but his merciful action must be voluntary.*

How does one person become vulnerable to the power of another person? Must the power of the person in the superior position be authorized, rightful, and legitimate? In legal contexts, these questions are easily answered. The vulnerable person is such because of wrongdoing or failure to fulfill an obligation. The power of legal authorities to exact punishment after due process of law is authorized, rightful, and legitimate. In personal contexts, the answers to these questions become murkier. Typically, we follow the legal paradigm and advance instances where the vulnerable person is such because of failure to fulfill a voluntarily contracted obligation to the person who now has the power to exact a penalty (for example, Antonio and Shylock enter into a loan arrangement, Antonio defaults on payment, and Shylock has the rightful power to enforce the penalty provision included in the contract).

But suppose an intruder forcibly invades your home, steals your money, binds you and your family with ropes, and sets your house on fire. As the structure burns, he suddenly turns softhearted and removes you and your family members from the blazing inferno. He leaves you safely bound away from the blaze and scampers into the distance. Should we conclude that the intruder has acted mercifully toward you and your family?

Clearly, the power of the intruder over you is not authorized, rightful, or legitimate. The only reason he has any power over you is that he lawlessly arrogated that position to himself. Yet he has voluntarily not used his power to the fullest possible extent. He recognized the vulnerability of you and your family—you would all perish in the fire if he did not act to prevent it—and he acted voluntarily to soften your vulnerability by removing everyone to safety. The intruder's act seems to fit squarely within the first element of our paradigm for mercy.

Yet, we may be troubled by those ushering him into the merciful hall of fame. But for his lawless action you and your family would not have been vulnerable to his power. Why should he glean credit merely for not being as cruel as he might possibly have been? If he does gain such credit, does not that imply that every criminal who stops short of being as cruel as possible is thereby merciful? After all, we can always imagine an even worse scenario to even the most gruesome murders. It would seem that only a criminal who inflicts the worst torture possible—whatever that is—that leads to inevitable death would not be merciful. Every other murderer would fall short of "using power to the fullest extent" and thus qualify as merciful to some extent. Such a conclusion is utterly zany.

Perhaps there is a way out of the conceptual quagmire. In my hypothetical case, the intruder had a good reason to leave you and your family in the burning home: to extinguish all witnesses to his criminality. He recognized your vulnerability to death and altered his plan in a way that eased your vulnerability: you and your family survive as a result. Should he be apprehended and convicted, legal authorities may well take into consideration his action of removing you and your family to safety. This would not make him eligible for a commendation but might well count in his favor to some degree at sentencing. Of course, his act of "mercy" must be placed in the larger context of how your vulnerability arose.

If we accept this as an act of mercy, the parade of horrors I described earlier does not automatically result. In other cases of criminal mayhem, the scenario of the lawless act, followed by extreme vulnerability of victims, recognition of that vulnerability by the criminal, and efforts by the criminal to ease the vulnerability of the victims does not occur. Merely refraining from doing the worst possible series of things you can do to one's victims—which would make every criminal "merciful" in a trivial sense—is insufficient to qualify as rendering mercy. The sequence of events and the other requirements of merciful actions will prevent criminals from automatically being merciful. I must conclude that the intruder in my hypothetical was merciful in the one respect noted.

Still, I am troubled by my conclusion. The prudential, studious criminal—if there is such a person—could set up his crimes with an element of "mercy" built in from the start. He could include ratcheting up the vulnerability of his victims only to alleviate part of that vulnerability just prior to departing the scene of the crime. Under my analysis thus far, such a contrived scenario would qualify as having a merciful element that somehow rebounded to the credit of the criminal.

Perhaps we should conclude that not all cases of mercy count in favor of the agent who performs them. Where the mercy is contrived, arises from the wrongful activity of the person in power, and serves only to alleviate a condition that the wrongdoer imposed, the merciful action does not automatically count in favor of the performing agent. Under such conditions, a case-by-case analysis, carefully attending to all relevant circumstances, is required to determine if the merciful act should count in favor of the performing agent.

Thus, our *second element: Should Shylock have power over Antonio, have reason to use his power to its fullest extent against Antonio but recognize Antonio's vulnerability and voluntarily refrain from doing so, Shylock's action may be merciful even though Shylock's power over Antonio was neither authorized nor rightful nor legitimate. But under such circumstances, special scrutiny must be given to determine whether Shylock's merciful action should count in favor of Shylock.*

In legal contexts, is mercy in conflict with justice? One might argue that the demands of retributive justice and bestowals of mercy point in different directions when determining the amount and type of punishment to inflict upon convicted wrongdoers. Retributive justice looks to what the wrongdoer deserves, while mercy is an appropriate response to remorse, repentance, atonement, and a host of other possible considerations. Mercy, then, is voluntarily exacting less than we are authorized or in a position to impose, or extending ourselves more than is typical given the situation. Compassion and empathy are crucial to a merciful mindset. Thus, mercy could be viewed as contrary to the principle of desert and to retributive justice.

In my view, however, such a judgment is misleading. The notion of desert, as previously sketched, is a slippery concept. At the legal level, an offender deserves punishment in accord with the gravity of the offense committed, the culpability of his mind-set (Did he perform the wrong intentionally, knowingly, recklessly, or negligently?), and the absence of justification or excuse. None of the factors inclining us toward dispensing mercy rise to the level of justifications ("I did what is typically wrong and was responsible for doing it, but in this case the act was permissible because of a special set of circumstances") or excuses ("I did what was wrong, but in this case I was not completely responsible for the act because of a special set of circumstances"). Of course, at a moral or psychological level, we can explore the notion of desert further: Does an extraordinarily severe socialization soften a person's responsibility for the ensuing deplorable character he displays? What follows normatively from the fact that none of us deserves our initial starting position in society or our genetic inheritance?

We are all the product of biological and social conditions that at least partly undermine our commitments to justice and salutary intimacy. Although existentialists remind us fondly that we have no excuses and we are condemned to our freedom, they tend to overlook or downplay the effects of our socialization and genetic inheritance and are too often overly scrupulous in holding us fully accountable for our characters. They spill much ink over the respective roles of facticity (our unalterable givenness) and transcendence (our freedom and capability of going beyond our current self-conceptions) but almost always end up glorifying our freedom, scolding us about taking more responsibility, and effacing the effects of our background, natural and social conditions.

What factors might incline us toward mercy? A perpetrator's sincere remorse or well-intended attempts at restitution; an offender's especially gruesome socialization that fueled his or her depraved character; particular circumstances that led a perpetrator to act lawlessly in this case but contrary to his or her general character; and cases where offenders have already suffered greatly for their misconduct and full additional punishment would seem disproportionate to the deed. In all such cases, what the miscreant legally deserves is unchanged. However, the inclination to be merciful centers on special hardships and circumstances that incline us toward meting out less punishment than legally deserved.

What are other typical grounds that lead someone to act mercifully? One reason would be that unless mercy were rendered the vulnerable person would suffer more than she should endure based on her general character and the nature of the act that rendered her vulnerable. For example, suppose a well-intentioned, generally decent person contracted to purchase a home at a time when lending institutions and the government were actively promoting such purchases. Soon thereafter, a widespread economic recession befalls the country and the person loses her job. She is unable to find a new position despite vigorous efforts and bereft of other ways to make her monthly mortgage payments, the bewildered person pleads for relief. Assume also that the rental market in her area is unpromising and foreclosure upon her home will cause her grave hardship. She seems to be a plausible candidate for mercy. That is, the lending institution holding her mortgage might well conclude that given the totality of circumstances it will voluntarily refrain from exerting the full force of its power over the struggling debtor. This conclusion would be strengthened should the lending institution recognize that exerting its full force of power over the struggling debtor (that is, foreclosing on the home) would benefit the lending institution meagerly—as possible purchasers of such homes are now few because of the recession—while the hardship to the debtor would be severe. Here the case for mercy is grounded in the debtor's lack of culpability for her misfortune, the circumstances which promoted her vulnerability, and the lack of commensurate benefit to the institution should it exert the full force of its power over the vulnerable debtor. Although the debtor lacks a right to mercy, those having power over her would do well not to exercise the full force of their legal prerogatives.

Another reason underlying merciful legal action is empirical: psychological and institutional vectors typically facilitate harsher punishments than deserved. For example, we tend to overestimate the role of individual character and underplay the role of natural and social conditions as causes of human actions (call this our "existential bias"); public relations campaigns against crime almost always ratchet up the rhetoric about getting "tough on crime"; legislators have enacted fixed penalties and mandatory sentences for a host of crimes; law-abiding citizens too often are drawn to such campaigns and enactments, and reward politicians identified as being tough on crime with their votes; and we tend to ignore any collective responsibility for the social conditions that nurture crime. In such an atmosphere, opportunities for dispensing mercy allow us to thwart injustice done in the name of justice.[9]

The call for mercy, then, flows from an appreciation that human beings are flawed, fallible creatures prone to sin and vice. Extending mercy underscores our solidarity with others and refuses to see ourselves as immune from committing common transgressions. Moreover, mercy is not limited to the domain of justice. That is, mercy emerges from our commitment to humanity and as an adjustment to our tendency toward harsh judgments. At times, dispensing mercy transcends considerations of justice. Furthermore, merciful actions underscore our vulnerability to the power of others and caution us against always exerting the full extent of the power we have over those vulnerable to us. In the spirit of Jesus, merciful actions remind us that a relentlessly legalistic or truculently formalistic approach to human relations eviscerates our souls and attenuates our sense of community.

If mercy is a value independent from justice, then conflicts between the two may arise. However, it does not follow that mercy is therefore unjust. Dispensing mercy need not ignore or wrongly trample upon the imperatives of justice. Instead, mercy is considered only after an offender's just deserts have been calculated. At its best, mercy can temper justice to arrive at the best overall normative result. Remember Aristotle's words: where justice is in place, friendship is still necessary; but where friendship is firm, justice is unnecessary.[10] Justice is crucial to, but not the exclusive component of, the best overall resolution. We should not take considerations of justice to be dispositive of the best normative outcome. Moreover, as we have seen, even determinations of moral desert—which are more refined than determinations of legal desert—provide only a reason, and often not a conclusive reason, for normative action. Clearly, even if Aristotle overstates the case, human relationships are grounded in normative considerations beyond those of retributive and distributive justice. Mercy is one such consideration.

Thus, our *third element: Whether in a legal or moral context, Shylock may have legitimate reasons to bestow mercy on Antonio, reasons that go beyond the determinations of what Antonio legally or even morally deserves.* Merciful action in such cases does not violate retributive or distributive justice, but acts as a corrective to our tendency to overestimate the role of individual character and underplay the role of natural and social conditions as causes of human actions. Moreover, as always, the principle of desert is only one of several considerations to be factored into determining the best overall normative result.

Unlike the case in legal institutions, in the private sphere, human beings have no prima facie obligation to inflict the full force of their power upon a party vulnerable to it. Thus, creditors may waive their rights to payment from a struggling debtor. Although entitled to such payment, the creditor may suspend, reduce, or relinquish his claim to it.

In the private sphere, is mercy merely an imperfect duty? That is, are we morally required to be merciful but the time, manner, and beneficiaries of the discharge of that duty are a matter of our discretion? On this approach, no one is required to show mercy in all the instances where plausible grounds for doing so exist. Moreover, no potential recipient possesses a right to our aid or to our mercy such that she can claim our help as her entitlement. But in order to fulfill our imperfect duty we must bestow mercy a sufficient number of times given our opportunities. Of course, to what a "sufficient number of times" amounts is contestable and will vary from person to person just as the number of opportunities to dispense mercy differs among people.

Unlike typical perfect duties that prescribe when, how, and to whom we owe moral concern, imperfect duties bestow upon us the authority to sculpt our own lives, while balancing consideration for others with our own specific projects, purposes, and interests. In effect, recognizing imperfect moral duties contributes to the development of our moral agency and to our possibilities for self-definition.

Imperfect duties, however, embody the same prescriptive power as do perfect duties. We must, among other things, contribute a reasonable amount of aid to the needy and extend mercy a sufficient number of times given our opportunities to do so, but we enjoy freedom as to whom, when, and how we fulfill our imperfect duties. However, possessing such leeway does not morally ratify every possible decision we might make in these regards. For example, should we refuse to aid a needy person or to extend mercy to her based only on her race, religion, ethnicity, gender, and the like, the grounds of our refusal are morally impermissible because they are unjustifiably discriminatory, all other things being equal. (There may be some occasions where taking into account such factors when allocating resources is morally relevant.) Thus, my personal preferences for aiding this rather than that person or for bestowing mercy upon one person instead of another cannot themselves be morally objectionable. Finally, the scope of imperfect duties is limited by the acceptability of avoiding excessive costs. Thus, we are not morally obligated to aid the needy if doing so would require heroic action, enormous risk, or great hardship. (Even Peter Singer at his most uncompromising invokes the bar of marginal utility as a permissible limit that defines excessive costs. As already discussed, he later relaxes that standard in deference to pragmatic concerns.)

However, recognizing a duty as imperfect may promote common human weaknesses. First, we tend to procrastinate: we can continue to postpone rendering the aid or mercy required by moral duty by assuring ourselves that we will do so vigorously and soon, but not today. Given human capabilities for rationalizing and conjuring excuses, the open-endedness of imperfect duties can nurture moral laxity. Second, the imprecision in the amount owed to others based on imperfect duties can result in moral agents concluding that minimal effort is sufficient to discharge our obligations. Still, these and other possible problems should be regarded as cautions, and we should remind ourselves to guard against the human weaknesses sketched. These problems do not undermine the moral power or demonstrate fatal flaws of the notion of imperfect duties.

Or is dispensing mercy not an imperfect duty but, instead, always supererogatory action? One might argue that mercy is praiseworthy (supererogatory) action when we are under no moral obligation to so act. Thus, the intruder of my previous hypothetical was not merciful because he was under a moral obligation not to murder his victims, and he was thereby obligated to remove them from the immolation he had created. Accordingly, even though he did not use his power over the vulnerable victims to the fullest extent, he was in this case morally obligated to not do so, and thus he was not merciful at all.

Such an approach has the virtue of removing mercy from all examples in which the power exerted is neither authorized nor rightful nor legitimate. In all such cases, the person who gains power over the vulnerable victim does so by contravening his moral obligations. On the approach under consideration, that would render any relaxing of that power over the vulnerable victim a welcome, but not merciful, event.

As tempting as this approach may be, I conclude that it should be rejected. I derive that conclusion from two considerations. First, imagine a person who was never merciful. Although in a position to extend mercy on numerous occasions, he always declines the invitation to do so. Would we want to say that such a person fulfilled his moral duties and merely failed to perform supererogatory actions? Or would we find such a person morally deficient—someone who failed in an important respect to be a morally decent human being? I would think that a person who never bestowed mercy although often in a position to do so is morally deficient; thus I am committed to an imperfect duty to be merciful. Second, the paradox that recognizing an action as merciful seems odd if the agent was only acting in accord with obligation can be unraveled without concluding that all merciful acts are supererogatory. We need only distinguish legal from moral obligation, and perfect from imperfect duties. While we are often under no legal obligation to relax the power we legitimately possess over a vulnerable victim, we may still have an imperfect moral obligation to do so that permits the determination that we have been merciful.

For example, in *The Merchant of Venice*, Shylock has no legal obligation to permit Antonio to renege on repayment of his loan. Let's suppose that Shylock has an imperfect moral obligation to render mercy on a sufficient number of occasions given his opportunities. Also suppose that Shylock, in the absence of Portia-Balthasar's judicial chicanery, chose not to exert the legal power he had over Antonio. Instead, Shylock decided to extend the time that Antonio had to repay the loan or even forgave the debt straightaway. If so, Shylock would be waiving one of his legal rights while fulfilling an imperfect moral obligation. To call Shylock's action merciful even though it was in accord with moral obligation is reasonable because that obligation did not demand that Shylock relax his legal power on *this* occasion nor did it require Shylock to relax his legal power to the *extent* that he did (in the event that Shylock forgave the debt entirely). Thus, Shylock's action can be viewed reasonably as merciful and to include both obligatory (fulfilling an imperfect moral duty) and supererogatory elements (going beyond the call of duty in the event that he forgave the debt entirely).

Thus, our *fourth element: Human beings have an imperfect moral obligation to be merciful. That is, are we morally required to be merciful but the time, manner, and beneficiaries of the discharge of that duty are a matter of our discretion?* No one is required to show mercy in all the instances where plausible grounds for doing so exist. Thus, in matters of mercy, no one is required to always treat like cases alike, but the reasons for declining to be merciful in a particular case must themselves be morally unobjectionable. Moreover, no potential recipient possesses a right to our aid or to our mercy such that she can claim our help as her entitlement. But in order to fulfill our imperfect duty we must bestow mercy a sufficient number of times given our opportunities.

THE PARABLE, FORGIVENESS, AND MERCY

The king's treatment of his servant's debt fits the rubric of *mercy* more closely than it does of *forgiveness*. The servant has contracted an enormous debt, probably tallied from a series of loans from the king. The king is entitled to full repayment, but he is not obligated, either legally or morally, to exact repayment. At this time and place, the king is also entitled but not obligated to consign his servant to debtor's prison or even to sell the debtor and his entire family into slavery should the servant fail to repay the loan. Thus, the king possesses serious power over

The Unforgiving Servant: "Shouldest Not Thou Also Have Had Compassion?" 107

the debtor-servant who is extremely vulnerable to that power. When the king discovers that the servant cannot remit repayment of the loans, the king's first instinct is to inflict the full measure of his power: sell the entire family into slavery, liquidate whatever resources the family held, and be done with the affair. The king, then, has reason to treat the debtor harshly.

But the struggling debtor saves the day by falling before the king, "worshipping" him, and pleading for an extension. The question is why, how, and for what purpose was the king moved? Did he suddenly understand the hardship that the man and his family would bear should the king exact the full punishment to which he was entitled? Was the king moved by the humility that the debtor demonstrated? Or was the king flattered by the obsequious display of "worship"?

Was it possible that the debtor's self-debasement reminded the king of the praiseworthy overall character of the man? Or was the debtor so pathetic that the king was suddenly ashamed of destroying so helpless a creature?

Some of these possibilities show the king in a better light than others. We lack sufficient details to know the precise answer. I will assume the most charitable possibilities: the king was reminded of the debtor's generally praiseworthy character; moved by the hardship that inflicting his full power over the debtor would produce; and cognizant that the benefit to him of inflicting that power would pale in comparison to the suffering incurred by the debtor and his family. Accordingly, the king acts mercifully and waives his right to the debt. Even though the debtor had pled only for an extension of time, the king's decision goes well beyond that request.

Assuming that the king had an imperfect duty to be merciful, his action demonstrates both a dutiful and a supererogatory element: he chose this occasion to extend his mercy thereby fulfilling his imperfect duty, and he went beyond the call of duty in that he waived the entire debt instead of merely granting the debtor an extension.

The case for understanding the king's action as one of forgiveness is less compelling. The servant-debtor has not wronged the king. True, he cannot repay his loans and thus cannot fulfill the positive duty he has contracted with the king. But from the available evidence, this situation was not nurtured by the servant's malice or evil intentions. That is, the servant did not scheme to transgress against the king. Obviously, given the king's power, such a plot would have been imprudent to say the least. Nor is it obvious that the servant was culpably negligent or reckless, except in his foolishness in acquiring so much debt (which foolishness the king ratified). The servant's mawkish display before the king is not so much an act of repentance as it is a plea for a merciful extension of time. Although he bemoans the fact that he cannot remit timely repayment of his loans, the servant does not repent a wrong. Thus, I take the king's initial reaction—liquidate family assets, sell the whole bunch of bounders into slavery, and wash my hands of the affair—as his best way to recoup part of his financial losses. He is less interested in legal retribution (for example, consigning the servant to debtor's prison) than he is in salvaging part of his loan.

But events soon change the king's perceptions. Directly after being the recipient of the king's mercy, the servant confronts one of his colleagues who owes him money, demands repayment, and physically assaults the debtor. His fellow servant falls to his knees in much the same way as the creditor-servant had done earlier with the king, begging for a time extension. The creditor-servant, learning nothing from the king's bestowal of mercy, exerts the full legal power he has over his desperate, vulnerable colleague and has him cast into debtor's prison. We might suppose that if the creditor-servant had been fully armed with contemporary moral understandings he might have argued, "I do not choose to fulfill my imperfect duty to be merciful at this time. Instead, on this occasion I conclude that I will exercise my full legal rights. Although I am not obligated to exercise my full legal rights, I am entitled to do so and choose to do so." We can only wonder whether the creditor-servant had in the past bestowed mercy upon those who were vulnerable to his power. The trajectory of the parable suggests that he had not.

Once the king learns from other of his servants about the creditor-servant's hard-heartedness, he withdraws his earlier bestowal of mercy: those who refuse to be merciful will be treated unmercifully, now and in the coming Kingdom of God. The servant is dispatched to debtor's prison, presumably to join the man whom he had consigned there. We must assume that the creditor-servant's actions were in character. Otherwise, we might conclude that one failure to fulfill an imperfect duty should not automatically result in the king's harsh response. After all, our assessments of when to be merciful typically include an overall evaluation of the character of the person who is vulnerable to our power, not merely recognition of one incident in his life.

But notice the parable's final line: "So likewise shall my heavenly Father do also unto you, if ye from your hearts forgive not every one his brother their trespasses." This line does not exude the language of imperfect duties. Instead, Jesus enjoins us to "forgive" *all* trespasses against us (or, more precisely, to be *merciful* to all those over whom we have rightful power and who are vulnerable to our full exercise of that power). If so, talk of the vulnerable person's overall character and of choosing to be merciful here but not there is wildly misplaced. Jesus seems to be demanding that mercy and forgiveness are *always required*. At the very least, they are always required where the vulnerable person would suffer significantly should we exercise the full power we hold over that person. The vulnerable person's need, not his character, is paramount. Our own ability to love our neighbor is put to the test in such cases.

Still, such a conclusion is too easy. Remember, the king ends up withdrawing his mercy in response to the creditor-servant's pitiless treatment of his debtor-colleague. As Jesus extols the king's actions as akin to the judgments of God, it would appear that there is one type of vulnerable person we need not forgive or bestow mercy upon: the person who refuses to be forgiving or merciful. Thus, at least one aspect of a vulnerable person's character is relevant after all: her history of forgiving and being merciful toward others.

Accordingly, we might conclude that the following captures Jesus' sentiments: Our default position should be forgiving and being merciful toward those vulnerable to our rightful power where exercising that power fully would place significant hardship on the vulnerable person—the vulnerable person's need should be our critical concern. But should the vulnerable person not be merciful or forgiving toward others, then we are not required to be merciful or forgiving toward him. Indeed, we are enjoined in such cases to treat such a person as he has treated his fellow man.

This rendering, however, remains unsatisfying. Suppose the parable were slightly different. On this version, the servant who was obliged to the king first was unmerciful to his colleague—as in the parable, he chokes his colleague; refuses to give him an extension of time to repay the loan; and relegates him to debtor's prison. After having done so, the servant is confronted by the king who demands repayment of the servant's debt. As in the parable, the servant throws himself at the feet of the king and begs for mercy. The question looms: Would the king have said, "Well, you did not give your debtor-colleague any consideration, so I will not render mercy to you"? If so, then perhaps my rendering of Jesus' sentiments is acceptable. Or would the king have extended mercy to the servant anyway? If so, then the crucial part of the parable is that the servant, *having been the beneficiary of mercy*, was then unwilling to extend mercy to his colleague-debtor in a situation much like the one in which he was benefited.

On this second reading, we might conclude that the following captures Jesus' sentiments: Our default position should be forgiving and being merciful toward those vulnerable to our rightful power where exercising that power fully would place significant hardship on the vulnerable person—the vulnerable person's need should be our critical concern. But should the vulnerable person, after having been the beneficiary of mercy, not be merciful or forgiving toward others in a like situation, then we are not required to be merciful or forgiving toward him. Indeed, we are enjoined in such cases to treat such a person as he had treated his fellow man.

The difference in the two principles is that the second rendering underscores the failure to pass merciful action forward. Any person who has benefited from merciful action but does not extend that benefit to others is doubly culpable: not only does he exhibit a hardness of spirit, but he has failed to appreciate sufficiently the way he was benefited in the past and refuses to emulate merciful behavior in the future.

The first rendering of the principle conjures a different temporal sequence of events. That is, it counsels that our first response to others should be forgiving and merciful but invokes a type of punitive Golden Rule in those cases where we know that a person has not been forgiving or merciful in the past: treat a person as they have treated others. This rendering of the principle seems to invoke the principle of desert: not having bestowed mercy or extended forgiveness of others in the past, the person at issue does not deserve to be forgiven or benefited by merciful action today.

I conclude that the second rendering is the more precise understanding of the parable, but it may still not be entirely accurate. If the king of the story is the analogue of God, the principle derived may be a description only of the way that those in the highest positions of authority—on earth and in the transcendent realm—will act toward people who receive their mercy, but who fail to act mercifully toward their fellow human beings. That is, instead of offering a parable from which we can extract a complex principle to guide our conduct toward our colleagues, the story may be only a report of how God will treat us. Assuming that we have all benefited from God's mercy in the past, we are not enjoined to forgive the trespasses of our fellow human beings. If we fail to do so, God will presumably judge us sternly. If this is correct, then the broad message for human beings is a recurrent theme in the New Testament: forgive others their trespasses against you, and be merciful when you are in a position of power over others—place the needs of those vulnerable to your authority above your inclination to exercise the full spectrum of your entitlements. On this view, the duty to be merciful is not imperfect; instead, we have a duty to be merciful that is not only as stringent as our other moral duties, but it is also not subject to our choices as to when and to whom we fulfill that duty. We might even go so far as to conclude that the needs of other people vest a right such that they are entitled to our mercy. Thus, being merciful is not a supererogatory act, although the *extent* of our mercy—how much of our entitlements we waive in deference to the needs of others—at times may well exceed duty.

But does this imply that we must *always* be merciful when in a position to do so? Does it suggest that we must *always* forgive those who transgress against us (at least when they have repented)? The message of the Parable of the Unforgiving Servant, especially when combined with other biblical passages where Jesus insists that we should forgive and be merciful toward other human beings, suggests the answer is "yes."

But even here we must be cautious. Although philosophers are driven to formulate general principles and rules that might be applied to future cases, Jesus, as always, does not appeal to formalistic renderings and code-book morality. His is an invocation of the life of love, which resists generalized cases that anticipate particular decisions. Thus we should be wary of capturing Jesus' prescriptions for living in neatly crafted, self-executing moral principles. Of course, the danger is that we may conclude that we are left with nothing more than our own conscience in deciding what the life of love requires in concrete circumstances. If we can rely only on unguided human judgment to determine the correct moral decision in every instance, then the life of love lacks sufficient substantive criteria. Even the entreaty of faith—"trust the Lord"—suggests that human beings are merely conduits or empty vessels through which God will work the divine will.

Perhaps the most charitable conclusion is also the most obvious: Jesus advises that either we must always be merciful and forgiving or, at least, that we should take that as our default position and vary from it for only the most compelling reasons.

But should we still not be cautious? Are there not serious dangers in forgiveness too easily rendered and mercy too readily bestowed? Might not Jesus' prescription unwittingly increase the possibility of serial transgressions? Might automatic forgiveness encourage wrongdoers to continue or amplify their wayward approach to life? Do those who forgive too easily suffer from a lack of self-esteem, intense guilt, or feelings of inferiority?

Surely, such considerations must be factored into whether we forgive and act mercifully toward others on particular occasions. But parts of Jesus' teachings on these topics were prefigured by numerous thinkers. For example, over four centuries prior to Jesus' birth, Socrates spread a radical moral message. A metaphysical dualist, he defined "harm" as that which impaired the human soul (or mind or psyche); what impaired the human soul were irrational, immoral actions that upset the soul's equilibrium; the soul's equilibrium was a state of harmony established by the correct relationship of the three parts composing the soul; that correct relationship depended on reason being in control of the other parts (spiritiveness and desire); no person can compel another to perform an irrational, immoral act; therefore, no harm could befall a good person without his collaboration.

Socrates' radical message was that bodily injury was in fact not a genuine harm as it need not produce disharmony in the soul. Obviously, other people may injure me physically without my consent, but the crux of genuine harm resides in the condition of my soul, which defines my identity. Thus, those who transgress against me by physically injuring me or by slandering my reputation or by pilfering my material goods or through mean-spirited behavior do not harm me unless I react in irrational, immoral ways—in which case I am responsible for harming my own soul by my thoughtless reaction.

A consequence of this ethic is a trajectory toward forgiveness and mercy, toward not responding to intended wrongdoing in kind, and toward placing prime value not on material well-being but on the condition of one's soul. Moreover, because Socrates also held that all wrongful actions arose from ignorance—as miscreants thought erroneously that their misdeeds would benefit them—victims of those wrongs should raise the epistemological awareness of their transgressors. Instead of reacting to others based on their intentions toward us and with punitive actions grounded in what they deserve because of their past deeds, we are better served by attending to our own internal condition and to theirs.

Several of Socrates' major assumptions are dubious, especially his commitment to metaphysical dualism; his understanding of the relationship between physical injury and mental distress; his supposition that all wrongdoing flows from ignorance; and his depiction of the nature of the human soul, mind, or psyche. But my point is that much of the trajectory of his moral thought is compatible with the life of love advocated by Jesus.

Perhaps where the appropriate cautions are taken—and these are typically contestable—and where what will best serve the well-being of transgressors is understood acutely, Jesus' radical moral message may still resonate: always strive toward mercy and forgivingness, and stray from that commitment for only the most compelling reasons. But we should not minimize how wildly the radical messages of those such as Socrates and Jesus deviate from conventional moral wisdom, in their times and in ours. Turning the other cheek to wrongdoers; rejecting the seemingly bedrock conviction that physical injury is genuine harm; forgiving always the trespasses of those who repent (even when we cannot be certain that repentance is sincere and even when trespassers are serial recidivists); forgiving often the trespasses of those who do not repent; being almost always merciful toward those vulnerable to our authority; and acting toward others not merely from a Kantian sense of moral duty but from inner affection, even love, do not seem our natural, in the sense of biological, default setting. Socrates and Jesus would argue that such precepts do capture our natural setting in another sense—that which would best facilitate human fulfillment and propel us toward our proper destiny.

If everyone were to adopt instantaneously the programs of Socrates and Jesus, then human relations would undoubtedly be elevated. In fact, in such a world much of what Socrates and Jesus advised would be unnecessary because human transgressions would dwindle drastically. But the more interesting question is whether being one of only a relatively few people to adopt such morally radical messages in a world where the overwhelming majority of people do not is wise. The answer to this question must address both moral and prudential concerns. Of course, neither Socrates nor Jesus would be moved an inch by this question. They would rejoin in unison, "The cultivation of your soul is not hostage to the like actions of others. The received opinions of the masses to the contrary must not be taken as an excuse for your turning away from the proper moral path."

In any case, the foundations of how Jesus views our world and our mission in it consist of his recurring general themes: he makes moral judgments from an Archimedean point of the Ideal Observer, God; as such, Jesus privileges the universal and the unconditional over the particular and contingent; from this perspective, what is common among human beings—their supposed spark of divinity and shared membership in the human community—is more important than factual inequalities that they embody; from this arises a commitment to radical egalitarianism such that we should extend our love and concern to everyone, especially to those with special needs. Jesus is suspicious of formalistic and mechanical application of moral law to specific cases. He cautions us against pursuing the flimsy glitter of material accumulation and celebrity in this world. His is a virtue ethic that places great emphasis on inner motives and intentions.

Throughout history, many writers have argued that existential tension is at the heart of human experience: our yearning for intimate connection with others and the recognition that others are necessary for our identity and freedom coalesces uneasily with the fear and anxiety we experience as others approach.[11] We simultaneously long for emotional attachment yet are horrified that our individuality may evaporate once we achieve it. If we experience too much individuality we risk alienation, estrangement, and psychological isolation. If we experience insufficient individuality we court emotional suffocation, loss of self-esteem, and unhealthy immersion in the collectivity. This disharmony may never be fully reconciled once and forever, and so we find ourselves making uneasy compromises and adjustments during our life's journey as we oscillate along the continuum whose endpoints are "radical individuality" and "thorough immersion in community," respectively. This existential tension replicates itself at numerous levels: the individual confronts family, the family confronts wider community, communities confront society, and society confronts the state.

By stressing our joint project of redemption and salvation, and through his relentless call for unconditional love and forgiveness, Jesus places himself squarely on the communitarian side of the continuum.

NOTES

1. The section on the interpretation of the parable has been informed by Klyne R. Snodgrass, *Stories with Intent* (Grand Rapids, MI: William B. Eerdmans Publishing Company, 2008); Craig L. Blomberg, *Interpreting the Parables* (Downers Grove, IL:

InterVarsity Press, 1990); Richard N. Longenecker (ed.), *The Challenge of Jesus' Parables* (Grand Rapids, MI: William B. Eerdmans Publishing Company, 2000).

2. Snodgrass, *Stories with Intent*, 66.

3. The section on the concept of forgiveness has been informed by Lucy Allais, "Forgiveness and Mercy," 27 *South African Journal of Philosophy* (2008): 1–9; Nicholas Wolterstorff, "Jesus and Forgiveness," in *Jesus and Philosophy*, ed. Paul K. Moser (Cambridge: Cambridge University Press, 2009); "Does Forgiveness Undermine Justice," in *God and the Ethics of Belief*, ed. Andrew Dole and Andrew Chignell (Cambridge: Cambridge University Press, 2005); Jeffrie G. Murphy, "Remorse, Apology, and Mercy," 4 *Ohio State Journal of Criminal Law* (2007): 423–49; Jeffrie G. Murphy and Jean Hampton, *Forgiveness and Mercy* (Cambridge: Cambridge University Press, 1988).

4. Wolterstorff, "Jesus and Forgiveness," 208.

5. Ibid.

6. The section on the concept of mercy has been informed by Martha C. Nussbaum, "Equity and Mercy," 22 *Philosophy & Public Affairs* (1993), 83–125; Andrew Brien, "Mercy within Legal Justice," 24 *Social Theory and Practice* (1998): 83–110; John Tasioulas, "Mercy," 103 *Proceedings of the Aristotelian Society* (2003): 101–32; Lucy Allais, "Forgiveness and Mercy," 27 *South African Journal of Philosophy* (2008): 1–9; Carol S. Steiker, "Murphy on Mercy," 27 *Criminal Justice Ethics* (2008): 45–54; Jeffrie G. Murphy, "Remorse, Apology, and Mercy," 4 *Ohio State Journal of Criminal Law* (2007): 423–49; Jeffrie G. Murphy and Jean Hampton, *Forgiveness and Mercy* (Cambridge: Cambridge University Press, 1988).

7. William Shakespeare, *The Merchant of Venice*, in ed. Hardin Craig and David Bevington, *The Complete Works of Shakespeare* (Glenview, IL: Scott, Foresman and Company, 1973), Act 4, Scene 1, Line 185.

8. See, for example, Brien, "Mercy within Legal Justice," 86.

9. Steiker, "Murphy on Mercy," 49–51.

10. Aristotle, *Nicomachean Ethics*, trans. by Martin Ostwald (Indianapolis, IN: Bobbs-Merrill, 1962), 1155a26–28.

11. See, for example, Raymond Angelo Belliotti, *Seeking Identity: Individualism Versus Community in an Ethnic Context* (Lawrence, KS: University Press of Kansas), ix–x, 157–58, 191–93.

FIVE

The Rich Fool: "Then Whose Shall Those Things Be?"

> And one of the company said unto him, Master, speak to my brother, that he divide the inheritance with me. And he said unto him, Man, who made me a judge or a divider over you? And he said unto them, Take heed, and beware of covetousness: for a man's life consisteth not in the abundance of the things which he possesseth. And he spake a parable unto them saying, The ground of a certain rich man brought forth plentifully: And he thought within himself, saying, What shall I do, because I have no room where to bestow my fruits? And he said, This will I do: I will pull down my barns, and build greater; and there will I bestow all my fruits and my goods. And I will say to my soul, Soul, thou hast much goods laid up for many years; take thine ease, eat, drink, and be merry. But God said unto him, Thou fool, this night thy soul shall be required of thee: then whose shall those things be, which thou hast provided? So is he that layeth up treasure for himself, and is not rich toward God.
>
> (Luke 12:13–21)

INTERPRETATION OF THE PARABLE

The opening of the parable is important in that Jesus refuses to be a "divider" as between a man and his brother.[1] He declines the opportunity to "judge" their respective inheritance claims. Jesus is not a legal official bound to render decisions over the proper division of property. The man's initial declaration to Jesus—"speak to my brother" is more in the form of a demand than a request. Jesus' testy response is understandable.

The man appears concerned more with his own gain than with his relationship with his brother or the needs of others. As is typical, the man amplifies what he deserves or is entitled to and ignores or deflates what is due to others. The connotation of "divider" here refers not only to the distribution of property but also to the separation of brothers. Implicit in the man's demand is that once the inheritance is divided according to law, he and his brother will have no further business; their fractured relationship will end. As Jesus' self-image is one of reconciler, he will not advance a judgment on a legal matter that will deepen a pre-existing estrangement. Underlying these themes is the connection between the pursuit of material accumulation, the development of robust relationships, and personal identity. Jesus makes clear that a human being is not defined by his or her material possessions: what a person has and who a person is are conceptually distinct. Moreover, amassing an abundance of material "things" is neither necessary nor sufficient for attaining an abundant life.

The core of the subsequent parable centers on a wealthy, seemingly fortunate man whose land is uncommonly fertile. So productive, in fact, that he has no more room to store his latest bounty. This seemingly constitutes his major problem in life: what to do with his excess wealth.

When I was an undergraduate, we dubbed one of our colleagues, "The Eye." He was so-named because virtually every sentence he uttered began with "I." Even in a sea of somewhat self-absorbed college students, his preoccupation with self stood out like an elephant in an ant colony. The wealthy man of the parable is reminiscent of The Eye. As he "thought within himself," in the space of fewer than four sentences, he refers to himself no less than eleven times.

Indeed, he literally thinks of no one but himself when concocting a way out of his "problem." As is typical, he assumes throughout that he and only he is entitled to the material abundance that his land has spawned.

In fact, the parable provides no evidence that the surplus that has befallen the already-wealthy man flows from his additional effort, ingenuity, or prudence. Instead, the land has been especially fertile, undoubtedly aided by fortuitous weather. We, then, must assume that good fortune has again smiled on the wealthy man. His only concern is how to preserve these unexpected material gifts for himself. The matters of communal need or gratitude for good fortune are not merely marginalized; they are pushed off the page of concern. Much as Plato cautioned centuries earlier, the man's wealth has become a prison: it has isolated him from the wider community and provided a false cocoon of security. Worse, his self-image is defined by his financial success.

The wealthy man concludes that the solution is simple: he needs larger barns with more storage capacity. So he will tear down his existing structures and construct "greater" storage facilities. He has claimed full possession over the gifts arising from good fortune. Once this is done, the wealthy man fatuously believes that he will achieve final serenity. For the remainder of his days, he will relax and "eat, drink, and be merry." That a material man will judge success only in sensual delights such as food, beverage, and merriment does not surprise. One wonders with whom, if anyone, the wealthy man will experience these supposed joys. If present during his soliloquy, would we not caution the man that his prescribed regimen will soon turn boring, unhealthy, and pitiful?

But life is not about taking our ease and taking care of ourselves. To be "rich toward God" means to live productively, reflecting the character of God in all our relations.[2]

God had heard enough and sharply informs the wealthy man that he is a "fool." The fortunate landowner has unwisely placed his faith in material accumulation as the path to the good life. In truth, the man has failed to understand how transitory, how subject to decay, and how spiritually unfulfilling his chosen path is. Worse, he has misunderstood the genuine goal of the good human life, which is hardly "eat, drink, and be merry." Ignorant of the proper end and employing the wrong means, how else might we describe the man other than as a "fool"?

The appellation "fool" is appropriate because the man is not an active agent of evil. He does not hatch plots to undermine others. We must assume that he does not violate his negative moral duties more than is typical among flawed human beings. But he surely neglects his positive moral duties to others, although not from venal motives. His is an ignorance nurtured by insensitivity and a miserly soul that sympathizes too little with the needs of others. The man is responsible for the self he has sculpted; his ignorance is willful.

God decides the man must die that very night. But the man is already dead in a more profound sense: he has crafted an isolated existence, estranged from the wider community, and distanced from spiritual value. He has in effect already killed himself through ignorance of the good. Once he dies biologically, others will possess his material holdings. Moreover, he will die alone and without knowledge of whom those others might be. The man has forged his own destiny by seizing upon material accumulation as his ultimate commitment, by using his wealth unwisely, by being oblivious to the common good and to the true nature of the good human life, and by failing to attend to his relationships with others and the divine. Finally, the wealthy man is utterly unaware of what he has done to himself; his ignorance burrows far below his surface and contaminates his very soul.

> The man is the antithesis of Jesus' teaching that a disciple is to deny self and that the one who wishes to save life . . . loses it. The real issue is the focus of life. The fool's focus was on preparing things for himself . . . Foolishness consists in thinking that responsibilities end with securing one's own economic future. Life should not be focused on self, but on God and his purposes.[3]

Sadly, the wealthy man had "layeth up treasure for himself, and [was] not rich toward God." He has labored to feather his own material nest instead of striving to enrich others and thereby offer gifts to God. The wealthy man failed to grasp what now emerges as the theological point of the parable: human lives and material possessions are gifts from God; when, like the wealthy man in the parable, human beings assume, ignorantly, their ownership over both, they sow the seeds of spiritual disaster.

> [Jesus'] words called for a response that is immediately possible for both rich and poor. They must awaken to the illusory nature of ownership. Even the poor will find their security only in God, not in clothing, food, or drink.[4]

We should not take the moral lesson to be restricted only to accumulation of material goods. Seeking wealth is only a metaphor for any path of ignorance that inexorably leads to the results depicted in the parable: an isolated existence that is estranged from robust relationships and without spiritual value. Accordingly, even those who are not wealthy can focus their lives on the pursuit of material possessions or other ersatz goals that facilitate an impoverished life.

The major philosophical issue flowing from the parable centers on the place, if any, of material accumulation in leading a good human life. This invites a more general discussion of the nature of such a life. The most promising starting point to develop these themes in a context where philosophy and religion overlap lies in examining the question, "Was the historic Jesus a Cynic philosopher?"

WHO WERE THE CYNICS?

More than four centuries prior to the birth of Jesus, an uncommonly interesting, idiosyncratic series of philosophers called the Cynics arose. Not bound together as a school or by a set of formal dogmas, the Cynics were loosely identified by a shared approach toward life. The derivation of the term "Cynics" is from the Greek term for "dog" and was applied to certain philosophers both for their self-consciously minimalist way of life and for their sometimes bestial exhibitionism.

To attribute the "founding" of Cynicism to one person is inappropriate because of the explicitly unorthodox stance toward philosophy and collective thought that those described as Cynics embodied. The two earliest Cynics may have been Antisthenes (c. 445–c. 365 BC) and Diogenes of Sinope (c. 412–c. 323 BC). Later Cynics include Crates of Thebes (c. 360–c. 280 BC), his spouse Hipparchia of Maroneia, Bion of Borysthenes (c. 335–c. 235 BC), Menippus of Gadara (first half of third century BC), and Dio Chrysostrom (c. 40–112).

Diogenes of Sinope is by far the most colorful and well known of the group. Stories, either historically accurate or utterly fictitious, about him abound. Even those tales that are probably apocryphal are instructive in that they depict critical aspects of his personality and his approach toward life.

I'll relate three by way of illustration. The first chronicles his meeting with the conquering militarist Alexander the Great. Impressed by accounts of Diogenes he had heard and by his capability of reveling in minimalism, Alexander tells Diogenes that he is prepared to fulfill any desire that Diogenes expresses. At the time, Alexander was standing over Diogenes while the Cynic was apparently sunning himself. Diogenes' response was immediate and telling, "Stand out of my sun." In one fell swoop, Diogenes had established his complete independence from the authority of Alexander, affirmed that he could fulfill his only needs through natural objects, and refused to be tempted by the material comforts that a successful militarist might provide. Moreover, he did not bother with the conventional pleasantry of saying "please." Diogenes would bow before no man, not even a world conqueror with the power to slay him instantly without reprisal.

The second story is short but telling. Diogenes comes upon a child drinking water from his hands. The Cynic immediately casts his own drinking cup away and utters, "A child has defeated me in frugality." Even the ultimate minimalist had been lured into luxury. Having been reminded by the actions of the child, Diogenes tossed aside his clutter.

The final story concerns Diogenes' search for a genuine human being. Traveling to the marketplace with a lighted lantern at high noon he cries out that he is trying to find such a person. The implication was that his task was impossible: mass society drains the authenticity from us all.

These tales, along with those that describe Diogenes using an empty storage vat for wine as his bed and masturbating in public, provide examples that allow us to sketch an outline of characteristic attitudes and lifestyle nuggets that identify Cynicism to the extent that is possible.

Crates describes Diogenes in glowing terms:

> Diogenes put on a cloak not just once but throughout his life, he was superior to both toil and pleasure, he demanded his support but not from the humble, he abandoned all necessities, he had confidence in himself, he prayed that he might never attain to honors out of pity but as a revered man, he trusted in reason and not in guile or bow, he was brave not only at the point of death but was also courageous in his practice of virtue.[5]

Human Fulfillment and Personal Character

The Cynics were convinced that human excellence ("virtue" in a much wider sense than "moral action") and self-realization are grounded in distinguishing the distracting values of society—such as pursuit of material goods; high reputation; hedonistic gratification; fulfilling conventional obligations connected to family, religion, and nation—from the salutary values of personal independence, freedom, and self-sufficiency. The conventional understandings of mass society imprison human beings in a fruitless cycle of desire, dependence, and ignorance. The more intensely we yearn for society's baubles the more tightly we are ensnared in an unrelenting vulnerability that nurtures only long-term misery. Lacking an antecedent notion of the amount of goal-attainment that would constitute happiness, we are lured into an endless pursuit in which we can always fantasize that we are entitled to more of society's prizes than we possess. Unable to fully control the responses of other people and the vicissitudes of fortune, we become increasingly dependent on currying favor as a means of maximizing our chances for worldly success. In so doing, we become unwitting collaborators in our own degradation.

The Cynic antidote to this common malady consists of three countermeasures. First, minimize your yearnings for material objects and for particular kinds of responses from people and nature: to desire nothing is to ensure that you lack nothing. Second, become more divine by aspiring to spiritual, physical, and material independence. Third, concentrate on developing a strong mind and body such that the physical and mental hardships that force lesser human beings (that is, the vast majority of mass society) to cower with fear are readily absorbed without a loss of independence, freedom, and self-sufficiency.

The program requires a complete distancing of the self from conventional wisdom, but the Cynics did not seek isolation. Instead, they strode confidently into the heart of society, often badgering, mocking, and shocking their self-chosen adversaries. In that vein, Diogenes was renowned for public exhibitionism involving sexual and bodily functions. Many Cynics actively sought public attention as a venue for espousing their superiority and underscoring their distance from society's pieties. They took the mythological Hercules as their hero and sought to emulate his capability of overcoming extreme hardship in service of freedom and self-realization.

Robust Sense of Entitlement

To describe the Cynics as humble, modest, or self-effacing would be a mistake. Those who placed themselves above the authority of society also refused the duty of earning their keep (providing for their undeniable need for food, clothing, and shelter) through wage labor. The Cynics are sometimes described as beggars, but that will not do. Those who beg are typically supplicant and even obsequious; they request the generosity of their potential benefactors. On the contrary, the Cynics approached societal paragons with a robust sense of entitlement; they neither applied for supererogatory action nor cast themselves down in an effort to elicit sympathy. Instead, they jauntily confronted society's minions in the spirit of receiving their due. Those who contributed to the Cynics' coffers were merely relinquishing that to which these philosophers were entitled.

But why, one might well inquire? Why should the Cynics be entitled to a piece of what other people had earned through their labor, while the Cynics seemingly did nothing except ridicule the lifestyles of those from whom they later claimed an entitlement? Diogenes had an argument that neatly summed up the Cynics' case: "All things belong to the gods. The wise (the Cynics) are friends of the gods, and friends hold things in common. Therefore, all things belong to the wise (the Cynics)."[6] Thus, a "begging" Cynic was only expropriating that which he by right owned. Of course, this was a self-serving, ego-saving posture, especially for philosophers such as the Cynics whose acceptance of the gods was highly ambiguous.

Some nuances, however, appear. For example, Crates wrote:

> Beg only from those men and accept gifts only from those who have been initiated into philosophy. Then it will be possible for you to demand back what belongs to you and not to appear to be begging what belongs to others. . . . For it is not begging that is base, but not showing oneself as worthy of what is given . . . do not take the same amount from everyone, but accept a triobol [1/2 drachma] from the prudent and a mina [100 drachmae] from spendthrifts . . . do not approach and beg from everyone, for you will not receive anything from them, but beg only from the wise men.[7]

Moreover, the Cynic accepted the symmetry of Diogenes' argument on common ownership of everything by the wise: "Heed the argument and do not be angry whenever you are asked for a triobol by wise men. For you are giving back not what is yours but what is theirs."[8]

Embrace of Minimalism

Cynics laid deed to no property or other worldly possessions with the exceptions of their cloak, staff, and satchel. Nevertheless, Cynics were often clearly identifiable by their common appearance.

> The Cynics scoffed at the customs and conventionalities of others, but were rigid in observance of their own. The Cynic would not appear anywhere without his *wallet, staff,* and *cloak,* which must invariably be dirty and ragged and worn so as to leave the right shoulder bare. He never wore *shoes* and his *hair* and *beard* were long and unkempt.[9]

The Cynics aspired to turn worldly values on their head. According to mass society, poverty, lack of hedonistic gratification, and joblessness were viewed as horrifying deprivations; whereas, for the Cynics they formed the cornerstone of personal salvation. Instead of homelessness and impoverishment making someone a candidate for charity, pity, or disgust, the Cynics took such conditions to be the badges of wisdom. The musical slogan "freedom is another word for nothing left to lose" could well have served as the chorus of the Cynic anthem. The warm embrace of minimalism presumably led to a fearlessness and self-sufficiency that nurtured the broadest freedom imaginable. Moreover, an implication of the Cynics' position is that the so-called socially downtrodden are not proper candidates for pity.

> The Cynics did not express any sympathy for the poor for, in their opinion, the poor possessed the conditions of happiness, freedom, and virtue [personal excellence]. Neither were they friends, advocates, and defenders of the poor, as they have sometimes been said to be. The possession of property was an encumbrance and disadvantage. The Cynics' repudiation of possessions led them to ignore the property rights of other men and explains their thievery. . . . The Cynics [took themselves to be] free to take anything they wanted and could lay their hands on.[10]

Crates sums up the power of Cynic minimalism: "We possess nothing, we have everything, but you [the wealthy], though you have everything, really have nothing because of your rivalry, jealousy, fear, and conceit."[11]

Freedom and Kingship

This is why Diogenes had no need for Alexander to bestow gifts upon him. The Cynic, unlike the overwhelming majority of human beings, was utterly indifferent to, actually disdainful of, everything Alexander could offer him. Diogenes, not Alexander, was the genuine king because the Cynic was spiritually secure and the master of his domain in a fashion that Alexander could never attain. Diogenes needed next to nothing, while Alexander needed everything.

This precept—that those who need the least are most akin to the divine—sums up the Cynic creed better than any other single slogan. The person who accepts material deprivation as a blessing and who is invulnerable to both personal insults and social acclaim attains maximum freedom. Moreover, adopting such a code relegates the race for material accumulation, the proclivity for class oppression, and the yearning for military conquest to the dustbin of irrelevancy at best and unwitting enslavement at worst. From the vantage point of Cynics, the typical paths to personal glory—success in military and political adventures—were strewn with the broken glass of dependency on the whims of other people and the painful gravel of abject vulnerability to ever-changing fortune. For Cynics, to have virtually nothing and to need no more than that opens the way for common people to attain freedom and self-sufficiency, qualities that were thought previously to be embodied only by earthly kings and divinities.

For this reason, Hellenic Cynicism, always a fringe movement, became even less popular during the time of the ascent of the Romans. Only in the Greek-speaking Eastern provinces did the Cynics retain a presence.

> [T]raditional Roman virtues could not accommodate the Cynics anarchic individualism: Cynic shamelessness was incompatible with Roman *gravitas* and *decorum*; Cynic irreverence with Roman *pietas*; Cynic contempt for custom with Roman respect for the *mos maiorum*. In brief, high-minded but worldly Romans might find Cynicism antisocial, even cynical, self-indulgent, unpatriotic, and ineffective.[12]

Repudiation of Social Conventions and Customs

Of course, the very reasons why Romans built their empire on the cornerstones of the pursuit of military and political glory, reverence for the traditions of a sentimentalized past, respect of social discipline, veneration of a hierarchy of merit, and the inculcation of patriotic zeal were precisely the reasons why Cynics steered the opposite course. By their mere presence, the Cynics sought to repudiate the social conventions, customs, and values that vivified Roman imperialism.

> [T]he Cynic avoids traditional clothes, jewelry and bodily adornments for his own "uniform"; he restricts his diet; does not live in a house; derides bathing, sports, the Games; scoffs at festivals, sacrifice, prayer and religious life generally; does not marry, dodges work and steers clear of the courts, assembly, army and other arenas of political participation. He even strives to bust out of old patterns of talking, and tosses up for himself a wild new language . . . [this approach to life] becomes synonymous with critical reason and the refusal to live according to mere habit and entrenched opinion.[13]

Although the Cynics sneered at conformity, they were readily identifiable by their appearance: a cane or staff could be used to assist mobility, to ward off assailants, and to gesture pointedly to underscore rhetorical claims; a simple cloak, invariably soiled, provided some protection from the elements and symbolized Cynic austerity; bare feet underwrote physical hardiness and material minimalism; a satchel contained a few Cynic necessities such as beans, bread, and reading material; long, unkempt hair and a beard signaled Cynic scorn of cultivating a pleasing physical appearance in order to appear alluring to others; and a nomadic existence that rejected domesticity and settled abode. Claiming to learn from the animals, Cynics insisted that any space, public or private, could be used for any natural purpose: if a dog indulged in a certain natural function in public, so too could a human being. Most important, was the Cynic bearing: accusatory, prophetic, uncompromising, and proud. Again, the Cynics were not itinerate beggars supplicating themselves before their "betters" in the hope of appealing to charitable instincts and eliciting pity.

Instead, as the self-proclaimed wisest and most self-sufficient citizens of the cosmos, they demanded their entitlements.

Moreover, dominant moral understandings were merely another set of social conventions. As such, they were subject to grave suspicion if not outright rejection. What Cynics took to be the natural life (in the normative, not biological, sense of that term) was simple, liberated from social conventions, ascetic, free, self-sufficient, and firmly rooted in immediacy. The Cynics aspired to create a citadel of the self, an inner power so robust that they were invulnerable to external events. Personal excellence assumed pride of place over fulfillment of conventional moral pieties. Embedded in apparent Cynical anti-socialism was a radically democratic message: class privileges grounded in wealth, birth, education, and the like are utterly baseless. One's merit is determined only by his ability to attain the Cynic values of freedom and self-sufficiency, goods available in principle to everyone.

Ambiguous Relationship to Religion

Cynics tended to trade on religion when doing so served their interests. Thus, Diogenes highlighted the alleged "divine" aura of Cynicism: freedom, self-sufficiency, minimal needs, and refusal to conform to mass opinion. Moreover, he claimed that as the wisest of human beings, Cynics were "friends of the gods" and thereby entitled, as were the gods, to everything human beings accumulated. Acknowledging the obvious—that fervent belief in gods was widespread and invocation of the gods was often a powerful rhetorical tool—the Cynics alluded to gods and to the ancient adages of religion in order to illustrate their lifestyle, justify their indolence, and highlight their supposed entitlements.

But the entire culture surrounding religion was taken as yet another series of social conventions to scorn. Fear of divine retribution; elaborate sacrifices, rituals, and prayers in supplication to the gods; veneration of sacred places and forums; deferential treatment of oracles and soothsayers; assiduous preparation for the afterlife—these were taken by most Cynics as baseless superstitions worthy only of disdain.

Sense of the Dramatic

Cynics were far from shrinking violets. In ancient times, if a Cynic was in your midst he would make you well aware of his presence.

> [W]histling to the crowd, eating beans nosily, farting, belching, urinating, defecating in public, masturbating, rolling about in the sand, embracing snowy statues, carrying a tuna or bowl of soup across a crowded marketplace, sleeping in a [abandoned wine vat or tub], carrying a lantern around at noon, and innumerable other contortions,

twists and shapes: all these loudly trumpet the brazen freedom and antinomianism of the Cynics.[14]

The Cynics distanced themselves from fancy learning—math, philosophy, music, and astronomy were deemed useless for harmonious, daily living. Oddly, they were concerned with the process of dying and how the way a person died often revealed the merit of his character. Later Cynics reveled in the death stories of the likes of Socrates and Cato.

WAS JESUS A CYNIC PHILOSOPHER?

To describe the historical Jesus as a Cynic philosopher could mean any of the following:

- We can note similarities in attitude, teaching, and general approach to life between the Greek Cynics and those attributed to Jesus by the early Christians.
- We can interpret the teachings of Jesus from the vantage point of Cynic philosophy (and this is what first-century Christians did).
- We should interpret Jesus as a self-conscious Cynic philosopher, as taking Cynicism as one of the cornerstones of his teaching.
- We should interpret Jesus as a Jewish version of a Hellenic Cynical philosopher, even if Jesus was unaware of Cynic philosophy.
- We should understand Jesus as a Cynic philosopher, as someone who arrived independently at Cynical views even though he was unaware of Cynic philosophy in the Hellenic world.
- Jesus' teachings, as transformed and adjusted by early Christian leaders, would have been understood in the first century as examples of Cynic philosophy.

Obviously, some of these descriptions are stronger than others. That is, some of these theses tie in Jesus with Cynicism much more directly and explicitly than other of these theses. I'll begin with the general case that has been or could be advanced to connect Jesus with Cynicism.

THE CASE IN FAVOR OF IDENTIFYING JESUS WITH CYNICISM

Even secular philosophers who are unconcerned about proving conclusions about the historical Jesus have noted a connection between Cynicism and Christianity. For example, Farrand Sayre writes:

> The Cynics did much to prepare the way for Christianity by destroying respect for existing religions, by ignoring distinctions of race and nationality and by instituting an order of wandering preachers claiming exceptional freedom of speech. Tertullian says that the early Christian preachers adopted the Cynic cloak.... Augustine mentioned the club

> or staff as the only distinctive feature of the Cynics. . . . Julian mentioned the similarity of methods of the Cynics and the Christians in their public discourses and their collections. . . . Lucian describes cooperation between Cynics and Christians. . . . The early Christians worked side by side with Cynics for three hundred years and were to some extent influenced by them. . . . Early Christian orders of priesthood accepted celibacy and poverty as virtues.[15]

First, the early Christians, like the Cynics, intentionally adopted appearance and garb that distanced themselves from conventional lifestyles of their time: "And [Jesus] commanded them that they should take nothing for their journey, save a staff only; no scrip, no bread, no money in their purse" (Mark 6:8). Exuding a dignified poverty was the calling card of the Cynics and the first followers of Jesus. But to conclude that the historical Jesus sought to emulate the uniform of the Cynics would be too facile. Other biblical passages suggest differences between the two groups: "Nor scrip for your journey, neither two coats, neither shoes, nor yet staves [staffs]: for the workman is worthy of his meat" (Matt. 10:10); "And [Jesus] said unto them, Take nothing for your journey, neither staves, nor scrip, neither bread, neither money; neither have two coats apiece" (Luke 9:3); "Carry neither purse, nor scrip, nor shoes: and salute no man by the way" (Luke 10:4). Whereas Cynics typically bore a cloak, satchel, and staff, Jesus and his first followers apparently dispensed with the satchel and may or may not have carried staffs. Both groups traveled shoeless.

In an effort to homogenize the two groups, sometimes it is argued that Cynics carried staffs only as a concession to old age. Such efforts are misguided, in my view. Given the sketchy and sometimes conflicting historical information we have about the Cynics, to assert confidently that the two groups embraced the same default position—no staffs unless strictly necessary for mobility—is hasty and unnecessary. What is significant about the parallels between the two groups is not that they bore precisely the same uniform, but that their dress and appearance conveyed similar messages: the need for people interested in personal salvation to distance themselves from conventional understandings of success; the call to champion the cause of material minimalism; the distrust of societal purification and cleansing rituals; and the information conveyed by the nomadic lifestyle that Cynics and early Christians were citizens of the world but of no particular place. Regardless of whether the two groups adopted the same dress and accoutrements, the more important conclusion to draw is that the trajectory of their appearance dispatched a similar set of messages about living a good human life.

Second, the most general theme of the two groups is similar: strive toward becoming more divine by distancing yourself from the arbitrary authority of humanly created hierarchies of social power. Despite their ambiguous relationship to the gods, the Cynics accepted the conception of the gods as worthy of emulation: the closer one came to complete freedom, self-sufficiency, invulnerability, and needlessness, the closer one approximated the highest ideal. Jesus and the early Christians explicitly devote themselves to discerning and practicing a life based on proper worship of God. Both groups object strenuously to entrenched hierarchies of social and political power as obstacles to their respective missions. Moreover, the Parable of the Rich Fool and the deductive argument attributed to Diogenes arrive at similar conclusions: everything in fact belongs to God (or the gods in Diogenes' version). Although we might well contest the sincerity of Diogenes' posture—Was it, after all, only a way to cadge food and material goods that Diogenes declined to secure through his own labors? Was this not the perfect example of the Cynics invoking the divine only when doing so suited their purposes?—the notion that genuine ownership transcends the human world of artificial property rights is shared by the two groups.

Third, both groups acted in ways that underscored their rebellion to societal conventions. Jesus did not comply with Jewish purification rituals, consorted with those thought to be undesirables (for example, tax collectors, prostitutes, lepers, and sinners), and refused formalistic interpretations of Jewish law. His actions brought scorn from vested authorities: "And when the scribes and Pharisees saw him eat with publicans and sinners, they said unto his disciples, How is it that he eateth and drinketh with publicans and sinners? When Jesus heard it, he saith unto them, They that are whole have no need of the physician, but they that are sick: I came not to call the righteous. But sinners to repentance" (Mark 2:16–17). Likewise, the Cynics sought out those in need of a spiritual cure. When the Cynic Antisthenes was asked why he scolded his pupils so harshly, he replied, "Physicians are just the same with their patients."[16] When he was criticized for keeping company with evil men, he replied, "Well, physicians are in attendance on their patients without getting the fever themselves."[17] Both groups, then, understood that people were capable of reimagining and remaking their lives where their wills were resolute and took themselves to be physicians of the soul in possession of the proper medicine to energize the transformation.

Fourth, both groups gained their moral authority not simply because they expounded certain philosophies of life, but because they exemplified their theories by their practice. That is, both groups lived their preaching. Even the grandest figure of the world of the early Cynics, Alexander the Great, had heard of Diogenes and admired his uncompromising approach to life so much that he was willing to grant him any wish. Was this a test—a way of seeing if Diogenes at bottom was just as desirous of material aggrandizement as were other men? Or was Alexander secretly hoping that Diogenes would spurn his invitation as cavalierly as he is reported to have done? In any case, that Diogenes was not even tempted by Alexander's offer highlights the Cynic's rigorous commitment to the lifestyle he extolled to others. If the Alexander story is apocryphal then it still illustrates what the Cynic's followers were convinced Diogenes would have done if put in that position.

Jesus was willing to accept crucifixion as his penalty for threatening Jewish authorities and Roman imperialists. Moreover, countless early Christians accepted martyrdom rather than repudiate their faith. Such heroism undoubtedly advanced their cause as bystanders were drawn to investigate Christianity further as a result of these examples.

Fifth, both groups taught moral lessons through parables, aphorisms, and stories rather than crafting sophisticated philosophical principles and arguments. Many of these tales or barbs contain strong rebukes to those with a misplaced sense of superiority. In that vein, Jesus scolds the Pharisees when they comment on his failure to fulfill the purity ritual of washing prior to eating: "Now do ye Pharisees make clean the outside of the cup and the platter; but your inward part is full of ravening and wickedness. Ye fools did not he that made that which is without make that which is within also? . . . Woe unto you, scribe and Pharisees, hypocrites! For ye are as graves which appear not, and the men that walk over them are not aware of them" (Luke 11:39–40, 44). Objecting lawyers fared no better: "Woe unto you also, ye lawyers! For ye lade men with burdens grievous to be borne, and ye yourselves touch not the burdens with one of your fingers . . . for ye have taken away the key of knowledge: ye entered not in yourselves, and them that were entering in ye hindered" (Luke 11:46, 52).

For his part, Diogenes mocked rhetoricians as "thrice human" meaning "thrice wretched"; he called an ignorant wealthy man "the sheep with the golden fleece"; and upon seeing a for-sale sign on the home of a profligate man uttered, "I knew well that after such surfeiting you would throw up the owner."[18] Historian Diogenes Laertius summed up the Cynic's approach thusly: "He was great at pouring scorn on his contemporaries. The school of Euclides he called bilious, and Plato's lectures waste of time, the performances at the Dionysia great peep-shows for fools, and the demagogues the mob's lackeys."[19] In all such cases, both Christians and Cynics were emboldened to speak strongly and directly in service of their spiritual mission: the transformation of human souls.

Sixth, both groups eschewed traditional family values. In opposition to the dominant ideas of their time and place, the Cynics broke existing family ties, advised against marriage, fled from domesticity, and refused to view children as a hedge against mortality. At most, they agreed with Diogenes who "advocated community of wives, recognizing no other marriage than a union of the man who persuades with the woman who consents. And for this reason he thought sons too should be held in common."[20] Diogenes dismissed the common idea that children should be grateful to their parents: "One need not thank one's parents, either for the fact of being born, since it is by nature that what exists came into being; or for the quality of one's character, for it is the blending of the elements that is its cause. Furthermore, no thanks are required even for the things done by deliberate [parental] choice or willed purpose."[21] Going even further, Diogenes concluded that marriage and children were simply more trouble than they were worth, even if the consequence of acting on his advice was the end of the human species:

> One should not wed nor raise children, since our race is weak and marriage and children burden human weakness with troubles. Therefore, those who move toward wedlock and the rearing of children on account of the support these promise, later experience a change of heart when they come to know that they are characterized by even greater hardships . . . But even if the human race should fail [from lack of reproduction], would it not be fitting to lament this as much as one would if the procreation of flies and wasps should fail?[22]

Jesus also repudiated the conventional understandings of the role of family in his culture: "If any man come to me, and hate not his father, and mother, and wife, and children, and brethren, and sisters, yea, and his own life also, he cannot be my disciple" (Luke 14:26); "Verily I say unto you, There is no man that hath left house, or brethren, or sisters, or father, or mother, or wife, or children, or lands, for my sake, and the gospels', But he shall receive an hundredfold now in this time, houses, and brethren, and sisters, and mothers, and children, and lands, with persecutions; and in the world to come eternal life" (Mark 10:29–30). Moreover, Jesus publicly snubbed family members: "There came then his brethren and his mother, and standing without, sent unto him, calling him. And the multitude sat about him, and they said unto him, Behold, thy mother and thy brethren without seek thee. And he answered them, saying, Who is my mother, or my brethren? And he looked round about on them, and said, Behold my mother and my brethren. For whosoever shall do the will of God, the same is my brother, and my sister, and mother" (Mark 3:31–35). In sum, both groups not only distanced themselves from traditional family values, but also expected that their revolutionary moral messages would be rejected by those closest to them (see, for example, Mark 6:4 and 3:20–21).

Seventh, much of the specific moral message of the two groups is similar. For example, both groups renounce the typical human responses of revenge, retaliation, and resentment for perceived wrongs. Like several other Hellenistic moral movements, the Cynics define genuine harm as that which corrupts the soul while taking physical assaults as producing "only" pain. Pain as such need not undermine a person's quest for spiritual salvation and is thus not strictly speaking a harm at all. Thus, to respond to physical assaults or theft of property or slander by retaliating in kind is to collaborate unwittingly in one's own corruption. Cynic freedom requires that one not relinquish self-sufficiency by being lured into negative reactions to the hostility of other people. In that vein, Diogenes advises that we should treat friends and enemies the same.[23] Again, we observe the distinction between what is biologically natural (avenging perceived slights and wrongs) and what is normatively natural (what facilitates the salvation of the soul: eschewing retaliation and revenge). In that vein, Diogenes writes, "But be aware that although Diogenes' body was beaten by the drunkards, his virtue was not dishonored, since it is in its nature not to be adorned or shamed by evil men. . . . Really, through the foolishness of one person foolish men throughout the populace come to ruin, since they plan improper actions and wage war when they should be at peace."[24]

Jesus' admonitions to love enemies, to extend the circle of your concern beyond immediate friends and loved ones, and to forgive the trespasses of others are well known and have been sketched earlier in this work: "But I say unto you which hear, Love your enemies, do good to them which hate you, Bless them that curse you, and pray for them which despitefully use you. And unto him that smiteth thee on the one cheek offer also the other; and him that taketh away thy cloak forbid not to take thy coat also (Luke 6:27–29); "And forgive us our debts, as we forgive our debtors" (Matt. 6:12).

> This Christian and Cynic approach to wrongdoing is not confined to an individual's dealing with wrongs done to her or him. It goes along with a refusal to stand in judgment. It should be clear beyond question . . . that such abstention from censoriousness does not mean that "anything goes." The standards are high. In fact the refusal to condemn others is at the heart of the very exacting ethic that Cynics and Christians proposed.[25]

Eighth, both groups stress the importance of sharing material goods and necessary foodstuffs. Although I have questioned the Cynics' motivation in appealing to the gods when seeking donations from others, Diogenes reportedly said that "we ought to stretch out our hands to our friends with the fingers open and not closed."[26] Moreover, the Cynic Crates liquidated his property and gave it all away: "So he turned his property into money—for he belonged to a distinguished family—and having thus collected about 200 talents, distributed that sum among his fellow-citizens."[27] Such a stance is the logical offshoot of material minimalism, the creed of both groups. In that vein, Jesus consistently counseled generosity to others: "But love ye your enemies, and do good, and lend, hoping for nothing again; and your reward shall be great, and ye shall be the children of the Highest: for he is kind unto the unthankful and to the evil" (Luke 6: 35); "Give to every man that asketh of thee; and of him that taketh away thy goods ask them not again" (Luke 6:30).

Thus, John Dominic Crossan writes,

> The historical Jesus was a *peasant Jewish Cynic*. . . . His strategy . . . was the combination of *free healing and common eating*, a religious and economic egalitarianism that negated alike and at once the hierarchical and patronal normalcies of Jewish religion and Roman power. And, lest he himself be interpreted as simply the new broker of a new God, he moved on constantly, settling down neither at Nazareth nor at Capernaum. . . . Miracle and parable, healing and eating were calculated to force individuals into unmediated physical and spiritual contact with God and unmediated physical and spiritual contact with one another.[28]

Ninth, both groups highlight that the value of material minimalism lies in its voluntary nature. To be impoverished because one had no choice or was the victim of cruel fate is one thing. To proactively choose material minimalism as one's path for philosophical or religious reasons is quite another. A person such as Crates who is born into wealth and privilege but rejects both in service of higher ideals and personal salvation glistens with Cynic resolve. Such choices signal acceptance of freedom, self-sufficiency, and invulnerability to others that form the crux of the Cynic recipe for soul crafting. For Jesus, disciples must divest themselves of not only familial but also financial ties. As with the Cynics, poverty is a choice made for spiritual reasons. With both groups, wealth is viewed as not merely irrelevant but a genuine impediment to personal salvation. The starkest examples of this position occurs when Jesus says, "It is easier for a camel to go through the eye of a needle, than for a rich man to enter into the kingdom of God" (Mark 10:25); and "Woe unto you that are rich! For ye have received your consolation" (Luke 6:24). No ambiguity here.

The dangers of wealth are manifold: pursuing wealth distracts human beings from higher concerns; pursuing wealth lures us into the quagmire of desire such that our yearning for more can never be satisfied; pursuing wealth often leads us to trampling the just claims of other people; the accumulation of wealth invariably produces wrongful social hierarchies of power and privilege; the pursuit of wealth makes individuals dependent on the reactions of other people and the vicissitudes of chance; disparities in wealth nurture further exploitation; and, most important, the pursuit of wealth distorts our sense of identity as we define ourselves in terms of what we have in contrast to who we are in terms of our relationships with others and with the divine. Cynics and early Christians reject accumulating wealth, along with promoting high culture, advancing scientific understanding, and fostering grand creativity. The overriding objective of both groups is personal salvation grounded in particular notions of individual freedom and robust relationships (although the Cynic rendering of relationships is much thinner than that of the Christians).

Tenth, both groups are more open to accepting women as fuller participants in the human drama than the degree permitted by the dominant understandings of their cultures. Thus, Antisthenes observes that "Virtue is the same for women as for men. Good actions are fair and evil actions foul."[29] Crates writes that "Women are not by nature worse than men. The Amazons, at any rate, who have accomplished such great feats, have not fallen short of men in anything."[30] Women take a more prominent role in Jesus' ministry than one would expect at that time. The scriptures of Luke and Mark mention several women who followed Jesus: Mary Magdalene, Joanna, Susanna, Mary "the mother of James the less," "and many others" (Luke 8:2–3; Mark 15:40–41); women discover the empty tomb of Jesus and are instructed by an angel that Jesus has risen from the dead (Matt. 28:1–7); a host of unidentified women approach Jesus at various times and are received warmly (Mark 5:25–34; 7:25–30; Luke 10:38–42); and Jesus extends the Jewish understanding of adultery — which had hitherto been taken as an offense only against the husband — to include offenses against women (Matt. 5:27–28, 31–32).

Eleventh, the philosophies of both groups threatened the political hegemony of Rome. As noted previously, the Cynic litany of values were antithetical to the foundational values of Rome: the call for indolence, exhibitionism, mocking of traditions, individualism, peace, and dismissal of personal insults coalesced uneasily with Roman pride, work ethic, militarism, seriousness, veneration of tradition, unabashed aristocracy, and pursuit of worldly glory in what was taken as an inevitable international zero-sum contest: win or become subservient to those who did. Christian meekness, humility, withdrawal from political and military affairs, rejection of vengeance and retaliation, repudiation of arbitrary class hierarchies, and submission to divine authority fared no better when judged from prevalent Roman understandings.

> [Cynics and Christians] confronted established authority and the aims and ideals of the possessors of wealth and power, challenging them by their dress, their lifestyle, their ideas. They stressed action over theorizing, learning over teaching. They had little truck with polite convention, sure they had divine backing for their offer of new possibilities for human living, accepting they were likely themselves to get hurt in the attempt to share what they had for sharing. Yet for all their abrasive style, they lived and proclaimed an openness to foe and friend alike, across all barriers of possessiveness and fear. Simplicity was to be the setting where friendships could richly flourish, and the wealthy were to be rescued, as well as the poor.[31]

To supplement these eleven similarities between the Cynics and early Christians, we can also point to historical and geographical factors that join the groups in common cause. Although the Jesus tradition is generally taken to be non-Hellenic, Cynic teachings had reached Gadara, a town only six miles from Galilee and Sepphoris, located about three miles northwest of Nazareth. Thus, Jesus and those within the regions he preached may well have had opportunity to learn of Cynic teachings.

Moreover, Jesus, like the Cynics dismissed flatterers and, as always, material accumulation: "There came one running and kneeled to him, and asked him, Good Master, what shall I do that I may inherit eternal life? And Jesus said unto him, Why callest thou me good? There is none good but one, that is, God . . . go thy way, sell whatsoever thou hast, and give to the poor, and thou shalt have treasure in heaven: and come, take up the cross, and follow me" (Mark 10:17–18, 21). Also, Jesus, like the Cynics, repudiated artificial hierarchies of authority: "Ye know that they which are accounted to rule over the Gentiles exercise lordship over them; and their great ones exercise authority upon them. But so shall it not be among you: but whosoever will be great among you, shall be your minister: And whosoever of you will be the chiefest, shall be servant of all. For even the Son of man came not to be ministered unto, but to minister, and to give his life as ransom for many" (Mark 10:42–45). Finally, Jesus, like the Cynics, rejects the prevalent view that entrenched power structures are ratified by divine authority as a reward for uncommon virtue:

> It is not simply that their style of power is refused; they themselves cease to be acknowledged. The system is no longer seen as having God's backing. Wealth is no sign of divine approval, and neither is political power. Once the wealthy and the powerful are no longer seen as "benefactors" they can only appear as parasites. The structures of society as they stand have no claims on the allegiance of Jesus' followers.[32]

Like the Cynics, Jesus associates easily with those stigmatized as outcasts by the dominant judgment of society. Both the Cynics and Jesus take such outsiders as double victims of the larger community: first, by being exploited by those with access to greater means and influence and, second, by thereafter being rejected as viable members of the community that has used them so cavalierly. When Jesus sketches a more salutary lifestyle forthcoming in the Kingdom of God, he invites his followers and his audience to prefigure that way of living by adopting it in the present. Most strikingly, the teachings of the Cynics and Jesus converge on a stunningly radical conviction: the construal of "harm" as injury to the soul and the call for forgiveness at times even where repentance is absent. The belief that genuine harm is not the result of physical assault, theft of property, slander, and the like, but only action that corrupts the human soul was as difficult to sell in the first century as it is today. To enjoin victims to forgive their trespassers after these miscreants had repented is one thing—most religious and moral figures would accept such a proposition even though they would be wary of distinguishing feigned repentance from the real thing—but to ask victims to create unilaterally the distance between a sinner and his misdeed is quite another. "And forgive us our sins; for we also forgive every one that is indebted to us (Luke

11:4); "And forgive us our debts, as we forgive our debtors. . . . For if ye forgive men their trespasses, your heavenly Father will also forgive you: But if ye forgive not men their trespasses, neither will your Father forgive your trespasses" (Matt. 6:12, 14–15). Given the biological naturalness of deep feelings of revenge, retaliation, and resentment when human beings recognize that others have transgressed against them, to enjoin a normative naturalness of reflex forgiveness is beyond radical.

If one accepts the similarities between Cynics and the early Christians, and between Cynics and Jesus, what can account for such parallels?

> These early Christians, with their Christ, proposed a variant of Cynic social subversion. . . . Then, either they effectively conspired to change a non-Cynic Jesus into one who would be consistently Cynic in ethos while remaining (unaccountably) Palestinian Jewish in appearance, or there actually was such a Jesus. The latter seems much the more likely. We must then conclude that the only "historical Jesus" available to us is this Jewish-Cynic teacher. If the Cynic material is removed . . . there is practically nothing left. . . . The Jewish-Cynic Jesus . . . did not think he was God incarnate; it cannot be imagined that such a thought ever crossed his mind.[33]

Another source of possible evidence binding Jesus and Cynics is the work of Josephus, a first-century Jewish court historian, appointed by the Roman emperor, Vespasian. In his *The Jewish War* and *The Antiquities of the Jews*, Josephus describes activities in first-century Palestine. Among other things, he describes four religious and philosophical sects prominent during the time of Jesus. Although most Jews did not belong to any of the four sects, these small groups were socially and politically powerful in Palestine. All four groups subscribed to basic Jewish religious views: they believed in what they took to be the one, true God, who created the world; they believed the nature and workings of that God were revealed in Holy Scripture; they believed they were God's chosen people whom God would protect in return for their worship of him and obedience to his laws. The groups differed in their interpretations of what practices were required by religious laws, of what reactions and postures were prudent in the face of foreign (Roman) occupation, and in their understandings of the genealogical purity of high priests.

The best-known and largest sect was the Pharisees. Numbering about six thousand, they were strongly committed to formalistic renderings of God's law as revealed in the Torah. The letter of the law was primary in discovering proper devotional practices. Where the letter of the law was ambiguous, the Pharisees arrived at rulings that served as oral traditions that supplemented the Torah. By about two centuries after the death of Jesus, these oral traditions were compiled by rabbis into the *Mishnah*, which would form the core of the Talmud, a major collection of Jewish learning. Although the later Christian tradition stigmatized the Pharisees as hypocrites, that characterization is uncharitable. Certainly, Jesus often interpreted Jewish religious law more in terms of its spirit than its letter. Jesus did not subscribe to formalistic renderings as did the Pharisees. But from this it does not follow that the Pharisees were insincere or hypocritical, only that their theological interpretations and judicial decisions would sometimes differ from those of Jesus. To conclude that the Pharisees were thereby hypocrites fails to distinguish a difference in integrity from a difference in judgment.

The Sadducees did not leave any writings. They arose from the aristocratic classes and many of them were priests in the Jewish Temple. Although relatively small in number, this group emerged as the most powerful in first-century Israel. The chief priests, who represented the interests of the Jews to the Roman authorities, emerged from the ranks of the Sadducees. The Sadducees, unlike the Pharisees, were uninterested in promulgating oral traditions. Instead, they stressed the propriety of sacrificial rituals conducted in the Temple. These were taken as crucial to proper worship of God. The Sadducees were willing to accommodate Roman imperialism so long as the foreign authorities did not interfere with the sacrifices in the Temple. Of course, Jesus' understanding of the best religious priorities differed from that of the Sadducees.

Numbering around four thousand, the Essenes were convinced that most Jews had fallen away from the righteous religious path. They produced a collection of writings that were discovered in the twentieth century and dubbed the "Dead Sea Scrolls." After examining these writings, scholars conclude that the Essenes embodied an apocalyptical vision: a final battle would soon take place between the forces of good and the forces of evil; those aligned with God would emerge victorious and enter into God's blessed kingdom. In preparation for this battle, the Essenes began their own community and sought to preserve their ritualistic purity in the wilderness. This strategy was required to avoid the spiritual contaminations afflicting the Jewish masses. The Essenes conferred privilege of place upon their ritualistic purity as the centerpiece of their relationship to God. Just as he distanced himself from the Pharisees' formalist renderings of law and the Sadducees' traditional sacrifices, Jesus was unimpressed with the Essenes' ritualistic purity.

Josephus called the fourth group the "Fourth Philosophy." Josephus may have conferred this title because the Pharisees were thought to be somewhat Stoic, the Essenes somewhat Pythagorean, and the Sadducees akin to the Epicureans.[34] Although I am convinced all three parallels are overdrawn, Josephus might well have thought that the fourth group should also be viewed in the light of Hellenic philosophy. Characterizing this sect, or hodge-podge of groups, is difficult, but Josephus wrote:

> The fourth of the Jewish philosophical schools had Judas of Galilee as its self-appointed leader. At most points this school shares the views of

> the Pharisees. But they have an unconquerable love of freedom, totally convinced that God alone is their one and only leader and master. They care little about dying all sorts of death themselves, or of letting retribution fall on family and friends, so long as they may avoid calling any human master. . . . Judas assured his followers that the deity would be eager to help them if, with their minds set on great things, they did not shrink from painful effort.[35]

These words have led some scholars, such as F. Gerald Downing, to conclude that the Fourth Philosophy was Cynical.[36] The notions prevalent among those subscribing to the Fourth Philosophy—radical freedom, indifference to death, refusal to supplicate oneself before others, distance from family, acceptance of painful effort, bold expression of one's views, and recognition of the divine as an exemplar—appear similar to basic Cynical convictions.

> Taken in the light of the Cynic insistence on going everywhere, and of the fact that some eminent Cynics actually originated in the Decapolis near to Galilee, the evidence in Josephus may reasonably be taken to show that the idea of Cynic influence there would at least not have seemed unreasonable at the time.[37]

To conclude, however, that the Fourth Philosophy influenced Jesus or, even more, that his teachings were included within it would be imprudent. One of main features of the Fourth Philosophy was active resistance to foreign domination.

> The view that characterized these sundry groups [composing the Fourth Philosophy] was that Israel had a right to its own land, a right that had been granted by God himself. Anyone who usurped that right, and anyone who backed the usurper, was to be opposed, by violent means if necessary. Among those who took this line in the mid-first century were the "Sicarii" . . . a group whose name comes from the Latin word for "dagger." These "daggermen" planned and carried out assassinations and kidnappings of high-ranking Jewish officials who were thought to be in league with the Roman authorities. Another group . . . were the "Zealots." These were Jews who were "zealous" for the Law and who urged armed rebellion to take back the land God had promised his people.[38]

Such groups eventually led a revolt against Rome around AD 66 that led to a war of over four years against Rome that ended in the destruction of Jerusalem and the burning of the Temple. More important for my purposes, however, is that the call for armed resistance mirrors the teachings of neither Jesus nor the Cynics. Moreover, the invocation of God's desire as a motivating force for armed resistance is alien to Jesus and the Cynics as well. Finally, the parochialism of the groups comprising the Fourth Philosophy—their adherence to strict tribal lines, their lodging territorial claims grounded in such lines, and their exclusion of competing claims from alleged outsiders—differs markedly from Cynicism's ideal of the global citizen and Jesus' openness to gentiles.

However, one may argue that the Fourth Philosophy's connections to violence generously postdated Jesus. In the *Jewish War*, Josephus understands the Fourth Philosophy as being utterly dissimilar to the other Jewish sects. In the *Antiquities*, he understands the Fourth Philosophy to be in agreement with the Pharisees on everything except their extraordinary passion for freedom. On either rendering, the Fourth Philosophy does not seem to reflect the teachings of Jesus.

The resistance of the Fourth Philosophy to Roman imperial rule emerged from four concerns. First, paying taxes to Rome constituted a type of slavery for the Jews, a form of tribute to foreign dominators. Second, submission to Rome intruded upon the Jewish tradition of striving to live directly under the rule of only God. Third, that human beings are responsible for living in accord with the will of God and resistance to foreign domination, even if that meant suffering and death to self and family, was more in line with that calling than serving human masters. Fourth, such resistance might well contribute to the bringing about of the Kingdom of God.[39]

The nature of the resistance of the Fourth Philosophy is contestable. The links of the Fourth Philosophy to the violence of the Sicarii and Zealots took place decades after the death of Jesus. The original strategy of the Fourth Philosophy was focused on resistance to foreign rule and refusal to docilely accept taxation, both in order to sever homage to foreign masters. Although Josephus reports that the effect of this strategy was to unsettle the nation, he supplies no evidence that the Fourth Philosophy engaged in violent rebellion. That is, the early strategy of the Fourth Philosophy paved the way for more virulent resistance decades later but did not enact such violence itself. Instead, the adherents of the Fourth Philosophy asserted their willingness to suffer and die in order to illuminate the righteousness of their cause and to facilitate the coming Kingdom of God. As such, theirs was an aggressive, but nonviolent form of resistance to Rome.[40]

Still, even the Fourth Philosophy's apparent nonviolent resistance in the early stages of its existence is not easily attributed to Jesus. When asked by the Pharisees, "Is it lawful to give tribute to Caesar, or not?" Jesus asks for a coin and replies, "Whose is this image and superscription?" When the Pharisees answer "Caesar's," Jesus advises, "Render to Caesar the things that are Caesar's, and to God the things that are God's" (Mark 12:14–17; Matt. 22:17–21; Luke 20:22–25). This exchange might be interpreted as a clear instruction that paying tribute to Rome was merely returning to the imperialists what was theirs: coinage minted by and celebrating the Romans. But does the instruction also enjoin paying tribute with coinage that was not Roman? That is unclear; and not all coinage circulating in Israel was minted by Rome. Moreover, the tagline "to God the things that are God's" might well be taken to mean "everything," as all belongs to God. Jesus' answer, then, is not as transparent as one might first conclude. But one would expect that if Jesus was an adherent to the early strategy of the Fourth Philosophy his answer would have resounded with a clear admonishment to resist foreign taxation as an example of refusing to collaborate with foreign domination that interferes with direct service to God. Moreover, if Jesus subscribed to the Fourth Philosophy we should expect that he would otherwise clearly advise active, even if nonviolent, resistance to Rome. But we do not find such advice in the words attributed to him in the canonical scriptures. Although his prescribed way of life defies numerous Jewish and Roman conventions, values, and societal understandings, Jesus does not seem to mirror the early strategies, much less the later violent approaches, of the Fourth Philosophy. So too, the Fourth Philosophy does not mirror closely the general understandings of Cynic philosophy. Accordingly, to conclude that the Fourth Philosophy demonstrates the intersection of Cynic philosophy and Jesus' teachings is certainly misguided.

THE CASE AGAINST IDENTIFYING JESUS WITH CYNICISM

Two differences between the typical Cynic and Jesus were context and audience. Cynics invariably confronted others in urban marketplaces, whereas Jesus often met with rural peasants in agricultural settings. Moreover, although identifiable by common themes, approaches, and dress, the Cynics were not as much of a self-defined, disciplined group as were Jesus and his followers. Also, Jesus and his disciples were self-consciously geared toward communal transformation, whereas the Cynics repudiated society without any genuine hope of wholesale change. By far the most striking difference between Jesus and the Cynics was their respective approaches to God. Whether one interprets the historical Jesus as an apocalyptic prophet heralding the imminent Kingdom of God or as the son of God sent to redeem the world or as a peasant Jewish Cynic philosopher, at the core of each understanding is the primacy of God. Jesus takes established Jewish law and social practice and refashions it into what he takes to be a better rendering of the imperatives of God. For their part, the Cynics had an ambivalent relationship to the gods. They invoked Zeus when doing so helped them illustrate a philosophical point or justify their lifestyle, but they distanced themselves from the typical rituals, sacrifices, and worship prevalent at their time. Unlike Jesus, they did not stress the importance of earning eternal life nor did they allude to a blissful afterlife as a reward for righteous living or the bestowal of divine grace. In short, the Cynic view of the gods seemed more expedient than reverential, more utilitarian than devout. While both the Cynics and Jesus took the ways of life they espoused as wise and valuable immediately, only Jesus and his followers expressed the further benefits of eternal life.

Moreover, those who are unconvinced that Jesus can be categorized neatly as a Jewish Cynic philosopher point out that he was raised in the rural village of Nazareth and spent his entire life in such settings prior to his climatic trip to Jerusalem that set into motion the events that ended his life (see, for example, Mark 1:45; 3:7; 4:1; 6:6; 6:31). Also, no trips undertaken by Jesus to nearby Hellenically influenced cities such as Sepphoris and Gadara are recorded in the canonical Gospels. Finally, Cynics were not reputed to embody special powers or to be capable of performing miraculous deeds, whereas Jesus was thought by his followers to glisten with such powers and capabilities. Scriptures chronicle numerous episodes of Jesus performing miracles, healings, exorcisms, and the like.

> Cynicism was an urban phenomenon that, paradoxically, encouraged both an unyielding antisocial individualism and yet, at the same time, begging for sustenance. The Jesus movement, on the other hand, appears to have been largely a rural Galilean phenomenon that encouraged strong community bonds and included the sharing of ministry, food, and other resources according to need. Finally, it is important to note that two of the activities central to the ministry of Jesus—healing and exorcism—afford no real parallels with ancient Cynicism.[41]

One would expect that if Jesus was a self-conscious Cynic that references to that philosophy would appear in scripture. But that is not the case. Although the Epicureans and Stoics appear as philosophers in Athens, the Cynics do not (Acts 17:18). Early Christian literature is also devoid of references to the Cynics.

> It is only the second-century Apologists who comment on the Cynics, albeit in a hostile way. Pagan attacks against Christianity, however, make use of similarities between Christian and Cynic preachers . . . such comparison . . . was a stereotypical anti-Christian propaganda tool, used then also by Christians themselves against "heretics" . . . Comparisons of Cynics with Jesus are rare. Lucian characterizes Jesus . . . as founder of a mystery cult, not as a Cynic.[42]

Those who perceive Jesus as a Jewish Cynic philosopher sometimes assume parallels exist between the Cynic tradition and the Q source. Q is a document that does not exist, but which scholars are quite sure did exist at an earlier time. That the Gospels of Mark, Matthew, and Luke contain so many of the same stories and accounts of Jesus' life and teaching is thought to be the result of an early source, the Q document. Assuming, as most scholars do, that the Gospel of Mark was the first to be written, that neither Matthew nor Luke copied his account from the other, and that in the Gospels of Matthew and Luke is material not found in Mark, leads to the conclusion that the Q document once existed, possibly around AD 50. Strictly speaking, Q is thought to consist of material common to Matthew and Luke, but not contained in Mark (from which Matthew and Luke might have copied). Q, then, is thought to be the earliest account of the historical Jesus. Its reconstruction consists mostly of sayings of Jesus and parables. The Cynic tradition was also transmitted largely by collections of sayings, stories, epistles, and biographies.

But we should resist the temptation to make too much of possible parallels between Q and the Cynic tradition. The Cynic tradition is a mixture of Socratic and Stoic elements, wrapped together with distinctive Cynic seasoning. Q is a hypothetical document that can be reconstructed in ways that seem more or less Cynical, depending on the interpreter's antecedent commitments. Even where parallels exist between Q and Cynicism, the problem of causation and correlation arises: from the fact that a particular set of sayings in Q correlate closely to Cynic philosophy, it does not automatically follow that Cynic philosophy was the cause or source of the sayings in Q.

Another problem confronting those who identify the historic Jesus as a Cynic philosopher is the diversity that characterized individual Cynics. For example, not all Cynics were as flamboyant as Diogenes is reputed to have been in performing public demonstrations of bodily functions. Obviously, this was not an aspect of Jesus' teachings or the behavior of his followers. The malleability of Cynicism permits either of two conclusions: that here is a stark contrast between Jesus and Cynicism; or Diogenes' antics were not central to Cynicism, so the difference is irrelevant in assessing whether the historical Jesus was a Jewish Cynic philosopher. This is but one of numerous examples of how a possible difference between the two groups can be handled. Here are three other examples in this vein: Jesus and his followers were also not as overtly hostile to those they confronted as were the Cynics; Jesus and his followers did not beg with the same sense of entitlement as did the Cynics; Jesus and his followers were more consistently warm and charitable to the disenfranchised than were the Cynics (despite some of their rhetoric). In each of these cases, the diversity of individual Cynics permits plausibly drawing either the conclusion that evidence against the Jesus-was-a-Jewish-Cynic thesis is present or the conclusion that the matter at hand differs depending on which Cynic philosopher we are considering. In such situations, the antecedent convictions of the interpreter are paramount.

Thus, William Desmond observes:

> It is unclear, for example, to what extent Hellenism had penetrated Galilee. Even if Jesus spoke some Greek, it was not his native language and surely he did not speak Greek to Peter the fisherman. Moreover, the depiction of Jesus as a Cynic rebel against *nomos* [social conventions] should not be exaggerated. He may have opposed Pharisaic legalism, questioned laws of diet and purity, "worked" on the Sabbath day and so forth, yet he still recognized the Sabbath as a special day, celebrated Passover as a holy time, and did not quip, like Crates, that

> for him *every* day was a festival day. Although not a Pharisee, Jesus did argue from scripture, thus showing his respect for tradition that needed to be reformed, not rejected outright. . . . Jesus ministered to his own people, and was not exile or homeless beggar. He preached to large crowds but did not harangue random passers-by.[43]

In that vein, those who insist that Jesus was a Jewish Cynic peasant philosopher invariably include the works of those not commonly categorized as Cynics to make that point. For example, they point out similarities in the teachings or lifestyle of Jesus to thinkers who are taken by professional philosophers to be Stoics such as Epictetus, Musonius Rufus, and Seneca.[44] That methodology fuzzes up the claim that Jesus was a Cynic because it expands the notion of Cynicism beyond its recognized academic borders. Moreover, that both ancient Cynics and Jesus employed aphorisms and stories to articulate their views is hardly newsworthy. Numerous traditions, including the Jewish and eastern, did likewise. In fact, "one of the most characteristic forms of Jesus' teaching style—the parable—has no real Cynic parallels and is a fundamental *Jewish* form. In short, there is no need to postulate a *Cynic* background to Jesus' styles of communication."[45]

The Cynics were renowned for boldly confronting strangers encountered in their journeys, either to beg from or harangue them. But Jesus is reported to have cautioned his disciples: "Salute no man by the way" (Luke 10:4). While the Cynics espoused an extreme personal freedom and *self-sufficiency*, Jesus did not so much challenge Jewish law as offer several deeper interpretations of it. He distanced himself from strictly formalist understandings of the law in order to highlight its profound spirit. In so doing, Jesus underscored the *dependency* of human beings on God.

> Jesus also passed up numerous opportunities to challenge social conventions that any good Cynic would have jumped at: for example, religious sacrifices, religious and governmental taxes, and the civil institution of marriage. Furthermore, there are absolutely no indications that Jesus practiced the sort of "doggish" shamelessness that characterized the Cynics' public behavior. Rather than Cynic self-sufficiency, Jesus' life and teachings attest both to one's absolute dependence on God and mutual self-giving within community.[46]

Most important, understanding Jesus as a Jewish Cynic makes it difficult to account for the most critical aspects of his life story: he greatly annoyed Jewish leadership, threatened Roman imperialism, was crucified as a result, gathered a host of followers, and after his death was the rallying point for an enormously influential religious movement. No Cynic philosopher had a parallel narrative. Remember, the power broker of the Hellenic world, Alexander the Great, actually admired Diogenes. The Cynics in general were perceived with wry amusement, overt disgust, or recurrent curiosity. They were seen as petty annoyances and, less frequently, as admirable social outcasts. But Cynics were not taken so seriously that their presence threatened the political, social, and moral status quo so deeply that they were subject to governmental terror.

> A Jesus who went around saying wise and witty things [like a Cynic philosopher] would not have been threatening enough to have been crucified during Passover when he was surrounded by hundreds who liked him. A Jesus who was a religious genius who helped people in their relationship with God and was kind, compassionate, and gentle would not have been crucified either. A social revolutionary would have been crucified (and this partly explains Jesus' death, in my view), but it is doubtful that such a revolutionary would have given birth to a church that was hardly a movement of social revolution.[47]

Perhaps much of the form the church assumed after the crucifixion of Jesus can be attributed to stylizations fashioned by Jesus' disciples and the early Christians. That is, perhaps much church doctrine, creed, ritual, and self-understanding arose not from the explicit design of Jesus, but from the work of his followers. Still, much of the point remains: unlike a typical Cynic philosopher, Jesus threatened the status quo severely and was met with the harshest reprisals. Sure, philosophers were sometimes exiled for spreading heretical doctrines in the Hellenistic world, and later Roman emperors occasionally banished philosophers en masse when it suited their purposes. But Jesus' collection of loyal followers, climactic confrontation with Jewish and Roman authorities, and subsequent crucifixion are beyond what Cynic philosophers endured. If Jesus was merely a Jewish Cynic peasant philosopher we would not expect such a result. Because of its austerity and apparent conflict with our biologically natural mind-set, Cynic philosophy was simply not perceived as having revolutionary implications for the military and political status quo. Only a few, seeming crackpots, would be so deranged as to renounce family and all material comforts, take up the staff, satchel, and cloak, and roam about haranguing or begging from other people.

In sum, the claim that Jesus was mainly or solely a Jewish Cynic peasant philosopher is highly contestable. While revealing the genuine historical Jesus is well beyond the scope of this work—Was the historical Jesus the exemplar of mainstream Christian religion who self-consciously understood himself to be the Son of God sent to redeem the world? Was the historical Jesus a Jewish Cynic philosopher? Was the historical Jesus an apocalyptic prophet who was convinced erroneously that the Kingdom of God was imminent? Or was the historical Jesus something else?—certain conclusions seem reasonable.

First, that Jesus was directly familiar with particular Cynic philosophers and their work is almost certainly false. Second, that Jesus was *only* a Cynic philosopher is almost certainly false. Third, that some followers of Jesus and the early Christians could discern parallels between some of

Jesus' teachings and the positions of Cynic philosophers is probably true. Fourth, that we can from our contemporary understanding draw such parallels is certainly true. Fifth, extracting Jesus from his Jewish context and portraying him retrospectively as a Hellenistic philosopher is certainly misguided. Sixth, that we can evaluate Jesus' moral message independently of appealing to Cynic philosophy is certainly true.

To this task we will now turn.

NOTES

1. The section on the interpretation of the parable has been informed by Klyne R. Snodgrass, *Stories with Intent* (Grand Rapids, MI: William B. Eerdmans Publishing Company, 2008); Craig L. Blomberg, *Interpreting the Parables* (Downers Grove, IL: InterVarsity Press, 1990); Richard N. Longenecker (ed.), *The Challenge of Jesus' Parables* (Grand Rapids, MI: William B. Eerdmans Publishing Company, 2000); Kenneth E. Bailey, *Poet & Peasant Through Peasant Eyes* (Grand Rapids, MI: William B. Eerdmans Publishing Company, 2000).
2. Snodgrass, *Stories with Intent*, 401.
3. Ibid., 399.
4. Stephen I. Wright, "Parables on Poverty and Riches," in Longenecker, *The Challenge of Jesus' Parables*, 223–24.
5. Crates, "The Epistles of Crates," in Abraham J. Malherbe, *The Cynic Epistles* (Missoula, MT: Scholars Press, 1977), Epistle 19.
6. Diogenes Laertius, *Lives of the Eminent Philosophers*, trans. R. D. Hicks (Cambridge, MA: Harvard University Press, 1925, 11th edition, 2005), 6.37.
7. Crates, "The Epistles of Crates," Epistles 2, 17, 22, 36.
8. Ibid., Epistle 27.
9. Farrand Sayre, *The Greek Cynics* (Baltimore: J. H. Furst Company, 1948), 18.
10. Ibid., 16.
11. Crates, "The Epistles of Crates," Epistle 7.
12. William Desmond, *Cynics* (Berkeley: University of California Press, 2008), 45.
13. Ibid., 78.
14. Ibid., 122–23.
15. Sayre, *The Greek Cynics*, 27.
16. Diogenes Laertius, *Lives of the Eminent Philosophers*, 6.4.
17. Ibid., 6.6.
18. Ibid., 6.47.
19. Ibid., 6.24.
20. Ibid., 6.72.
21. Diogenes, "The Epistles of Diogenes," in Abraham J. Malherbe, *The Cynic Epistles* (Missoula, MT: Scholars Press, 1977), Epistle 21.
22. Ibid., Epistle 47.
23. Diogenes Laertius, *Lives of the Eminent Philosophers*, 6.68.
24. Diogenes, "The Epistles of Diogenes," Epistle 20.
25. F. Gerald Downing, *Jesus and the Threat of Freedom* (London: SCM Press Ltd., 1987), 81.
26. Diogenes Laertius, *Lives of the Eminent Philosophers*, 6.29.
27. Ibid., 6.87.
28. John Dominic Crossan, *Jesus: A Revolutionary Biography* (San Francisco: HarperSanFrancisco, 1994), 198.
29. Diogenes Laertius, *Lives of the Eminent Philosophers*, 6.12.
30. Crates, "The Epistles of Crates," Epistle 28.
31. Downing, *Jesus and the Threat of Freedom*, 124.

32. Ibid., 142.
33. Ibid., 147–48, 159.
34. Ibid., 133.
35. Josephus, *Jewish Antiquities*, trans. Louis H. Feldman (Cambridge, MA: Harvard University Press, 1965), 18.13, 18.5.
36. Downing, *Jesus and the Threat of Freedom*; see also Crossan, *Jesus: A Revolutionary Biography*; *The Historical Jesus: The Life of a Mediterranean Jewish Peasant* (San Francisco: HarperSanFrancisco, 1991); B. Mack, *A Myth of Innocence* (Philadelphia: Fortress, 1988).
37. Downing, *Jesus and the Threat of Freedom*, 136.
38. Bart D. Ehrman, *Jesus: Apocalyptic Prophet of the New Millennium* (New York: Oxford University Press, 1999), 114.
39. Richard A. Horsley, *Bandits, Prophets & Messiahs* (Harrisburg, PA: Trinity Press International, 1985), 192–94.
40. Ibid., 196–99.
41. Paul Rhodes Eddy, "Jesus as Diogenes? Reflections on the Cynic Jesus Thesis," *Journal of Biblical Literature* 115 (1996): 449, 462.
42. Hans Dieter Betz, "Jesus and the Cynics," *The Journal of Religion* 74 (1994): 453, 460–61.
43. Desmond, *Cynics*, 214–15.
44. See, for example, Downing, *Jesus and the Threat of Freedom*.
45. Eddy, "Jesus as Diogenes?" 461.
46. Ibid., 463.
47. Scott McKnight, "Who Is Jesus?" in Michael J. Wilkens and J. P. Moreland, eds., *Jesus Under Fire* (Grand Rapids, MI: Zondervan Publishing House, 1995), 61–62.

SIX

The Unjust Steward: "Because He Had Done Wisely"

And he said unto his disciples, There was a certain rich man, which had a steward; and the same was accused unto him that he had wasted his goods. And he called him, and said unto him, How is it that I hear this of thee? Give an account of thy stewardship; for thou mayest be no longer steward. Then the steward said within himself, What shall I do? For my lord taketh away from me the stewardship: I cannot dig; to beg I am ashamed. I am resolved what to do, that, when I am put out of the stewardship, they may receive me into their houses. So he called every one of his lord's debtors unto him, and said unto the first, How much owest thou unto my lord? And he said, An hundred measures of oil. And he said unto him, Take thy bill, and sit down quickly and write fifty. Then he said to another, And how much owest thou? And he said, An hundred measures of wheat. And he said unto him, Take thy bill, and write fourscore. And the lord commended the unjust steward, because he had done wisely: for the children of this world are in their generation wiser than the children of light. And I say unto you, Make to yourselves friends of the mammon of unrighteousness; that, when ye fail, they may receive you into everlasting habitations. He that is faithful in that which is least is faithful also in much: and he that is unjust in the least is unjust also in much. If therefore ye have not been faithful in the unrighteous mammon, who will commit to your trust the true riches? And if ye have not been faithful in that which is another man's, who shall give you that which is your own? No servant can serve two masters: for either he will hate the one, and love the other; or else he will hold to the one, and despise the other. Ye cannot serve God and mammon.

(Luke 16: 1–13)

INTERPRETATION OF THE PARABLE

The steward is most likely an agent of the wealthy landowner.[1] He manages the estate and receives a fee. The debtors rent parcels of the land and pay the landowner the amounts of produce specified in their leases.

> [Agents] then, as now, were vulnerable and especially so given the cutthroat nature of the oppressive system within which they worked. They were unpopular with the peasants because they collected the landlord's tribute, which included a cut for themselves. But they could also arouse the suspicions and resentment of their masters if they began to look too powerful or wealthy. Furthermore, peasants struggling to survive might well make trouble between a manager and a landlord as a ruse to improve things a bit for themselves. No party would have operated in a world of moral ideals.[2]

The parable begins with the landowner's suspicion that the steward had squandered his goods. He had heard as much from sources unnamed in the story. How might the steward have done this? He might have embezzled money from the landowner through fraudulent account ledgers. He might have been lax in enforcing the lease agreements. He might have been incompetent and made a host of costly errors. In any event, the landowner has been informed that the steward has wasted his goods, and he confronts his underling. The steward apparently is silent, which confirms the truth of the allegation. He issues no denials, makes no excuses, and conjures no justifications for his actions. Neither does he express regrets, offer contrition, or beseech his patron for mercy. The steward's silence is puzzling in that almost anyone else in his situation would have responded in some way.

We would expect that the landowner would summarily discharge the steward at this point, probably after a stern reprimand. The landowner would also have legal recourse against the miscreant steward but apparently foregoes that option. However, the timing of the steward's presumed firing is unclear. On one hand, the agent muses over what he should do "when I am put out of the stewardship," which suggests that his dismissal is imminent but not yet in place. On the other hand, the agent also moans that "For my lord taketh away from me the stewardship," which suggests that he has already been fired. Moreover, we would not expect that a landowner would permit an incompetent or dishonest agent to continue on for a few days as steward after he has admitted his serious malfeasance. In any case, what is clear is that if the steward has been fired that event is unknown to the public; the steward is assumed by the debtors he soon contacts to still have the authority to represent the landowner.

Instead of constructing rationalizations for his actions or expressing remorse for his misdeeds, the steward focuses only on his self-interest.

How is he to survive now? He judges himself both unfit and unwilling for grueling manual labor. He could resort to begging, but, just as the conventional wisdom of his time and place would conclude, he finds such action shameful.

His only viable action is to hatch a scheme whereby he might ingratiate himself to others with the means to "receive me into their houses." The others in question are the debtors with whom he regularly interacts. The expression, "they may receive me into their houses," should not be construed literally. The steward does not embody the zany aspiration of becoming the Middle East's perpetual house guest—bouncing from home to home; enjoying ongoing but brief hospitality, food, and lodging in gratitude for past service rendered. Instead, the more likely plan is that he might secure employment from one of the debtors as reciprocation for whatever benefits he confers upon the debtors through his contemplated scheme.

What is the scheme? Quite simply, the plan is to lower the amount of rent that each debtor owes the landowner. As the debtors assume that the steward still speaks for the landowner, they are overjoyed. They receive a one-sided, beneficial adjustment to their leases. Moreover, we must assume that the steward gently suggests that this adjustment is due to his influence with his patron. After all, if the steward is reporting only a benefit that the landowner conferred independently, there is no reason for the debtors to be grateful to the steward. The amounts specified in the leases are considerable, and the relief offered by the steward is significant.

> One hundred *baths* of oil (bath is a unit of measurement) would be equivalent to about 800 or 900 gallons, the yield of possibly 150 olive trees and equivalent to the wages of about three years for the average worker. One hundred *kor* of wheat would be almost 1100 bushels, probably enough to feed 150 people for a year, the produce of 100 acres, and equivalent to seven and one-half years of labor for the average worker. In each case the steward reduced the bill by the same amount, about 500 denarii or the wages of more than two years for a day laborer. The parable tells of fairly large business dealings. None of the people involved are poverty-stricken peasants or even people with average incomes.[3]

At first glance, we are astounded by the steward's apparent moral obtuseness. After being justly accused of malfeasance and fired (or about to be fired) from his job, he doubles down on fraud: he continues to represent himself as the landowner's agent; he falsely asserts that he is empowered to lower the rents of the lease-holders; he takes credit for allegedly convincing his patron to authorize these reductions in anticipation of the debtors' grateful response; and he thereby, once again, squanders the goods of his employer in service to his own self-interest.

We would expect that upon discovering this treachery that the landowner would immediately expose the unjust steward, rescind the fraudulent lease adjustments, and pursue maximum legal action against his former employee. Instead, the landowner "commended the unjust steward, because he had done wisely." We scratch our heads and wonder, "What is the wisdom in fraud?"

Our common initial reaction is captured well by Charles C. Torrey:

> [The Parable of the Unjust Steward] brings before us a new Jesus, one who seems inclined to compromise with evil. He approves a program of canny self-interest, recommending to his disciples a standard of life which is generally recognized as inferior: "I say to you, gain friends by means of money." This is not the worst of it; he bases the teaching on the story of a shrewd scoundrel who feathered his own nest at the expense of the man who had trusted him; and then appears to say to his disciples, "Let this be your model."[4]

Why, then, does the landowner not only permit the lease reductions but also praise the unjust steward for his wisdom? One line of thinking is as follows: once the debtors enjoyed what they thought was authorized relief from the steward, word spread, and the landowner's reputation flourished. What, then, were the landowner's choices once he discovered the steward's chicanery? He could reveal his steward's recurring fraud, rescind the changes to the leases, and deflate his blossoming good will and the spirits of the debtors; or he could ratify the changes to the leases, tip his hat to the crafty, unscrupulous steward, with benefits accruing to all (although those rebounding to the landowner would come at a monetary cost—the loss of a portion of his entitlements under the leases). On this view, the steward, although unjust, earns the landowner's commendation because he has managed to salvage his fate from a seemingly impossible predicament.

Still, can "wisdom" be grounded in fraud? Although the steward has manifested skill and craft aimed at self-preservation, the means he has used hardly merit the honorific title of "wisdom." Once his initial squandering of the landowner's goods was discovered, could not the steward have repented his incompetence or wrongdoing, thrown himself on the mercy of his patron, and sought forgiveness (or, at least, a strong letter of recommendation that he might parlay into a future job)? As it was, the fraudulent scheme he hatched still depended for its success on the good graces of the landowner. Intuitively, under comparable circumstances, how many betrayed employers would have reacted with the generous spirit displayed by the landowner? How many, after being twice played for a fool by a seemingly ungrateful employee, instead would have exacted the maximum personal and legal response?

Another line of thinking contends that the steward did not act unjustly when he amended the leases.[5] The reductions were merely deletions of interest contained in the leases, interest payments which were not permissible charges under Jewish law. Thus any deprivation incurred by the landowner and by the steward (who thereby forfeits the usurious portion of his commission) was not money to which they were legally entitled from the outset. On this view, the steward's wisdom lies in disgorging only that which was wrongfully included in the leases with the result that great benefit flowed to him (the gratitude of the debtors and a commendation from the landowner), his patron (the landowner gains a reputation for righteousness), and the debtors (a significant reduction in their debt). The steward's wisdom, then, arises from his understanding that doing the right thing correlates with everyone's self-interest.

However, the problems with this rosy account are clear. First, the parable supplies no evidence that the landowner is greedy, unscrupulous, or exploitive. On the contrary, the parable provides strong support for the landowner's merciful and warm disposition: when he discovers that the steward has squandered his goods, he neither reprimands nor presses legal charges against him; when he learns of the steward's lease reductions, he neither scolds him for exceeding his authority nor threatens him with legal action. Given that the lease agreements are explicit and public, that the landowner would include hidden illegal usury fees is highly unlikely. Second, the parable is of the "unjust" steward, not the agent who saw the light and did the right thing in order to serve everyone's interests. That his "injustice" derives from his actions pertaining to the lease reductions is the most likely explanation for the title of the parable. Indeed, we cannot be completely confident that his initial wasting of his patron's goods was due to "injustice." The steward may simply have been incompetent or reckless. Third, the lease reductions are significant, which suggests they are greater than illegal interest charges would have been.

Possibly, the steward's wisdom emerges not from his slick deceptions, but from his perception of his patron and his use of money to advance the common good. Although most employers would undoubtedly have reacted more harshly toward the steward regarding both sets of his transgressions, the steward staked his well-being on the tender mercies of the landowner. He knew that his patron would not react in commonplace fashion once he understood the benefits to all that were possible. The steward knew well that the landowner would judge that relinquishing material goods for the sake of the common good was a prudent bargain. Moreover, when we place the parable in the context of the historical Jesus as apocalyptic prophet—as heralding the imminent transformation of the world into the Kingdom of God—we may well conclude that part of the message is that material goods should be used now in order to prepare for that transformation: instead of obsessing over material accumulation, use your money to advance the common good and increase your prospects for a warm reception in the coming age.

Such an interpretation exudes currency, but at least one puzzle remains: Have we not separated means and ends too neatly? Surely, Jesus does not adopt an "ends justify the means" ethic. While the ends of the steward's act may be commendable—as all parties benefit and the only person who has seemingly been deprived, the landowner, by his own calculations in the long run gains more than he relinquishes—the means employed are unworthy. The steward deceives the debtors about his own authority to continue as an agent; he lies to the debtors about having convinced the landowner to permit reductions in the leases; and he alters the lease agreements to the benefit of the debtors. His is a premeditated fraud with only one evident purpose: to salvage the steward's own well-being. If the steward had any genuine concern about the burden to the debtors or his employer's reputation for righteousness why had he not approached the landowner earlier and suggested that reducing the lease payments might be an effective strategy for advancing the common good? Of course, the answer is that the steward could not have cared less about the common good until promoting it would advance his only abiding interest: his own self-preservation. So the steward maneuvers the landowner into a situation such that the steward strongly suspects the landowner will "do the right thing." But should not "wisdom" be spawned from finer cloth?

Although we may well be inclined to credit the steward's slyness and shrewdness—for even, perhaps especially, villains can concoct worldly artifices—why should we commend the steward's "wisdom," a term that connotes the marriage of sound judgment and virtue? Unless we fall back on the dubious possibility that the steward was not unjust when modifying the leases because he was only reducing his own illegal profits and the illegal usury of his employer, we must conclude that in the court of morality we have a serious ends-means problem in the parable.

Perhaps the easiest, but still unsatisfying, conclusion is that "wisdom" was simply a poor choice of words. The landowner was merely commending the steward for his cunning and acuteness; he was not in fact exalting his "wisdom" in the fullest sense of that term. That is, the landowner was not endorsing morally both the means and ends employed; instead, he was only commending the steward's ingenuity and effectiveness in refashioning his prospects. Instead of taking umbrage at the steward's presumption, the landowner appreciates his keen wit and sharp understanding of the source of his salvation—the landowner's expansive mercy. Ultimately, the "wisdom" of the unjust steward is not in his methods but in his perception in knowing where his redemption resided—in the character of his patron.

Some commentators point out that understanding the audience of the parables is clarifying. Jesus preached to his disciples and to crowds, most of whom were Jewish peasants. To such an audience the theme of the Parable of the Unjust Steward would resonate.

> Many earlier commentators worried over how Jesus could use a dishonest man as an example. But this need not delay us. The Middle Eastern peasant at the bottom of the economic ladder finds such a parable pure delight. Nothing pleases him more than a story in which some David kills a Goliath . . . the Western listener/reader is surprised at the use of a dishonest man as a hero. The Eastern listener/reader is surprised that such a hero is criticized.[6]

Stigmatize me as an obtuse "Western reader," but I am still unsatisfied. If the suggested analogue is that human beings, even unjust ones, should entrust their very lives to boundless divine mercy and rest assured that God will pay any price for our redemption, then our ends-means problem persists. Surely the parable is not intended to suggest that human beings should strive to outfox God by hatching schemes that will compel his mercy. But this is precisely the strategy of the unjust steward. Unlike the prodigal son, the unjust steward did not repent his earlier malfeasance whereby he squandered his patron's goods; he did not offer to make restitution; he uttered no contrition. Most important, he did not petition the landowner for a merciful resolution. Instead, the steward, who from the textual evidence regretted only that his transgression had been exposed, conjures a scheme designed to *compel* the landowner's mercy. To argue that "this clever rascal was wise enough to place his total trust in the quality of mercy experienced at the beginning of the story"[7] is not persuasive. I would submit that if the steward was genuinely trustful he would have gone to the landowner, hopefully after realizing and repenting his own wrongdoing, and petitioned for the landowner's mercy. Instead, the steward, employing the arts of fraud and misdirection, maneuvered the landowner into a position wherein being "merciful" was in the landowner's best long-term interests.

Is this sequence of events an appropriate model for human beings who are counseled to entrust everything to boundless divine mercy? Would not the saga of David's slaying of Goliath have been less heroic if it included David's fraudulent drugging of Goliath prior to their battle?

While the Parable of the Unjust Steward may have provided succor to the Eastern audience to which it was first addressed, we may wonder why Jesus, who consistently excoriated the customs and values prevalent in his world, would pander to his audience's predilection for cheering "the clever fellow who won out over the 'Mister Big' of his community."[8]

Perhaps, though, the point of the parable is that if the unjust steward benefited so greatly from the mercy of an employer whom he had betrayed twice, then righteous human beings can expect much greater benefit when they place their faith in the boundless mercy of the divine.[9] Given the oppressive economic system that provides the backdrop of the parable, we might charitably interpret Jesus' story as not designed to pander to his audience, but to flow from a realistic socioeconomic context that they would understand all too well.

> The praise of the children of this age, however, is an accusation against the children of light. The steward, as a child of his age, knew how to handle the system to his best advantage, but the children of light do not know how to live wisely within *their* "system." That is, they do not know how to live in keeping with the kingdom already present.[10]

What, then, are the underlying messages of the parable consistent with Jesus' other teachings? First, human beings should have faith in the boundless mercy of the divine. By eschewing the means of the unjust steward, we can attain a far more glorious result than that achieved by the conniving agent. Second, instead of amassing wealth as an end in itself, we should use our money prudently to advance the common good and increase our prospects for a warm reception in the coming age ("Make to yourselves friends of the mammon of unrighteousness; that, when ye fail, they may receive you into everlasting habitations."). Third, more strikingly, human beings cannot successfully serve God while being obsessed with material accumulation ("Ye cannot serve God and mammon."). That is, we cannot at once make both God and pursuit of wealth our ultimate commitment. Fourth, the abatement and remission of debts, both material and spiritual, plant the seeds of personal transformation. In the parable, the softening of debts opens possibilities for salutary change for all parties, but in particular for the steward and the landowner.

From a philosophical standpoint, the parable invites us to reflect more deeply on the entire moral message of Jesus.

WHAT IS THE CONTEXT OF JESUS' MORAL MESSAGE?

What we take to be the context of Jesus' moral message depends on how we understand the historical Jesus. For example, those who insist that the historical Jesus was an apocalyptic prophet conclude that Jesus' moral teachings are short-term pronouncements, not ethics for the long run. As the present age is thought by those subscribing to this view to be dominated by the forces of evil, God will dispatch soon the Son of Man, a cosmic adjudicator, to destroy those opposed to God. This will open the way for the establishment of the Kingdom of God, a special sort of paradise:

> [F]or the hitherto poor and oppressed, as well as for all who heard Jesus' message and turned completely to God, determining in their hearts to love God above all else and to love their neighbors as themselves. Those who refused to accept this message were to be condemned—even if they, like the Pharisees, followed the Torah of God [to the letter], or maintained the purity regulations of the Essenes, or remained faithful to the sacrificial cult of the Temple promoted by the Sadducees. In fact, religious leaders among these various groups, and

the institutions they represented, would be destroyed at the coming of the Son of Man. So, too, would the Temple itself.[11]

Understood in this way, Jesus was sent by God to announce upcoming events. Although not himself a divinity, Jesus would rule over his twelve disciples who would rule on twelve thrones once the Kingdom of God was in place. As such, Jesus' moral message is not intended to extol a radically egalitarian society attainable through acting in accord with his revolutionary moral teachings.

> [T]here is little to suggest that Jesus was concerned with pushing social "reform" in any fundamental way in this evil age. In his view, present-day society and all its conventions were soon to come to a screeching halt, when the Son of Man arrived from heaven in judgment on the earth. Far from transforming society from within, Jesus was preparing people for the destruction of society. . . . [The Kingdom of God] would not arrive through the implementation of new social reform programs. It would arrive with a cosmic judge, the Son of Man, who would overthrow the evil and oppressive forces of this world.[12]

Still, in my view, Jesus' moral message is important even if one subscribes to the position that he was an apocalyptic prophet lacking a mission of social reform from within. To agree, for the sake of argument, that Jesus' moral message embodies the ideals of the Kingdom of God which will be achieved by other means should not lead us to minimize the importance of that message. Surely, Jesus intended that people of good will should prefigure the Kingdom of God *now*. That is, Jesus intended that his contemporaries should embrace enthusiastically Jesus' moral message and act in accord with it even though doing so would not of itself establish the Kingdom of God. Establishing the Kingdom of God is one thing—the Son of Man will presumably take care of that—but internalizing and acting upon the moral imperatives and ideals of that Kingdom can and should be done now by those aspiring to love God above all else. Moreover, from our vantage point today, we can say assuredly that if Jesus was an apocalyptic prophet he has been proven incorrect on the timing of events. The world of evil has not been destroyed, the Son of Man is tardy, and the Kingdom of God awaits us still. Given that we must continue to live in this vale of tears, how should we live our lives? For the followers of Jesus, his moral teachings must guide our efforts. Accordingly, even if the historical Jesus' original understanding of how the Kingdom of God would be established is described accurately by those who believe he was only an apocalyptic prophet, his moral message remains paramount, and its evaluation is critical today.

For those who view the historical Jesus as primarily or only a Jewish Cynic peasant philosopher his moral message also invites evaluation. Under this interpretation, Jesus offered a recipe for personal transformation directed at either morally reforming society from within or at providing a blueprint for those yearning to distance themselves from conventional wisdom. In either case, his was a long-term social message about how human beings ought to live their lives.

Finally, for those who understand the historical Jesus in terms of institutionalized Christianity, embracing his moral message is critical to our quest for eternal salvation. Taking the historical Jesus as the Son of God and Redeemer of all human beings, Christians must conclude that Jesus' moral message is the best guide for achieving our highest destiny.

Accordingly, although trying to establish the one genuine interpretation of the historical Jesus goes beyond the scope of this work, under the three main contenders for that title, evaluating the moral message of Jesus is paramount. By assessing Jesus' teaching on a host of social matters of enduring concern we can also weave together the findings of the earlier chapters of this work.

SEX AND MARRIAGE

Jesus has relatively little to say about sex and marriage. What he does say strikes contemporary readers as inflexible and unrealistic. For example, upon questioning from the Pharisees, Jesus repudiates adultery and insists that a man may divorce his wife only if she is guilty of fornication. Moreover, should a man divorce his wife for reasons other than fornication and marry someone else, then he is guilty of adultery as is any man who marries the divorced woman. In an age when men could divorce their wives relatively easily, Jesus advocates what he takes to be the original intent of God's law.

First, the general prohibition against divorce: "For this cause [marriage] shall a man leave father and mother, and shall cleave to his wife: and they twain shall be one flesh? Wherefore they are no more twain, but one flesh. What therefore God hath joined together, let no man put asunder" (Matt. 19:5–6).

Next, the Pharisees object that Moses instructed the Jews that divorce was permissible. Jesus, however, is unmoved and suggests that Moses was influenced by practicalities: "Moses because of the hardness of your hearts suffered you to put away your wives; but from the beginning it was not so" (Matt. 19:8). Does the "hardness of hearts" suggest that but for permissible divorce men no longer willing to stay married might commit mayhem, perhaps slaying their undesired mates? Does this mean that Moses unilaterally adjusted God's law to fit more comfortably with human practice? One would hope not.

In any case, Jesus reasserts what he takes to be God's law from the beginning: "And I say unto you, Whosoever shall put away his wife, except it be for fornication, and shall marry another, committeth adultery: and whoso marrieth her which is put away doth commit adultery"

(Matt. 19:9; 5:32). Jesus distinguishes fornication from adultery. Fornication seemingly indicates consensual sexual relations between unmarried parties, whereas adultery connotes consensual sexual relations between parties, at least one of whom is married. On this interpretation, a man may divorce his wife only if she is discovered to have fornicated—to have engaged in consensual sexual relations while she was unmarried. Should he divorce ("put away") his wife for any other reason and remarry, he is guilty of adultery because in the eyes of God he remains "one flesh" with his first wife. In that vein, any man who marries the first wife is guilty of adultery for the same reason—the first couple remain wed in the eyes of God.

All of this is described from the male perspective. Although this is not surprising in the heavily patriarchal context of Jesus' time and place, it leaves unanswered questions. Suppose a wife engages in adulterous relations, does her husband then have legitimate cause to seek divorce? The wife did not fornicate, in the literal sense of that term, but she surely sinned against God and her husband. When, if ever, do wives have the right to divorce their husbands? Perhaps in a thoroughly patriarchal society the answer is "never." If a man unjustifiably "puts away" his wife, but then dedicates himself to chastity and never remarries, has he sinned even though he does not commit adultery? What is the moral force of the "one flesh" doctrine beyond the sin of adultery? We would suspect that divorcing one's wife on illegitimate grounds is itself a sin independently of future sexual conduct ("let no man put asunder"). What if a man marries a woman who is supposedly a widow, but whose first husband divorced her illegitimately and remains alive? Is the second husband an adulterer even though he married the supposed widow in good faith? And is the wife at the mercy of the actions of her husband? If he wrongfully divorces her, should she remarry it appears that her new husband is guilty of adultery, but is she guilty also?

Elsewhere in the Bible, the writers attribute related but somewhat different positions to Jesus: "Whosoever shall put away his wife, and marry another, committeth adultery against her. And if a woman shall put away her husband, and be married to another, she committeth adultery" (Mark 10:11–12). Also, "Whosoever putteth away his wife, and marrieth another, committeth adultery; and whosoever marrieth her that is put away from her husband committeth adultery" (Luke 16:18). These passages extend the divorce prohibition to women and remove the fornication exception clause.

Accordingly, Jesus clearly repudiates fornication and adultery. His view on divorce is either that it is (a) strictly prohibited, or it is (b) permitted only if the wife is found to have fornicated prior to the marriage, or, possibly, that it is (c) permitted only for reasons of fornication or adultery. He takes Moses' more permissive view of divorce as a concession to social practice that does not reflect God's original intent. Jesus' understanding appears grounded in the metaphysical doctrine of "one flesh"—that sex and certainly marriage join two people who were once separate into one flesh that should not be severed.

But Jesus is not finished. A person can commit adultery in the absence of sexual contact: "But I say unto you, That whosoever looketh on a woman to lust after her hath committed adultery with her already in his heart" (Matt. 5:28). Thus, merely lusting after a woman without any further action constitutes serious sin. "Lusting" must mean more than simply "being attracted to." Lusting, I would think, is more than a first reaction to the appearance of another person. It must also involve contemplating a desire, enjoying the possibility, and, perhaps, imagining a consummation. Moreover, we must conclude that to amount to adultery the perpetrator must be married. (Does that mean that an unmarried male can lust in his heart without sin? Or would such a man merely be exempt from committing the specific sin of adultery? Would he be guilty of the sin of fornication of the heart?)

Could a rapacious sexual marauder reason, "Well, I have already committed the sin of adultery by my lusting; I may as well try to consummate the act. What do I have to lose?" We must conclude such a strategy of doubling-down on lust would be unsuccessful. The agent who executed such a strategy would be guilty of both adultery of the heart and adultery in deed, thereby deepening his moral deprivation. In any case, if lusting after another person constitutes adultery, then the legion of serial sinners increases exponentially.[13]

In any event, in the area of sex and marriage, Jesus' interpretation of existing Jewish law is radically conservative. Bart Ehrman concludes that Jesus' position on marriage and divorce merely invokes his paramount guiding principle of love.

> In Jesus' time, when women were not able to go out to find a second job, but were for the most part reliant, by necessity, on the men in their lives (fathers, husbands, and sons), divorce could lead to abject poverty and misery. Jesus' understanding of the Law (with love as the guiding principle) forbade the practice altogether—even though the Law itself allowed it! Thus love for others means radicalizing the Law.[14]

We should not accept this conclusion too facilely. Why would Jesus' motives for "radicalizing the Law" be primarily economic? After all, Jesus is a material minimalist who does not otherwise seek to enlarge the gross national product. Would not God provide for destitute divorcees? Moreover, if economics were the main reason to resist divorce, then changes in the law permitting divorce could include what we now term alimony and child support. Perhaps levying a stiff economic burden on men seeking divorce could soften the problem of divorcees' "abject poverty." My point is that viewing Jesus' radicalization of Jewish law as grounded in economic concern flowing from love obscures other aspects of Jesus' position, the most important of which is the "one flesh" doctrine.

Apparently two people become "one flesh" through sexual intercourse. God "joins two people together" in the sense that once sexual intercourse occurs the participants are considered one flesh in the eyes of God. More precisely, God acknowledges that the two are now one more than God actively performs the joining. The act itself is tantamount to a lifelong commitment. Only fornication and perhaps adultery—which themselves trigger other unions of the flesh—can justify divorce, which formally severs lifelong commitment. (And on the strictest reading of Jesus on divorce, even fornication and adultery are insufficient.) Concluding that the act of sexual intercourse is even more important than a formal wedding in joining two people as "one flesh" is reasonable.

The metaphysical doctrine of one flesh retains some contemporary currency. Robust love relationships do extend the subjectivities of the participants. We no longer view our interests and well-being as fully distinct from the interests and well-being of our partner. While the metaphor of "two hearts beating as one" is overblown, the notion that we are no longer parties at arms length resonates. Marital partners may not be "one flesh," but surely they are no longer fully independent agents.

The problem with the doctrine from a contemporary standpoint is its irrevocability. Once joined, the parties cannot sever their relationship even by mutual consent. No exceptions to the prohibition on divorce are permitted for mistakes, errors in judgment, changes in the parties, or human fallibility. Instead, the doctrine of one flesh insists that a person's first act of sexual intercourse binds that person and his partner *forever*. In effect, human beings are deemed sexually infallible. To place so much importance on the act strikes the contemporary reader as indefensible. Other than the invocation "this is what God decrees" what could justify the one flesh doctrine? Why would God make such a decree in the face of human fallibility? Why would Jesus take such an absolutist or near absolutist position against divorce when he is otherwise nonformalistic in interpreting Jewish law?

Jesus nowhere stigmatizes erotic impulses as inherently evil. Preaching a law of love and assessing people on the basis of their inner motives and intentions, Jesus castigates sex and the material world as obstacles to eternal salvation only when they assume the role of idols.[15] As we have already seen, against the rigid legalism of the Pharisees, Jesus preached a philosophy of love which appealed to factors internal to humans as the criteria of moral virtue: inner attitudes and motives. Further, Jesus advanced the novel doctrine that God's love extends to all human beings, regardless of their earthly deeds. Rather than underscoring reward for the virtuous and retribution for the evil, Jesus stressed that sinners may require greater divine concern based on their greater need. Human beings themselves should love and pray for friends and enemies alike. Human concern and love should emulate divine benevolence. Again, unlike the legalistic Pharisees, Jesus at times abrogated conformity with general, abstract principles in deference to specific compelling circumstances.

Interpreted in light of these general inclinations—emphasis on inner motives, universal love, and anti-legalism—what can be said about Jesus' teachings on sex? The problem here, of course, is that another's inner attitudes and motives are rarely transparent and thus it is difficult for society, saddled inherently with fallibilism and partial information, to base its ethic on criteria which are fully accessible only to God.

That human action is not necessarily dispositive of human inner attitudes is clear. Is the married couple who stay together and who violate no obvious societal sexual prohibitions, while inwardly despising one another, morally virtuous? Is the unmarried couple who do not live together but who share an abiding consummated love thereby sexually immoral? How would Jesus evaluate such questions? On the basis of whether a sincere, mature love was present? On the criterion of whether the couple was officially (or unofficially) married? On the principle of whether sex is consummated with one and only one sexual partner? On the basis of the reasons why sex was consummated? On the criteria of whether the parties kept their word to the other: they married, remained so, were faithful, and shared a measure of love? The answers to such questions are not contained unambiguously in the recorded words of Jesus.

Those who antecedently long to interpret Jesus' words in nonconventional fashions may seize upon his anti-legalism and appeal to the contextualism of inner motives. Accordingly, they may argue that contemporary Christian sexual morality is at best a concession to society's epistemological inability to discern accurately the inner attitudes of sexual partners; while at worst it is a distortion of the spirit of Jesus' teachings and a reversion back to the discredited legalism of the Pharisees. Those who antecedently yearn to interpret Jesus' words as the seeds from which contemporary Christian sexual morality blossomed may appeal to the absolutism of Jesus' specific teachings on divorce and adultery. Thus, they may argue that divorce and adultery are strictly prohibited and that even lusting after another is morally tantamount to consummating the forbidden act.

We may say with confidence, however, that Jesus nowhere stigmatizes erotic impulses as inherently evil. Never accepting the most extreme forms of asceticism extant in the Greek world, Jesus castigates sex and the material world as obstacles to eternal salvation only when they assume the role of idols.[16]

FAMILY RELATIONS

In the Mediterranean world during Jesus' time, the family was firmly entrenched as the fundamental social unity. Jesus apparently had as many as four brothers and more than one sister (Matt. 13:55–56; Mark 6:3).[17] Yet Jesus often distances himself from family affiliations in deference to wider community membership. For example, when informed that his mother and brothers have arrived, Jesus replies that those who comply with God's will are his brothers and mother (Mark 3:31–35). When a woman in a crowd proclaims how fortunate his mother was to have born and raised him, Jesus responds that "rather blessed are they that hear the word of God, and keep it" (Luke 11:27–28). Jesus informs a multitude of people that he has not come to confer peace on earth, but division among families: "The father shall be divided against the son, and the son against the father, and the daughter against the mother; the mother-in-law against her daughter-in-law, and the daughter-in-law against her mother-in-law" (Luke 12:51–53; Matt. 10:35). He instructs his followers that they must "hate" (probably meaning "abandon") their families and their own lives in order to be genuine disciples (Luke 14:26–27; Matt. 10:37). Moreover, scripture alleges that Jesus' own family did not fully believe in what Jesus was doing and were even offended by him: "A prophet is not without honor, but in his own country, and among his own kin, and in his own house" (Mark 6:3–4; Matt. 13:55–57).

Several explanations for Jesus' repudiation of established family values are available. First, Jesus may be underscoring his conviction that nothing, not even the supposed fundamental social unit of the family, is more important than proper worship of God and compliance with God's will. If allegiance to family takes on the role of idolatry, it, too, is an obstacle to salvation. Second, a corollary of that conviction is Jesus' commitment to opening the boundaries of community. The Parable of the Good Samaritan instructs us that our "neighbors" are not simply those who share our religion, ethnicity, race, and tribe. So, too, our family is not restricted merely to parents, siblings, and blood relatives. All "those who comply with God's will" are our siblings, parents, and relatives. The community of God is accessible in principle to everyone. Thus, everyone in principle is our kin. Third, abandoning one's family may entail more than merely leaving one's home. It may mean that we discard conventional notions of hierarchy, authority, and deference in order to more closely emulate the salutary relationships embodied in the Kingdom of God. As the family is the initial locus of socialization, it is most likely to reflect the dominant societal ideas that Jesus aims to unsettle. As such, tight allegiance to the established family ethos promotes parochialism and conformity, both of which are antithetical to Jesus' revolutionary moral message.

Fourth, some commentators argue that the key to understanding Jesus' attack on family values is the passage in which Jesus declares his intent to divide families. The passage is often misread to mean that some family members will believe in Jesus' message, while others will not, and the resulting division will be ideological. But John Dominic Crossan points out that all the divisions mentioned are generational (older fathers, mothers, and mothers-in-law to younger sons, daughters, and daughters-in-law, respectively). He concludes that Jesus' repudiation of the traditional family is an effort to dislodge entrenched relationships of power.

> *The attack* [on established family values] *has nothing to do with faith but with power*. The attack is on the Mediterranean family's axis of power, which sets father and mother over son, daughter, and daughter-in-law.... The family is society in miniature, the place where we first and most deeply learn how to love and be loved, hate and be hated, help and be helped, abuse and be abused. It is not just a center of domestic serenity; since it involves power, it invites the abuse of power and it is at that precise point that Jesus attacks it. His ideal group is, contrary to Mediterranean and indeed most human familial reality, an open one equally accessible to all under God.[18]

Of course, the unsettling of established power relations as such cannot be the genuine goal of Jesus' efforts. Instead, it is better viewed as a means or instrument through which either wider social transformation becomes possible or greater access to the Kingdom of God blossoms for more people. Viewed in this light, established power relations are an obstacle to Jesus' revolutionary moral message and must be dissolved in order for that message to resonate with more people.

Fifth, those who interpret Jesus as an apocalyptic prophet deny that wider social transformation was his goal. Rather, they argue that Jesus' view of the family was predicated, as always, on his immediate concern: that people prepare for the imminent arrival of the Kingdom of God: "[Jesus] urged his followers to abandon their homes and forsake families for the sake of the Kingdom that was soon to arrive. He didn't encourage people to pursue fulfilling careers, make a good living, and work for a just society for the long haul; for him, there wasn't going to *be* a long haul. The end of the world as we know it was already at hand."[19]

On this view, Jesus' motivation for repudiating established family values (and much else) was purely expedient: nurturing family relations was a trivial pursuit given the impending apocalypse. Because the Son of Man would soon arrive and elevate the impoverished, meek, and oppressed, while deflating the wealthy and hitherto powerful, tending to long-range concerns such as family, occupation, and material accumulation was pointless. Now was the time to prepare spiritually for the coming age.

Still, in my judgment, those who are convinced that Jesus was "only" an apocalyptic prophet must concede that the way to prepare spiritually for the coming age was to prefigure the values and ideals of the Kingdom of God now. Regardless of whether the arrival of that Kingdom is imminent or sometime in the unknown future, those of good will should model their behavior on the appropriate values and ideals as soon as these are revealed. Thus, we have no reason to think that Jesus' moral message, particularly his views on proper family relations, would be different had he believed that the arrival date of the Kingdom of God was unknown or in the distant future. That is, I am not persuaded that the content of Jesus' moral message was driven by his alleged conviction that the Kingdom of God was imminent. Are we to believe that if Jesus was convinced that the arrival of the Kingdom of God was in the distant future that he would have counseled those of faith to adhere closely to traditional family values, to nurture assiduously their retirement pensions, to accumulate fervently wealth, and to pursue excitedly their secular careers? I do not think so. Whether the historical Jesus was only an apocalyptic prophet, a Jewish Cynic peasant philosopher, or the Son of God as understood by mainstream Christians, he would have extolled the values and ideals of the Kingdom of God and urged disciples to embrace and exemplify those values and ideals enthusiastically and immediately.

In any case, contra Jesus' position, we can amass a strong defense of the family unit and its values. Much of that defense simply parallels my defense of partialism against the claims of impartialism in chapter 1: conventional morality judges that we are permitted to advance the interests of family over those of strangers when we cannot fulfill the interests of everyone. As always, Jesus' contrary conclusion is grounded in his ethic of unconditional love and uttered from the moral standpoint of an Ideal, Impartial Observer, namely God. But human beings firmly seated in this world cannot easily ascend to such an Archimedean point. We are concrete individuals with specific biologies and biographies that largely constitute our identities; we are often grateful for and aspire to reciprocate past benefits that others have bestowed upon us; we develop personal relationships that facilitate our self-realization; we love a few other people in ways that cannot be extended to all human beings indiscriminately; and we understand well that but for the efforts of family we might well not even exist.

Families, cultural traditions, and national heritages are valuable because of their role in constituting personal identity. Human beings are valuable, and without social attachments and connections, of which some arise nonvoluntarily, we would all stand alone, naked before a terrifying and seemingly all-powerful universe. Not to belong to a nation, tribe, or parents—to be stripped of our metaphysical constituents—is to be nobody. We all draw strength from and are constituted by our inherited legacy, and to be uprooted, to belong to no place, is the great tragedy of displaced persons, refugees, and aliens. Such people suffer grave and frightening identity crises because they have lost some of their most valuable characteristics, those pertaining to membership and belonging. Thus our inherited legacy helps fulfill necessary psychological functions. A large measure of our inherited biological and biographical legacy often involves our families.

The self is given in and through a social context and is not a fixed and complete entity at a certain specified time. We enter the world already laden with history, traditions, prejudices, and community structures. Others make us who we are; we share and participate in a common identity and tradition which comprises one segment of the human heritage. Our concrete context of community memberships, cultural heritage, historical circumstances, core aspirations, attachments, and commitments are not always possessions or attributes we choose; instead, they partly constitute who we are. Their moral force results from the recognition that they are indispensable in forging the particular people that we are and in constituting the particular value we embody. At their best, certain interpersonal relations are characterized by intimate feelings—love, deep mutual affection, recognition that the interests of family members are part of my good as we experience forming subjectivities wider than ourselves.

We are also typically better placed to advance the interest of family members than we are to nurture the interests of strangers. To say that a moral agent is in a favored position to preserve and maintain value might suggest criteria relevant to resources such as wealth, or the possession of special skills and abilities, or situational advantages such as geographical proximity or being privy to certain information not accessible to everyone. But the more fundamental criterion here is one's metaphysical constitution. The values of a certain inherited legacy *are* "me," and as the repository of such values I am better placed than others to understand and preserve them simply by being who I am. In my view, one bears a special responsibility to the particular segment of the shared human heritage that one embodies and thus is in a position to cherish.

Our noninherited attachments, commitments, and properties are also important constituents of self. If others contribute to our personal identities intentionally, positively, and significantly—if they extend themselves in uncommon ways to us—then we are permitted to advance their interests over strangers in conflict situations. One ground for these moral requirements is a contractualist appeal to reciprocity; another arises from acknowledging the value of individuals. We all embody value—regardless of whether we are precisely who we would like to be, who we might have been, and in some cases regardless of the presence or absence of affection toward those who have contributed to our identities. We owe more to those who intentionally, voluntarily, and knowingly (and often at considerable sacrifice) made beneficial contributions to the person that we are and the value we thereby embody, as a demand of justice—returning value for value. Thus, our metaphysical constitution and our embodiment of certain value have moral implications in concert with generally accepted liberal principles of justice.

Our familial and other relationships are the core of life and morality. They provide the context for our deepest convictions, values, and normative moorings. The more radical and implausible versions of impartialism secure their universal prescriptions by plundering individuals of their distinctive metaphysical constituents, and they thereby impoverish our concept of personhood. Charges along these lines could be issued by the apostles of conventional morality against the unconditional love ethic of Jesus.

I must not, however, overly sentimentalize the tribalism of Mediterranean families prevalent during Jesus' life. Families then (and now) form bulwarks against the excesses of oppressive governments, hostile circumstances, and unreliable social relations. But they also reinforce to some degree the very estrangement from wider community from which their tribal ethic arose. Families both contribute to and mediate wider social injustice. The moral irony of family tribalism—its simultaneous promotion in the family and repression on other social levels of the cardinal virtues—is accompanied by a psychological irony: on the one hand, such family codes provide spiritual sustenance and the foundations of personal identity in an otherwise hostile world, while on the other hand, the codes facilitate lingering dependencies and help ensure that the outside world will remain hostile.

While I have emphasized the value of robust family relations, Jesus insists that these sentiments must be tempered by awareness that the family requires numerous myths, taboos, and tribal conventions that sometimes cultivate psychological distortions and impede full spiritual development. Accordingly, in Jesus' view, human beings must distance themselves from their families, at distinct times and often to extreme degrees, to actualize fully their potentials. Typically, Jesus' moral message will not be hostage to conventional understandings. His revolutionary view of the role of the family in attaining personal salvation resists my philosophical labors in defense of family values.

ASSOCIATING AND IDENTIFYING WITH UNDESIRABLES

Tax collectors exacted tribute from the Galilean population to be forwarded to Rome as payment for maintenance and security. Many were undoubtedly dishonest, charging excessive amounts from which they skimmed for their own benefit. All were in service of an imperialistic overseer, Rome, which had assumed dominion over land that God had presumably bequeathed to the Jews. As such, tax collectors, taken collectively, were not perceived as righteous. Yet Jesus consorted with them easily (Mark 2:15–16; Luke 19:1–10; Matt. 11:19). So, too, Jesus associated with other people stigmatized as undesirables such as demoniacs (Mark 5:1–20), lepers (Mark 1:40–42; Luke 17:12–19), Samaritans (Luke 17:12–16; John 4:4–40), and prostitutes (Luke 7:36–48; Matt. 21:31). Anticipating the ideals and values embodied by the Kingdom of God, wherein the haughty would be humbled and the oppressed would be exalted, Jesus ministered to those spurned as undesirables who both required and could benefit from his instruction the most.

In that vein, Jesus laments that John the Baptist was derided as demonic or demented for appearing on the scene austerely, neither drinking wine nor eating bread. But Jesus appears eating and drinking, and he is criticized as a glutton, a drunk, and a crony of tax collectors and sinners: "Ye say, Behold a gluttonous man, and a winebibber, a friend of publicans and sinners" (Luke 7:34; Matt. 11:19). In part, this was a reaction to another aspect of Jesus' ministry: his proclivity for and encouragement of eating and socializing with people without regard for existing social distinctions (Matt. 22:1–13; Luke 14:15–24). Prefiguring an egalitarian ideal of the Kingdom of God, Jesus refused to comply with the Jewish tradition of reflecting social hierarchy and division while eating: the recognized rules and customs of dining were microcosms of the more general regulations of association and socialization. Jesus softens the Jewish tradition in this regard by advocating

> an open commensality, an eating together without using table as a miniature map of society's vertical discriminations and lateral separations. The social challenge of such equal or egalitarian commensality is the [Parable of the Wedding Feast's] most fundamental danger and most radical threat. . . . Jesus lived out his own parable, [and] the almost predictable counteraccusation to such open commensality would be immediate: Jesus is a glutton, a drunkard, and a friend of tax collectors and sinners. He makes, in other words, no appropriate distinctions and discriminations.[20]

The radical egalitarianism of Jesus' theory and practice with regard to commensality, material possessions, and class structures threaten established social hierarchies and divisions that are so common that they are typically viewed as necessary to orderly social life. Imprisoned in what Jesus would take to be a false necessity, citizens too often conclude that the familiar is the inevitable. As such, they unwittingly collaborate in further entrenching the social forces that ensure their oppression. Jesus' invocation of love insisted that such distinctions are impediments to anticipating the ideals of the Kingdom of God. A precondition of opening our hearts to genuine love and loving is to break through false necessity and see social hierarchies for what they are: artificial barriers to creating robustly meaningful human relationships. As always, for Jesus, transforming our hearts and souls supersedes formalist renderings of traditional law and conventional social understandings of appropriate conduct: a new kind of human being is required in the Kingdom of God.

Jesus' proclamations about the transvaluation of values in the Kingdom of God, particularly the exaltation of the downtrodden and the humbling of the powerful, were not received warmly by the established community leaders. Moreover, Jesus' invocation to bestow unconditional love upon everyone (especially to those antecedently scorned as enemies) and forgiveness of all debts and transgressions (sometimes even in the absence of the perpetrator's repentance) threatened the foundations of society. Would not indiscriminate forgiveness condone past and encourage future wrongdoing? Would not unconditional love embolden enemies to amplify their malevolent schemes? Would not wholesale waiving of debts undermine the justice of restitution and retribution?

Jesus may have been swayed by his conviction that moral accounts would be squared during the Final Judgment. Instead of despising one's enemies now and responding to their malevolence in kind, we are better served by anticipating the ideals of the Kingdom of God, which require that we tend to the condition of our own hearts and souls, and strive to encourage our enemies to act likewise. Should our enemies rebuke our efforts, we would still retain our internal harmony while they will presumably meet cosmic justice during the Final Judgment. In any case, we would not have committed the most serious moral error—collaborating with or participating in evil that harms our soul. Moreover, by exemplifying the ideals of the Kingdom of God now we maximize our prospects for a felicitous judgment from the Son of Man in the future: to forgive others their trespasses now heightens the probability that our moral shortcomings will be forgiven later.

UNSETTLING ESTABLISHED RITUALS

As attested to by the Parable of the Good Samaritan, Jesus was willing to stray from the established Jewish purity rituals of his time. For example, the Pharisees and most other Jews always washed their hands prior to eating, as well as cups, containers, and cookware. This was not in deference to sanitation concerns, but to established traditions that stressed purity and cleanliness as critical for proper worship of God. Upon observing that Jesus and his disciples did not comply with the purity ritual, the Pharisees took Jesus to task (Mark 7:1–5). Jesus' response, in effect, is that what is more important that observing the purity rituals is how a person speaks, acts, and chooses: "There is nothing from without a man, that entering into him can defile him; but the things which come out of him, those are they that defile the man" (Mark 7:15; Matt. 15:11); "Woe unto you, scribes and Pharisees, hypocrites! For ye make clean the outside of the cup and of the platter, but within they are full of extortion and excess. Thou blind Pharisee, cleanse first that which is within the cup and platter, that the outside of them may be clean also" (Matt. 23:25–26; Luke 11:39–40). In sum, Jesus accuses the Pharisees, as usual, of not seeing the forest for the trees: they miss the big picture of what compliance with God's law entails because they are preoccupied with the minutia of formalist renderings of traditions and conventions.

This instruction is reinforced in the Parable of the Good Samaritan where the story's hero is an unclean Samaritan and the less noble figures are the priest and Levite who are overly scrupulous about observing the purity traditions. By refusing to act compassionately, the priest and Levite reveal that their internal condition does not match their external cleanliness, whereas the Samaritan, by acting compassionately, demonstrates that his heart and soul glisten even if he is judged by conventional Jewish standards to be externally contaminated.

Unlike the Pharisees, Jesus did not believe that fastidious compliance to formalist renderings of the laws of Torah was paramount to earning salvation in the Kingdom of God. Unlike the Sadducees, Jesus did not believe that scrupulous adherence to the rituals of worship and sacrifice in the Temple of Jerusalem was most important. Although Jesus may well have shared some of the Essenes' apocalyptic views and conviction that the Jews of the age had morally degenerated, he was not concerned with forming isolated communities focused primarily on maintaining their own purity. His rejection of the Sadducees, aristocratic leaders of the Temple, and his prophecy that God would soon destroy the Temple and transvalue existing values in the Kingdom of God—including humbling the self-righteous leaders of the Jewish sects—along with the threat Roman authorities perceived when he failed to deny that he was King of the Jews, undoubtedly led to his crucifixion by the Romans.

INTERROGATING PREVAILING NORMS OF JUST DISTRIBUTION

That Jesus distanced himself from conventional understandings of justice defined by the principles of desert and retribution is clear. In the Parables of the Prodigal Son and the Laborers in the Vineyard, the mean-spiritedness, jealousy, and envy of the older son and the first hired, respectively, are highlighted and repudiated. To assume that the undeserved good fortune of others amounts to an injustice to yourself is wildly misguided especially when you have received all to which you were entitled. Jesus teaches that in order to nurture our hearts and souls properly we must go beyond strict adherence to justice as defined by the principles of desert and retribution.

Aristotle observed that "Friendship unites the state. When men are friends, there is no need of justice, but when even if men are just, friendship is still necessary. Friendship is not just necessary, but also noble."[21]

Expand "friendship" to "love" and Aristotle's sentiments resound throughout the teachings of Jesus. To love our neighbor unconditionally requires that we go beyond appealing to justice, as defined by the principles of desert and retribution, when allocating goods and when responding to wrongdoing. Jesus points out that loving someone who loves you and benefiting someone who has aided you are not major accomplishments (Matt. 5:44, 46–47; Luke 6:27, 32–33). Instead, we should reflect God's willingness to be generous to the ungrateful and the wicked (Matt 5:45; Luke 6:35). In sum, lavishing unconditional love upon our neighbors requires an abundance of understanding, compassion, and affection that exceeds the imperatives of justice as defined by the principles of desert and retribution. Our typical notions of justice spawn resentment, competition, and invidious comparison. Moreover, as Aristotle intuited, our notions of justice are insufficient for robust human community. Where there is friendship (and unconditional love of neighbors) invocations of justice may be superfluous.

In the Parable of the Laborers in the Vineyard, from the standpoint of justice understood as distribution according to the principle of desert, the workers first hired have a strong case. But Jesus insisted that unconditional love does not bow before that principle of justice. Agape is not constrained by or reducible to the respective deeds of the beloved: the merits of the beloved are irrelevant to the distribution of social goods. However, I am still troubled that the vineyard owner demonstrated his generosity in connection with wage labor—he allotted the money to each of the groups hired at the end of the day and apparently for services rendered. I would think that had he paid each group of workers proportionate to the hours they worked but later gave monetary gifts to the last groups hired that equalized what each group received overall, then the first hired would have no basis for complaint. Instead, the vineyard owner muddled distribution according to proportionate desert with distribution according to need and distribution as gift. From a contemporary standpoint that conflation was unnecessary and leads to moral confusion. But from Jesus' vantage point the point of the parable may simply be the superiority of unconditional love to any humanly contrived principle of justice. Even where unconditional love and justice overlap, such as distribution according to need, it is the power of unconditional love that is paramount in determining how to proceed. The trajectory of unconditional love does not require identical treatment of everyone, but it does privilege needs over merits, spurns social hierarchy and division, and marginalizes factual differences among persons.

Of course, the problem is that we do not operate from a condition of universal friendship and unconditional love. Although it may well be true that should everyone adopt and act in compliance with Jesus' teachings our conventional notions of justice would be superfluous, what are we to say about our actual social condition—where only a tiny percentage of the population actually lives in accord with Jesus' teachings?

MATERIAL MINIMALISM

In the Kingdom of God a transvaluation of values will occur: "many that are first shall be last; and the last first" (Mark 10:31; Matt. 20:16; Luke 13:30). When the Son of Man renders judgment on our corrupt world, many of those who now revel in economic, social, and political power and privilege will be ousted and replaced by those who are now oppressed and disenfranchised. The implication is that many of those who now enjoy hierarchical advantage have benefited from and contributed to the evil that pervades the world.

As always, Jesus instructs that human beings should prefigure the Kingdom of God by unsettling the dominant values and social understandings that underwrite current corruption. Thus, instead of aspiring to the conventional indicia of a successful life—the accumulation of material resources, the attainment of political power, and the exercise of privilege—genuine disciples should dedicate their lives to community service. By relinquishing the competitive and material desires so common among human beings and by focusing our energies and efforts on service to other people, we can transform our own souls and anticipate social relations in the Kingdom of God: "For whosoever will save his life shall lose it; but whosoever shall lose his life for my sake and the gospel's, the same shall save it" (Mark 8:35). Instead of seeking to amplify and glorify ourselves as superior to others, we should humbly strive to advance the interests of other people, especially those paramount interests that nurture their souls. Alleviating the oppression and easing the exploitation of disenfranchised people is a prelude to facilitating the enrichment of their spirits.

Accordingly, material aggrandizement is either superfluous or an obstacle to personal well-being. Beyond garnering minimal material necessities, the pursuit of wealth distracts us from more important concerns. Jesus' message mirrors moral wisdom that generously predates his birth. About four centuries earlier, Socrates argued along similar lines (much of which reflected the spade work of Pythagoras): purifying the soul is the most important human mission; pursuit of society's rewards—wealth, honor, reputation, and privilege—distracts from or prevents the success of that mission; genuine harm is that which unsettles the harmony of the soul; service to others, in the form of philosophical illumination, is paramount; and those who ignore their souls and who lust for society's rewards will be barred from entering the everlasting bliss of the World of Forms.

Imagine, though, a world, nation, or community that self-consciously embraced the moral message of Jesus or Socrates. Would science and technology suffer? Would accumulated knowledge progress robustly? Would life be too simple and drab? Would the world, nation, or community be akin to an uninspiring Mennonite or Amish conclave?

To be fair, Socrates certainly emphasized the value of knowledge. Indeed, if knowledge truly does equal virtue (it doesn't), then the good human life and the purified soul depend on the pursuit of truth. While Jesus stresses only knowledge required to prefigure the values forthcoming in the Kingdom of God, surely he does not preclude the pursuit of nonreligious truth. Still, Socrates and Jesus are utterly indifferent to economic growth, scientific understanding, and even earnest labor. They clearly oppose the mind-set of the consumer society, which is grounded in value largely determined by goods that cannot be shared.[22]

> There is nothing in the teaching of Jesus as understood in the earliest days of the church or in the days of Jesus himself to give comfort to any kind of system that subordinates people to capital and to markets. Neither state, worker, nor "free enterprise" capitalism can draw any valid support from this Jesus. . . . The impossibility of a Jesus-style human flourishing being found where wealth is the controlling motive in society is an impossibility in logic. . . . It could be the case that the most appropriate response today is still to "drop out" ostentatiously, living an alternative life-style that dramatically puts in question the values of the wider society.[23]

Both Jesus and Socrates were convinced that their societies were firmly rooted in unfertile soil. Both concluded that a transformation of the human soul (or heart) was critical for personal salvation and societal advance. But the utopianism in both visions, and particularly in Jesus' anticipation of the Kingdom of God, rests uncomfortably with the exigencies of everyday life.

For example, Jesus' Sermon on the Mount includes, among other pieces of moral instruction, the following: "Whosoever therefore shall break one of these least commandments, and shall teach men so, he shall be called the least in the kingdom of heaven"; "But I say unto you, That whosoever is angry with his brother without a cause shall be in danger of the judgment"; "And if thy right eye offend thee, pluck it out, and cast it from thee . . . And if thy right hand offend thee, cut it off, and cast it from thee"; "whosoever shall smite thee on the right cheek, turn to him the other also"; "Love your enemies, bless them that curse you, do good to them that hate you" (Matt. 5:19, 22, 29, 30, 39, 44). Moreover, Jesus advises followers to sell all of their possessions and distribute the proceeds to the poor (Matt. 19:21; Luke 12:33, 18:22). These bits of moral instruction are wrapped within Jesus' most general imperative: unconditional love for everyone.

Jesus' moral instruction is devoid of self-executing bright-line rules that might be applied mechanically to individual cases. His life of the interior, embodying the injunctions of love, must inform our judgments when applying his thoughts to particular circumstances. But we may well be wary of relying totally on human judgment when seeking correct moral decision. Surely we must interpret Jesus' words as providing the guiding trajectory of moral decision making. Moreover, in borderline cases, we should incline toward the decision that better promotes the health of our souls and those of our neighbors.

Jesus' moral message inspired several later peasant socialist initiatives. For example, E. J. Hobsbawn describes the primitive social movement, millenarianism, in the following way:

> First, [millenarianism is characterized by] a profound and total rejection of the present, evil world, and a passionate longing for another and better one; in a word, revolutionism. Second, a fairly standardized "ideology" . . . the most important ideology of this sort before the rise of modern secular revolutionism, and perhaps the only one, is Judeo-Christian messianism. . . . What makes millenarians is the idea that the world as it is may—and indeed will—come to an end one day, to be utterly re-made thereafter. . . . Third, millenarian movements share a fundamental vagueness about the actual way in which the new society will be brought about.[24]

In the late nineteenth century, millenarianism was rife in western Sicily. Peasant alliances, called the "Fasci," largely under Socialist leadership, orchestrated riots and agricultural strikes that the Italian government suppressed militarily. The goal of the Fasci movement was radical egalitarian reform modeled on the words of Jesus. The Sicilians involved were overwhelmingly peasants for whom the Socialist-Christian vision constituted a new religion. Convinced that the teachings of Jesus had been betrayed by the institutional practices of organized Christianity and the mendacity of local priests, the Sicilian peasants organized in the name of a political return to the original intent of Jesus' teachings. The mind-set of the peasants was well represented by a woman from Piana dei Greci in the province of Palermo:

> We want everybody to work, as we work. There should no longer be either rich or poor. All should have bread for themselves and for their children. We should all be equal. I have five small children and only one little room, where we have to eat and sleep and do everything, while so many lords (*signori*) have ten or twelve rooms, entire palaces. . . . It will be enough to put all in common and to share with justice what is produced. . . . Jesus was a true Socialist and he wanted precisely what the Fasci are asking for, but the priests do not represent him well, especially when they are usurers . . . the object of the Fascio is to give men all the conditions for no longer committing crimes.[25]

When asked about the alleged presence of a criminal element among the Fascio, the peasant woman invoked the message of Jesus:

> Among us the few criminals feel that they still belong to the human family, they are thankful that we have accepted them as brothers in spite of their guilt and they will do anything not to commit crimes again. If the people were also to chase them away, they would commit more crimes. Society should thank us for taking them into the Fascio. We are for mercy, as Christ was.[26]

Given the apparent utopianism in his teachings, the question arises whether the totality of Jesus' moral message can be universalized. Supposing that everyone desires to follow Jesus' moral instructions, is it practically possible to do so? As Don Cupitt observes,

> [Jesus' ethic] seems to be economically impossible. We cannot all live like holy vagabonds ... and we cannot *all* of us sell up everything we have. Who would there be to sell *to*? There has to be settled life, there has to be land tenure, there has to be social infrastructure, there has to be economic exchange, and of course there has to be Piers Plowman, toiling away in the fields every day and carrying the rest of the world on his back. And in view of all this, is it not obvious that there will have to be some sort of compromise between the two moralities? The old theological morality of religious law binds everyone into maintaining the existing social order, while the dream morality is kept as "pie in the sky" and as a distant hope of future blessedness. . . . Economic necessity *versus* utopian humanism.[27]

Universal acceptance of Jesus' radical moral message has not occurred, even among those who describe themselves as Christians. Relatively few people are willing to distance themselves from their families; to renounce material goods and the pursuit of robust careers; to nurture forgiveness and mercy as their virtually default mind-set and response to those who transgress against them; to abrogate or at least soften appeals to retributive and restitutional justice; to seek out and minister to societal outcasts; to transcend distributive justice grounded in personal desert and production; to acknowledge the aggression and violence of others by offering compassion; to bestow unconditional love upon strangers and even those who perceive themselves as enemies; to embrace the one flesh doctrine and its implications for sex, marriage, and divorce; to promote impartial and thoroughly egalitarian relationships; and to understand harm as related primarily to injury of one's inner condition.

The Jesus-inspired Fasci movements in Sicily during the late nineteenth century, and others like them, met an all too predictable response: they were squashed by the governing military forces. Encircled by those who have internalized the dominant social message that zero-sum contests pervade international and national relations, those who embrace Jesus' moral message may well appear to be well intentioned, pure of spirit, but ultimately doomed by their naiveté. At least when laboring outside of established religious orders, such disciples may seem to be abject gulls in a wider society firmly entrenched in a much different ethos. If so, then Jesus' moral message is designed only for the personal salvation of those accepting the metaphysical background that animates Jesus' teachings: the existence of an all-knowing, all-powerful, all-benevolent God; the impending inauguration of the Kingdom of that God; and a human telos designed to exalt the inner citadel of the self by embracing and acting according to the imperatives of the divine will.

In any case, efforts to portray Jesus as an apostle of laissez-faire capitalism or patriarchal privilege or military adventurism are invariably strained. The words attributed to Jesus neither anticipate the economic wisdom of George Whatley, nor echo Aristotle's paean to patriarchy, nor paraphrase Homer's encomia to the warrior virtues.

We can speculate on Jesus' reaction to the branches of Christianity prevalent in our world, especially those that have accumulated vast chests of wealth by trading on his name. In the 1960s, an uncharitable slogan proclaimed that, "Billy Graham saves, saves every darn penny he can get his hands on." But the same could be said for other Christian denominations, televangelists, and a host of enterprising capitalists masquerading as religious prophets. While many Christian institutions and leaders do much charitable work that alleviates the recurring hardships of the least fortunate among us, we may wonder whether Jesus (or even Peter Singer) would approve of the amount of wealth they sometimes amass.

Conventional moral wisdom, in Jesus' time and in our own, cannot ratify his moral message. Much of Jesus' teachings in the parables and elsewhere in scripture will be judged inadequate when evaluated by dominant social ideas and practices. But no surprise, that. Unsettling dominant understandings was one of Jesus' paramount purposes. Accordingly, each set of ideas and practices will be viewed suspiciously by the other. Human beings are invited to choose one set or the other, or broker a compromise between them, or re-imagine and remake the possible combinations. As ever, no light matter is at stake, but the very fashion in which we will craft our souls and marshal our lives.

NOTES

1. The section on the interpretation of the parable has been informed by Klyne R. Snodgrass, *Stories with Intent* (Grand Rapids, MI: William B. Eerdmans Publishing Company, 2008); Craig L. Blomberg, *Interpreting the Parables* (Downers Grove, IL: InterVarsity Press, 1990); Richard N. Longenecker (ed.), *The Challenge of Jesus' Parables* (Grand Rapids, MI: William B. Eerdmans Publishing Company, 2000); Kenneth E. Bailey, *Poet & Peasant Through Peasant Eyes* (Grand Rapids, MI: William B. Eerdmans Publishing Company, 2000).

2. Stephen I. Wright, "Parables on Poverty and Riches," in Longenecker, *The Challenge of Jesus' Parables*, 224–25.
3. Snodgrass, *Stories with Intent*, 406.
4. Charles C. Torrey, *Our Translated Gospels* (New York: Harper, 1936), 59.
5. J. Duncan M. Derrett, *Law in the New Testament* (London: Darton, Longman and Todd, 1970), 48–77.
6. Bailey, *Poet & Peasant*, 105.
7. Ibid., 107.
8. Ibid., 105.
9. Ibid.
10. Snodgrass, *Stories with Intent*, 414.
11. Bart D. Ehrman, *Jesus: Apocalyptic Prophet of the New Millennium* (New York: Oxford University Press, 1999), 208.
12. Ibid., 190.
13. See, for example, W. G. Cole, *Sex in Christianity and Psychoanalysis* (New York: Oxford University Press, 1955), 17.
14. Ehrman, *Jesus: Apocalyptic Prophet of the New Millennium*, 173.
15. Cole, *Sex in Christianity and Psychoanalysis*, 12–31.
16. Ibid., 20.
17. Some Christian religious denominations, perhaps in order to preserve Mary's presumed virginity, insist that Jesus was an only child. Such denominations conclude that references to the "brothers" and "sisters" of Jesus in the Gospels of Matthew and Mark do not refer to biological siblings but to his wider community of disciples and followers.
18. John Dominic Crossan, *Jesus: A Revolutionary Biography* (San Francisco: HarperSanFrancisco, 1994), 60.
19. Ehrman, *Jesus: Apocalyptic Prophet of the New Millennium*, 244.
20. Crossan, *Jesus: A Revolutionary Biography*, 69.
21. Aristotle, *Nicomachean Ethics*, trans. by Martin Ostwald (Indianapolis, IN: Bobbs-Merrill, 1962), 1155a26–28.
22. F. Gerald Downing, *Jesus and the Threat of Freedom* (London: SCM Press Ltd., 1987), 48.
23. Ibid., 162–63.
24. E. J. Hobsbawn, *Primitive Rebels* (New York: Norton & Company, 1959), 57–58.
25. Ibid., 183.
26. Ibid.
27. Don Cupitt, *Jesus & Philosophy* (London: SCM Press, 1988), 98.

Bibliography

Allais, Lucy. "Forgiveness and Mercy." *South African Journal of Philosophy* 27, no. 1 (2008): 1–9.
Altizer, T. J. J. *The Contemporary Jesus*. Albany, NY: State University of New York Press, 1997.
Aristotle. *Nicomachean Ethics*, trans. by Martin Ostwald. Indianapolis, IN: Bobbs-Merrill, 1962.
Bailey, Kenneth E. *Poet & Peasant Through Peasant Eyes*. Grand Rapids, MI: William B. Eerdmans Publishing Company, 2000.
Barry, Brian. *Political Argument*. London: Routledge & Kegan Paul. 1965.
Belliotti, Raymond Angelo. "Blood is Thicker Than Water: Don't Forsake the Family Jewels." *Philosophical Papers* 18, no. 3 (1989): 265–80.
———. *Dante's Deadly Sins*. Oxford: Wiley-Blackwell, 2011.
———. *Good Sex*. Lawrence: University Press of Kansas, 1993.
———. "Honor Thy Father and Thy Mother and to Thine Own Self Be True." *Southern Journal of Philosophy* 24, no. 2 (1986): 149–62.
———. "Parents and Children: A Reply to Narveson." *Southern Journal of Philosophy* 26, no. 2 (1988): 285–92.
———. *Seeking Identity*. Lawrence: University Press of Kansas, 1995.
Betz, Hans Dieter. "Jesus and the Cynics." *The Journal of Religion* 74, no. 4 (1994): 453–75.
Blomberg, Craig L. *Interpreting the Parables*. Downers Grove, IL: InterVarsity Press, 1990.
Brandon, S. G. F. *Jesus and the Zealots*. New York: Scribner Books, 1967.
Brien, Andrew, "Mercy Within Legal Justice." *Social Theory and Practice* 24, no. 1 (1998): 83–110.
Buchanan, G. W. *Jesus: The King and His Kingdom*. Macon, GA: Mercer University Press, 1984.
Butterfield, Herbert. *Christianity and History*. London: Bell, 1949.
Cole, W. G. *Sex in Christianity and Psychoanalysis*. New York: Oxford University Press, 1955.
Cottingham, John. "Ethics and Impartiality." *Philosophical Studies* 43, no. 1 (1983): 83–99.
Crossan, John Dominic. *Jesus: A Revolutionary Biography*. San Francisco: HarperSanFrancisco, 1994.
———. *The Historical Jesus: The Life of a Mediterranean Jewish Peasant*. San Francisco: HarperSanFrancisco, 1991.
Cupitt, Don. *Jesus & Philosophy*. London: SCM Press, 1988.
Derrett, J. Duncan M. *Law in the New Testament*. London: Darton, Longman and Todd, 1970.
Desmond, William. *Cynics*. Berkeley: University of California Press, 2008.
Diodorus Siculus. *The Library of History*, trans. C. H. Oldfather. Cambridge, MA: Harvard University Press, 1933.
Diogenes Laertius. *Lives of the Eminent Philosophers*, trans. R. D. Hicks. Cambridge, MA: Harvard University Press, 1925, 11th edition, 2005.
Dole, Andrew and Andrew Chignell, eds. *God and the Ethics of Belief*. Cambridge: Cambridge University Press, 2005.
Downing, F. Gerald. *Jesus and the Threat of Freedom*. London: SCM Press Ltd., 1987.

Eddy, Paul Rhodes. "Jesus as Diogenes? Reflections on the Cynic Jesus Thesis." *Journal of Biblical Literature* 115, no. 3 (1996): 449–69.
Ehrman, Bart D. *Jesus: Apocalyptic Prophet of the New Millennium*. New York: Oxford University Press, 1999.
Feinberg, Joel. *Harm to Others*. New York: Oxford University Press, 1984.
———. *Doing and Deserving*. Princeton: Princeton University Press, 1970.
Feldman, Fred. "Desert: Reconsideration of Some Received Wisdom." *Mind* 104 (1995): 63–77.
Fiorenza, Elisabeth Schussler. *In Memory of Her*. New York: Crossroad, 1983.
Funk, Robert W., and the Jesus Seminar. *The Acts of Jesus: The Search for the Authentic Deeds of Jesus*. San Francisco: HarperSanFrancisco, 1998.
Goldstein, Morris. *Jesus in the Jewish Tradition*. New York: Macmillan, 1950.
Haidt, Jonathan. *The Righteous Mind*. New York: Pantheon Books, 2012.
Hillman, Robert A. "Debunking Some Myths About Unconscionability." *Cornell Law Review* 67 (1981): 1–49.
Hobsbawn, E. J. *Primitive Rebels*. New York: Norton & Company, 1959.
Hoistad, Ragnar. *Cynic Hero and Cynic King*. Uppsala: Bloms, 1948.
Hoover, Roy W., ed. *Profiles of Jesus*. Santa Rosa, CA: Polebridge Press, 2002.
Horsley, Richard A. *Jesus and the Spiral of Violence*. Minneapolis, MN: Fortress Publishers, 1987.
———. *Bandits, Prophets & Messiahs*. Harrisburg, PA: Trinity Press International, 1985.
Josephus. *Jewish Antiquities*, trans. Louis H. Feldman. Cambridge, MA: Harvard University Press, 1965.
Kekes, John. "Morality and Impartiality." *American Philosophical Quarterly* 18, no. 4 (1981): 295–303.
Kierkegaard, Soren. *Works of Love*, trans. Howard and Edna Hong. New York: Harper and Brothers, 1962.
Kleinig, John. "The Concept of Desert." *The Philosophical Quarterly* 8, no. 1 (1971): 71–78.
Kloppenborg, John S. *Q Parallels: Synopsis, Critical Notes and Concordance*. Sonoma, CA: Polebridge Press, 1988.
Lamont, Julian. "The Concept of Desert in Distributive Justice." *The Philosophical Quarterly* 44 (1994): 45–64.
Locke, Don. *A Fantasy of Reason*. London: Routledge, 1980.
Longenecker, Richard N. ed. *The Challenge of Jesus' Parables*. Grand Rapids, MI: William B. Eerdmans Publishing Company, 2000.
Mack, B. *A Myth of Innocence*. Philadelphia: Fortress, 1988.
MacMullen, Ramsay. *Enemies of the Roman Order: Treason, Unrest, and Alienation in the Empire*. Cambridge, MA: Harvard University Press, 1966.
Malherbe, Abraham J. *The Cynic Epistles*. Missoula, MT: Scholars Press, 1977.
Meier, John P. *A Marginal Jew*. New York: Doubleday, 1994.
Miller, David. *Social Justice*. Oxford: Oxford University Press, 1976.
Moser, Paul, ed. *Jesus and Philosophy*. Cambridge: Cambridge University Press, 2009.
Mo Tzu. *Basic Writings*, trans. Burton Watson. New York: Columbia University Press, 1963.
Murphy, Jeffrie G. "Remorse, Apology, and Mercy." *Ohio State Journal of Criminal Law* 4, no. 2 (2007): 423–53.
———, and Jean Hampton. *Forgiveness and Mercy*. Cambridge: Cambridge University Press, 1988.
Nozick, Robert. *Anarchy, State, and Utopia*. New York: Basic Books, 1974.
———. *The Examined Life: Philosophical Meditations*. New York: Simon & Schuster, 1989.
Nussbaum, Martha C. "Equity and Mercy." *Philosophy & Public Affairs* 22, no. 2 (1993): 83–125.
Outka, Gene. *Agape*. New Haven: Yale University Press, 1972.
Rachels, James. *Can Ethics Provide Answers?* Lanham, MD: Rowman & Littlefield, 1997.
Rajak, Tessa. *Josephus: The Historian and His Society*. London: Duckworth, 1983.

Rawls, John. *A Theory of Justice*. Cambridge, MA: Harvard University Press, 1971.
Sanders, E. P. *The Historical Figure of Jesus*. London: Allen Lane/Penguin Books, 1993.
———. *Jesus and Judaism*. Philadelphia: Fortress, 1985.
Sayre, Farrand. *The Greek Cynics*. Baltimore: J. H. Furst Company, 1948.
Scott, James C. *Domination and the Arts of Resistance*. New Haven, CT: Yale University Press, 1990.
Shakespeare, William. *The Merchant of Venice*, in eds. Hardin Craig and David Bevington, *The Complete Works of Shakespeare*. Glenview, IL: Scott, Foresman and Company, 1973.
Sher, George. "Effort, Ability, and Personal Desert." *Philosophy and Public Affairs* 8, no. 4 (1979): 361–76.
Sidgwick, Henry. *The Methods of Ethics*. London: MacMillan and Company, 1874, 7th edition. 1907.
Singer, Irving. *The Nature of Love, Volume 3: The Modern World*. Chicago: University of Chicago Press, 1989.
Singer, Peter. *Writings on an Ethical Life*. New York: HarperCollins, 2000.
———. *Practical Ethics*. Cambridge: Cambridge University Press, 180.
———. *Animal Liberation*. New York: Random House, 1975.
———. "Is Racial Discrimination Arbitrary?" *Philosophia* 8, nos. 2–3 (1978): 185–203.
Slote, Michael A. "Desert, Consent and Justice." *Philosophy and Public Affairs* 2, no. 4 (1973): 323–47.
Smart, J. J. C. and Bernard Williams. *Utilitarianism: For and Against*. Cambridge: Cambridge University Press, 1973.
Smith, Morton. *Jesus the Magician*. San Francisco: Harper & Row, 1978.
Snodgrass, Klyne R. *Stories with Intent*. Grand Rapids, MI: William B. Eerdmans Publishing Company, 2008.
Solomon, Robert C. *Love: Emotion, Myth, and Metaphor*. Garden City: Anchor Books, 1981.
———. *The Passions*. New York: Anchor Press, 1976.
———. *About Love: Reinventing Romance for Our Times*. New York: Simon & Shuster, 1988.
Stanton, Graham. *The Gospels and Jesus*. Oxford: Oxford University Press, 1989.
Steiker, Carol S. "Murphy on Mercy: A Prudential Reconsideration." *Criminal Justice Ethics* 27 (2008): 45–54.
Tasioulas, John. "Mercy." *Aristotelian Society* 103, no. 1 (2003): 101–32.
Thiering, B. *Jesus and the Riddle of the Dead Sea Scrolls*. San Francisco: HarperSanFrancisco, 1992.
Torrey, Charles. C. *Our Translated Gospels*. New York: Harper, 1936.
Wilkens, Michael J. and J. P. Moreland, eds. *Jesus under Fire*. Grand Rapids, MI: Zondervan Publishing House, 1995.
Williams, Clifford, ed. *On Love and Friendship*. Boston: Jones and Bartlett Publishers, 1995.
Wilson, Bryan R. *Magic and the Millennium*. New York: Harper & Row, 1973.
Wright, N. T. *Jesus and the Victory of God*. Minneapolis: Fortress, 1996.
Zaitchik, Alan. "On Deserving to Deserve." *Philosophy and Public Affairs* 6, no. 4 (1977): 370–88.
Zemach, Eddy M. "Love My Neighbor as Thyself or Egoism and Altruism." *Midwest Studies in Philosophy* 3, no. 1 (1978): 148–58.

Index

acts, supererogatory, 83; and Jesus, 85–87, 91
Aesop's fables, xvi
agape, 89; and abstractness, 52–57; and Parable of the Good Samaritan, 52–53; and Parable of the Prodigal Son, 41–45; and paradox, 45–49; and parental love, 49–52
Alexander the Great, 119, 122, 127–128, 141
Andolsen, Barbara Hilkert, 55
Antisthenes, 118, 127, 131–132
Archimedean point: and Jesus, 113, 161
Aristotle, 103, 166–167, 172

Badhwar, Neera Kapur, 46
Bion, 118
Buffalo Bills, 69

Cato, 125
Christian-Socialist movement, Sicily, xviii, 170–172
community, 31–32; and individualism continuum, 113
contract, 74–79; and procedural unconscionability, 74–75; and proportionate reward, 75–79; and substantive unconscionability, 74–75; and unequal bargaining power, 74–75; freedom of, 74–75
Cottingham, John, 25–26
Crates, 118–119, 121, 130–131
Crossan, John Dominic, xiv, 130–131, 160
Cupitt, Don, xiii, 171
Cynic philosophy, xiii–xiv, xvi, 33, 118–143; and freedom and knowledge, 122–123; and human fulfillment, 119–120; and Jesus, 125–143; and minimalism, 121–122;

and relationship to religion, 124; and sense of the dramatic, 124–125; and sense of entitlement, 120–121; and social convention, 123–124

desert, principle of, xvii, 33–34, 67–79, 87, 101
Desmond, William, 140–141
Dio Chrysostrom, 118
Diodorus the Sicilian, 9
Diogenes Laertius, 128
Diogenes of Sinope, 118–119, 121–122, 127–130, 140
Downing, F. Gerald, 136

egalitarianism, radical, 33–34, 52, 113, 164–165
Egypt, 9
Ehrman, Bart, xiv–xv, 156–157
entitlement, principle of, xvii, 33–34, 69–79
Epictetus, 141
Epicureans, 135, 139
Essenes, 135, 166

Final Judgment, xv, 165
forgiveness, xviii, 83–97, 108–113; and repentance, 84–92
Fourth Philosophy, 135–138
friendship, 167–168; and Aristotle, 166–167

Godwin, William, 18–19, 23, 30
Graham, Billy, 172

Haidt, Jonathan, 13
happiness, 119–120
Hercules, 120
Hipparchia, 118
Hobsbawn, E. J., 170–171

Homer, 172

ideal observer, 18–19, 32, 113
impartialism, 16–20, 23–34, 161
imperfect duties, 104–106
individualism: and community continuum, 113

Jesus: and contemporary philosophy, 13–34; and disciples, xv, 159, 165, 168–170; and family relations, 129, 159–163; and Final Judgment, xv, 165; and forgiveness, 86–91, 94–97, 108–113; and friendship, 167–168; and identifying with undesirables, 44–45, 48–49, 63, 131–132, 163–165; and interrogating prevailing norms, 133–134, 166–168; and Kingdom of God, 53, 149, 152–154, 160–161, 164–165, 168–169; and material minimalism, 118, 121–122, 130–131, 164, 168–171; and mercy, xviii, 97–113; and moral message, 152–154; and Parable of the Good Samaritan, xvii, 1–14, 16, 23, 159, 166; and Parable of the Laborers in the Vineyard, ix–x, xvii, 59–68, 74–79, 166; and Parable of the Prodigal Son, xvii, 37–49, 51–52, 57, 65, 90–91, 97, 166–167; and Parable of the Rich Fool, xviii, 115–118, 127; and Parable of the Unforgiving Servant, xviii, 81–82, 85–88, 106–111; and Parable of the Unjust Steward, xviii, 145–152; and principle of desert, xvii, 33–34, 67–79, 87, 101; and Socrates, 111–113, 125, 140, 168–169; and Son of Man, xiii–xvi, 152–154, 160–161, 168; and Sermon on the Mount, 154–159, 169–170; and sex and marriage, 154–159; and unconditional love, 45–52, 130, 166–168; and unsettling established rituals, 165–166; as apocalyptic prophet, xiii–xiv, xvi, 22, 149, 160–161; as Cynic philosopher, 22, 118, 125–143, 153–154; as Son of God, xiii, 154
John the Baptist, 164

Josephus, 134–137

Kant, Immanuel, 6, 112
Kierkegaard, Soren, 53
Kingdom of God, xiii–xvi, 2, 22, 27–28, 33–34, 53, 65–67, 79, 152–154, 160–161, 164–165, 168–169

love, unconditional, xvii. *See also* agape, and Parable of the Good Samaritan; agape, and Parable of the Prodigal Son

material minimalism, 118, 121–122, 130–131, 164, 168–171
Menippus, 118
Merchant of Venice, The, 98–99, 106
mercy, xviii, 97–113
Miami Dolphins, 69
Moses, 154–155
Mo Tzu, xvii, 17–19, 23–24, 26, 33–34
Musonius Rufus, 141

Nygren, Andres, 46–47, 49–50

Parables: of the Good Samaritan, xvii, 1–14, 16, 23, 159, 166; of the Laborers in the Vineyard, ix–x, xvii, 59–68, 74–79, 166; of the Prodigal Son, xvii, 37–49, 51–52, 57, 65, 90–91, 97, 166–167; of the Rich Fool, xviii, 115–118, 127; of the Unforgiving Servant, xviii, 81–82, 85–88, 106–111; of the Unjust Steward, xviii, 145–152
partialism, 18–34, 161
St. Paul, xv
Pharisees, 46, 127–128, 134–136, 152, 154, 158, 165–166
Plato, 116
punishment, 92–94; as deterrence, 92; as incarceration, 92; as rehabilitation, 92; as restitution, 92, 93–94, 102; as retribution, 92–93, 101
Pythagoras, 135, 168

Rachels, James, xvii, 20–23, 28–30
Rawls, John, 72–73
relations, family, 50, 129, 159–163

Index

repentance, 85–91. *See also* Jesus, and forgiveness
Romans, 123, 128, 132, 134, 136–138, 142, 163–164

Sadducees, 135, 166
Sartre, Jean Paul, 73–74
Sayre, Farrand, 125–126
self, 161–163
Seneca, 141
Sicarii, 136–137
Sidgwick, Henry, 13, 19–20, 33, 50
Singer, Peter, xvii, 13–17, 19–20, 23, 28, 30–33, 105, 172
Socialist-Christian movement, Sicily, xviii, 170–172

Socrates, 111–113, 125, 140, 168–169
Son of Man, xiii–xvi, 152–154, 160–161, 168
Stoics, 135, 139–141

Teresa, Mother, 52
Torrey, Charles C., 148

Vespasian, 134

Whatley, George, 172
Wolterstorff, Nicholas, 86–87

zealots, 117, 137
Zeus, 138

About the Author

Raymond Angelo Belliotti is a SUNY Distinguished Teaching Professor of Philosophy at the State University of New York at Fredonia. He received his undergraduate degree from Union College in 1970, after which he was conscripted into the United States Army where he served three years in military intelligence units during the Vietnamese War. Upon his discharge, he enrolled at the University of Miami where he earned his master of arts degree in 1976 and doctorate in 1977. After teaching stints at Florida International University and Virginia Commonwealth University, he entered Harvard University as a law student and teaching fellow. After receiving a juris doctorate from Harvard Law School, he practiced law in New York City with the firm of Barrett Smith Schapiro Simon & Armstrong. In 1984, he joined the faculty at Fredonia.

Belliotti is the author of fourteen other books: *Justifying Law* (1992); *Good Sex* (1993); *Seeking Identity* (1995); *Stalking Nietzsche* (1998); *What is the Meaning of Human Life?* (2001); *Happiness is Overrated* (2004); *The Philosophy of Baseball* (2006); *Watching Baseball Seeing Philosophy* (2008); *Niccolò Machiavelli* (2008), *Roman Philosophy and the Good Life* (2009), *Dante's Deadly Sins: Moral Philosophy in Hell* (2011); *Posthumous Harm* (2011); *Shakespeare and Philosophy* (2012); and *Jesus or Nietzsche?* (2013). *Good Sex* was later translated into Korean and published in Asia. *What is the Meaning of Human Life?* was nominated for the Society for Phenomenology and Existential Philosophy's Book of the Year Award. He has also published seventy articles and twenty-five reviews in the areas of ethics, jurisprudence, sexual morality, medicine, politics, education, feminism, sports, Marxism, and legal ethics. These essays have appeared in scholarly journals based in Australia, Canada, Great Britain, Italy, Mexico, South Africa, Sweden, and the United States. Belliotti has also made numerous presentations at philosophical conferences, including the 18th World Congress of Philosophy in England and has been honored as a featured lecturer on the *Queen Elizabeth II* ocean liner.

While at SUNY Fredonia he has served extensively on campus committees, as the Chairperson of the Department of Philosophy, as the Chairperson of the University Senate, and as director of general education. Belliotti also served as United University Professionals' local vice president for academics. For six years he was faculty advisor to two undergraduate clubs: The Philosophical Society and *Il Circolo Italiano*. Belliotti has been the recipient of the SUNY Chancellor's Award for Excellence in Teaching, the William T. Hagan Young Scholar/Artist Award, the Kasling Lecture Award for Excellence in Research and Scholarship, and the SUNY Foundation Research & Scholarship Recognition Award. He is also a member of the New York State Speakers in the Humanities Program.

main

JUL 11 2014

WITHDRAWN